The Oxford Book of Garden Verse

John Dixon Hunt is Academic Adviser to the Oak Spring Garden Library, Upperville, Virginia. He has been the editor of the *Journal of Garden History* since 1981. His many publications include *The Figure in the Landscape: Poetry, painting, and gardening during the 18th century* (1976), *Garden and Grove. The Italian Renaissance Garden in the English Imagination: 1600–1750* (1986), and editions of critical writings on Pope and Tennyson.

The Oxford Book of
Garden Verse

EDITED BY

John Dixon Hunt

Oxford   New York

OXFORD UNIVERSITY PRESS

1994

Oxford University Press, Walton Street, Oxford OX2 6DP

Oxford New York Toronto
Delhi Bombay Calcutta Madras Karachi
Kuala Lumpur Singapore Hong Kong Tokyo
Nairobi Dar es Salaam Cape Town
Melbourne Auckland Madrid
and associated companies in
Berlin Ibadan

Oxford is a trade mark of Oxford University Press

Selection, introduction, and notes © John Dixon Hunt 1993

First published 1993
First issued as an Oxford University Press paperback, 1994

British Library Cataloguing in Publication Data
Data available

Library of Congress Cataloging in Publication Data
The Oxford book of garden verse
edited by John Dixon Hunt.
p. cm.
1. Gardens—Poetry. 2. Gardening—Poetry.
3. English poetry. 4. American poetry. I. Hunt, John Dixon.
PR1195.G2096 1992 821.008'036—dc20 92-32260
ISBN 0-19-282338-8

1 3 5 7 9 10 8 6 4 2

Printed in Great Britain by
Biddles Ltd,
Guildford and King's Lynn

CONTENTS

CONTENTS

CONTENTS

CONTENTS

CONTENTS

CONTENTS

INTRODUCTION

These prospects and pavilions—even the rocks and trees and flowers will seem somehow incomplete without the touch of poetry which only the written word can lend a scene.

Jia Zheng, *The Story of the Stone*, Chinese, eighteenth century

The Groves of Eden, vanished now so long,
Live in description, and look green in song.

Alexander Pope, 'Windsor Forest'

The first book of the Bible tells of the first garden. Ever since, gardens and books have enjoyed a special relationship which this anthology both records and continues. Abraham Cowley thought gardens were God's poetry, in which collected works it was proper to read attentively before writing about them. Poets and certainly poetasters have often been seduced, variously, by a garden's preternatural spaces or by its call to hard labour: indeed, Roy Campbell's *The Georgiad* of 1931 mocks inert confusions between authoring and gardening:

Write with your spade, and garden with your pen,
Shovel your couplets to their long repose
And type your turnips down the field in rows,
Equal your skill, no matter which is which,
To dig an ode, or to indite a ditch . . .

There may well be poets who keep gardens alive and growing rather more easily in words than with green fingers on the ground; or they become so abstracted by gardens as to dream themselves the trees and be, as Hart Crane implies, no longer in need of the real thing.

From poems about gardens to reading in gardens is a short step: Richard Le Gallienne thought the greatest felicity was to have a library *in* the garden, and it is apparently only an eccentric who tries (as Robert Browning shows) to bury unappealing books in his garden. Some famous writers pretend to envy their gardener's workaday world—as does Boileau (in John Ozell's translation); some prefer—or say they prefer (like Pope)— the seclusion of their garden world to the nastier one of politics and public life; some cheerfully present themselves—like C. S. Lewis—as ordinary enough to manage without books provided that they can

water flowers and roll the lawn
And sit and sew and talk and smoke
And snore through all the summer day.

At the other extreme is W. H. Auden, also reclining in his garden chair, yet uneasily aware how those with the gift of language to write about flora and fauna are also those who experience loneliness.

Those are just a few of the many repercussions from encounters of poet and gardenist (a nice coinage of Horace Walpole's that includes garden designers as well as gardeners). Since poets often have their eye upon other poems, there is a bookish as well as a horticultural relish about many of the verses gathered here. The widespread versifying which undertook to celebrate the so-called English or picturesque garden in the second half of the eighteenth century is rife with echoes of Alexander Pope or John Milton, both credited with the invention of this landscape style *avant la lettre*. But then gardens, too, have copied and echoed other gardens, especially—because their myths were endlessly open to reinterpretation—the primordial Eden or the classical Hesperides. In modernist spirit, Edwin Morgan and Ronald Johnson make 'found poems' from the writings of gardenist predecessors.

The history of garden poetry follows, as in its turn it illuminates, the histories of both poetry and gardening. There is no room here for extended narratives of any of those three, but some hints of how poetry took its cue from contemporary gardens may be in order. It needs no advanced student of *Zeitgeist* to note the congruence of heroic couplets with regular gardening, the appeal of blank verse to those who championed the freer forms of picturesque landscaping, or the parallels between the conceitful performances of late Tudor and Stuart poetry and the intricate inventions of the knot garden, arbour, and other carpenter's work. It is of course relatively easy to read either poetry or garden in this tendentious fashion; nor is it necessarily uninteresting. But it does not always expand our thinking to explain one art in terms of what one already knows of another contemporary with it: thus it seems merely obvious to point to a modernist fascination with the art of *objets trouvés* in connection with Morgan's and Johnson's construction of poems from the casual debris of old garden correspondence, memoirs, or gossip.

It is perhaps more useful for the reader of this volume to ask what elements of the garden's vast repertoire of effects, forms, moods, and uses are brought into focus at any one time. The garden's infinite resources are there for the poet to tap for whatever serves his or her imaginative purposes. The garden's dream world, its potential for exploration, quest, and (self-)discovery attract the medieval poet; its rich exoticism enthrals the young Tennyson. Coleridge utilizes the small space of a garden arbour to consider a much wider landscape; this is a recognizable Romantic strategy, as it is also a situation sanctioned in contemporary design practice, like that of Humphry Repton. Beyond Coleridge's possible debt to contemporary ideas and habits is his fine exploitation of a garden's potential for meditation.

If I find a special richness and variety in twentieth-century garden poetry (however severely curtailed in this selection through pressures of space), it is not because writers have been responding to a parallel incidence of invention in landscape architecture. So we are left to find some other explanation of why these poets have exploited the range of garden ideas and forms as never before; maybe they were belatedly influenced by the eclectic fashions of garden design in the period leading up to the First World War; perhaps the late-twentieth-century passion for actual as well as historical gardens—witness the endless gardening books, articles, and programmes—has alerted them to gardens' inexhaustible resources as physical and metaphysical creations.

The remainder of this Introduction will seek to isolate some of the reasons why poets have entered gardens and what themes they have discovered or rediscovered there; equally, it will alert gardeners to the resources which poetry brings to some of *their* dearest concerns. I will review, briefly: space, time, work, pride and perfection, art and nature, stylistic changes and continuities, and the garden as metaphor.

Gardens are the prime art of milieu, the creation through natural and cultural means of an environment which has generally been judged to be in some way special. They are thus, first and foremost, a spatial art. Though some may be tiny—even as residual as the window-box or the roof garden—they possess length and depth and height, and as Octavio Paz reminds us, 'the sky is infinite' and all gardens look to the sky (which even the greenhouse or conservatory admits). The larger gardens are, the more likely are they to be subdivided. The discovery of these spaces constitutes one of the major experiences of gardens; when spatial surprise has surrendered to familiarity, there will still be excitements that come either from the endless permutations of route around even the smallest acreage or from the active, constantly changing, role of nature, including time, in the disposition of gardens.

Some of the earliest poems ('. . . as I wente . . .') to some of the latest ('Along the empty alley . . .') often re-enact movement through gardens; even when we think a garden can be appreciated at a glance, it takes time to explain and explore. Either way, poets bring special skills to such narratives; poetry, too, is an art of sequence. Milton gives to Satan a double experience that many of his contemporaries enjoyed in Italian gardens—in the first extract here, an enthralled overview, and in the second, his pursuit of Eve through the garden's spaces.

A garden's spaces will be marked in many different ways, and on many different scales. For Chaucer's or Lydgate's dreamer, the way will be punctuated and defined by temples or shrines that bring into gardens the sculptured presence of some apt deity; Venus and Priapus are guardians of gardens; another suitable inhabitant is Daphne, who was turned into laurel

(Marvell says that is the only reason Apollo chased her!). This mode of punctuating and defining garden spaces and giving them what came to be called 'character' also involved clearly marked sections or outdoor rooms, and it continued at least into the eighteenth century. The later, landscape garden marked its subdivisions by more subtle means, by controlling opening and closing shades, by moulding the ground, or with suddenly discovered full or hinted vistas. In the smaller gardens where modern poets seem to spend their time, the scale of spatial demarcation may be smaller but is no less palpable: 'the strength of sunlight | on the yellowed bricks', or the inch-by-inch changefulness of moss in a Japanese garden.

All these spatial markers focus for the garden owner and visitor alike a special sense of place: overall place, and/or local places within the larger. *Genius loci*, as Pope most famously made clear, is at the very centre of garden-making and garden poetry. Locations where gardens are established can already have this special sense of place, so that the landscape architect's job is to bring that identity out; or it can be specially contrived for them; the best gardens probably enjoy both devices. The lover will ape this gardenist strategy by saying his lady makes the place what it is, though Suckling turns this tactic on its head at Hampton Court, and Marvell will invoke the same conceit for the ex-General Fairfax and his Yorkshire flower-garden. Place is what you make it in poems as in gardens. Sometimes the poet's imagination extends the garden's spaces and thus augments their *genius loci* by invoking other places, other gardens, other persons who have been in the garden before him, or even—with Vita Sackville-West enthralled over nursery catalogues during winter evenings—other plantings.

Time is the fourth dimension and a special ingredient of gardens in ways essentially different from the other arts. Of course, poets have never had to wait to find themselves in gardens in order to brood upon time. Some, indeed, have pretended that in gardens they could escape its tyranny, together with the contingencies and accidents of the sublunary world: this is what Marvell pretends, until as his visit to 'The Garden' ends he is confronted with the gardener's *pièce de resistance* which turns out to be some kind of floral clock. But more usually poets have acknowledged in gardens a strong incidence of temporal themes and occasions. They know that they need time to explore gardens fully, and the narrative instinct that resides or is discovered in gardens (far more than in buildings) relies upon it too. More crucially, times of day and seasonal change can deliver the very same garden in myriad forms, although this ineluctable changefulness is, for Swinburne, 'alone the changeless lord of things'.

As 'The Forsaken Garden' insistently reminds us, however, with its rhythm checking the verbal richness like a metronome, time's endless threat to a garden is that it will kill off its plants, let its trees outgrow, encourage its weeds to obliterate the ordering and shaping endeavours of man or woman until they are lost to sight; then it is only 'the ghost of a garden'. Hence a sundial is the garden's habitual *memento mori*; but compost, too, makes Whitman 'terrified at the earth'. Death also haunts the garden in the ghosts that many poets detect there—for Waller, Penshurst is haunted by Sidney (though his verses, in their turn, by Jonson's); for Symons, remembering Verlaine, there are the *revenants* out of Watteau; while Sassoon imagines a former landowner returning to witness the decay of his estate.

Yet some poets, like gardeners, resist decay and dissolution. Thomas Hardy, with a characteristic sense of the *longue durée* of history, notices that gardens sometimes outlast their creators; while he is weeding, Michael Hamburger reflects upon who will ultimately 'overrun the earth'. Pope, too, knew that making landscape gardens like Stowe meant enjoying a visionary confidence in their coming to maturity long after their creators' deaths. And it is one of the enduring paradoxes of garden poetry that it is to the world of transience and fragility, 'of lilies rusted, rotting', that the unhappy, battered, and bruised have looked for solace. From *The Flower and the Leaf*—

> There is no heart, I deem, in such despair
> Nor with thoughts froward and contraire
> So overlaid, but it should soon have bote [relief],
> If it had once felt this savour soote [sweet]

—to the modern hospital gardens of Randall Jarrell or Anne Sexton (and others not here), we may trace the long confidence in a garden's solacing balm. Even if the poet sees it a duty to underline the ironies of that tradition, as Sewell does in 'Soliloquy', behind and beyond this scepticism we perceive an enduring human recourse to the sustenance, repose, and innocent soli(ci)tude of gardens where time heals as well as ravishes.

Marvell's witty celebration of the garden as retreat and solace is not, even in his own poem, the last word. Besides that quietist perspective, there is the alternative strategy of work. They even cohabit, as Grimald notices in praising the 'marvellous . . . mixture . . . of solace and gain'.

You can hold off the worst of time's predations by work; you can imagine, indeed convince yourself, that sweat and energy will keep at bay a garden's more voracious natural enemies. And such hard work can be offered, as in Armstrong's poem on *The Art of Preserving Health*, as suitable exercise for those unwilling to pursue blood sports. Anyone who keeps a garden knows that work is fundamental. Yet early poets, doubtless themselves either sufficiently well-to-do to let their servants do the gardening for them, or visiting as guests gardens where the labour was taken care of (behind the scenes, too, no doubt), often give the impression of maintenance-free gardens. Part of the magic of much early garden verse is indeed its celebration of an effortless world. But when the taste for gardens and the opportunities of having them spread to less-patrician parts of society, or when poets turned their attention to vernacular forms, then the gardener and his labouring become conspicuous themes. Gardens where work has always been at a premium as well as highly visible are those which are not much studied by garden historians, largely owing (one must presume) to lack of adequate documentation. But recent poets seem more at ease in all forms of vernacular gardening, those ordinary worlds of allotment, greenhouses, vegetable gardens, or the nondescript spaces where William Carlos Williams, for instance, finds a bed of tulips, or where Patrick Kavanagh knows that children have their best adventures. It is, not surprisingly, a contemporary poet, Douglas Dunn, who lends a voice to those who toiled in earlier gardens. Elsewhere in modern garden verse it is work that predominates: weeding, transplanting, turning the sod, taking cuttings, grubbing out ground elder, making compost (though Walt Whitman rises above its actual composition), rolling the lawn—all these are explicitly addressed; for many poets these are the glory of the garden and of gardening. Though Henry Jones turns his destroyed pea crop to ethical advantage, his is still a rare early example in verse of the hands-on gardener, nowadays a ubiquitous phenomenon.

One of the gardener's perennial absorptions is to outdo the neighbours. Armstrong, while recommending gardening for those who do not want to hunt or fish, still wryly accepts its competitiveness. Jones's ruined pea crop was a hubristic instance of 'Ambition's pride' that spurred his gardener 'All gard'ners to excell'.

Beyond such personal ambition, however, has been the garden's role of recovering the horticultural plenitude that was the Garden of Eden's, where we are told the Lord God 'planted every tree'. In medieval poetry gardens are credited with the same fullness: 'trees . . . Each in his kind' are matched only by the birds that sing on *every bough*. In Renaissance botanical gardens, newly discovered specimens from all over the world were accommodated in an effort, as John Rea put it, to 'Rifle the treasure of old *Paradise*', or, as John Evelyn, 'to be as a rich and noble Compendium of what the whole Globe of the Earth has flourishing upon her bosome'. That the availability of plants far exceeded the capacity of those gardens to fit them all in did not, however, diminish the idea that a garden should collect within its relatively limited spaces a conspectus of the world's flora. When neither biblical nor scientific authority urged this attempt at plenitude, it seems never to have been within the gardener's temperament to accept just what comes up in the spot wherever he or she happens to be gardening. All gardeners are what Neil Curry calls 'workers for Eden'.

Of course, as well as by their planting, gardens have always used architectural and sculptural imagery to invoke many other worlds—Chinese temples, Turkish tents, Egyptian pyramids, Greek temples, Gothic ruins, Japanese lanterns, Roman urns and columns, Swiss chalets, American gardens. This has often provoked the mirth of more down-to-earth gardeners like James Cawthorn, who deplore the rash of foreign references:

> Formed on his [the Mandarin's] plans, our farms and seats begin
> To match the boasted villas of Pekin . . .
> In Tartar huts our cows and horses lie,
> Our hogs are fatted in an Indian sty . . .

None the less, such wide-ranging references to other cultures in landscape and estate architecture have been defended by invoking a garden's need for completeness; or the garden's appeal to a perfection lacking in its own society, as with the Italianate garden in New York State in Williams's poem. Pope (following Sir William Temple) recommends Homer's description of the gardens of Alcinous for containing 'all the justest rules and provisions which can go toward composing the best gardens'.

The often vast cost to the real gardener, though, of implementing a range of such cultural or horticultural references can be achieved with much more economy on the printed page. Modern poets' increased attention to foreign gardens may be the result of more opportunities for travel and of media attention; but surely it also derives from the same instinct to extend a garden's range, to enjoy all manner of modes and forms, to increase perfection, in the traditional gardenist spirit of emulation. To increase the garden's potential and scope in the early eighteenth century Pope wanted to 'call in the country' (what the Chinese, in their turn, refer to as 'borrowed scenery'). What we see in twentieth-century verse are borrowed gardens, real or imagined foreign examples, called into the poetry: Rich at Versailles; several poets in Italy (Anthony Hecht at the Villa D'Este, the most rewarding of all these visits); Enright and Leithauser in Japan; Stevenson in the south of France. And there were always gardens to visit in other literatures: Stevenson and Porter look to Martial, Pope to Homer, Waley to the Chinese, Symons to Verlaine.

The presence of these borrowed examples at certain moments in the history of gardens, or of poetry, marks a cultural need for fresh visions, new perfections. One can only guess, but is not the delight in Italian garden art, expressed by so many modern poets here against the very grain of an Anglo-Saxon predilection for naturalness, a reaction against the blandness of current landscape architecture? Is it not the rage for some garden order after the insipid permutations of the so-called English style?

The gardener's striving for what Horace Walpole, praising the 'modern' or English landscape style, termed the 'more perfect perfection', has always involved calling art to the assistance of a flawed nature. Though there are many who resist the idea, the wildest cottage garden is, in fact, carefully contrived; even the sweeps and declivities of 'Capability' Brown are calculated. Yet gardens have endlessly been the battlegrounds of art and nature, or rather more often of their proponents. These have always tended to elicit sterile debates, refusing to acknowledge that gardens exist, as Robert Fergusson put it in the 1770s, to 'Give nature a fanciful look' or, as John Hollander in 1981, to be 'significant versions of the meaningless'.

Gardens are inevitably compounded of both human intervention—art, design, or technology—and natural ingredients. The aesthetic confrontations on this issue, though they never resolve matters once and for all, enable us none the less to adjudicate the local circumstances, conditions, and concerns which determine the exact values and proportions of art and nature in any one society, or any one group of people, or even—given the idiosyncrasy of poets and gardeners—individuals.

The strain of protest against luxurious gardens and their too conspicuous art is long and strong: Spenser's wandering knights can be censured for their seduction by art's vanities; for Shirley, the gardener's art purchases nature only at a price; Marvell produces the wittiest advocacy of the natural perspective ('' tis all enforced, the fountain and the grot'); Joseph Warton rejects Stowe and heads for the countryside. Against even the naturalistic pretensions of the landscape garden, Geoffrey Grigson can invoke the imagery of modern earth-moving technology.

On balance the proponents of art do not come out as strongly here as the naturalists; few landscape designers write verses about their art. Yet it is strange that poets cannot respond more to another art's control. The only modern poet who honours by name the designer of a garden, Anthony Hecht saluting Pirro Ligorio for the Villa D'Este, has also (unsurprisingly, therefore) a rare vision of what exactly motivates the garden's tension between art and nature:

> Controlled disorder at the heart
> Of everything, the paradox, the old
> Oxymoronic itch to set the formal strictures
> Within a natural context, where the tension lectures
> Us on our mortal state, and by controlled
> Disorder, labors to keep art
> From being too refined.

By contrast, suspicion of too much (especially foreign) art unites with a grave appeal to indigenous nature to commit Anglo-Saxon garden verse firmly to nature's side. In the United States, too, Wallace Stevens can resist 'Order, the law of hoes and rakes', and incline towards the ultimate order of decomposition, and Howard Nemerov is rebuked by the great seagull for rescuing his garden ('miserable regimen') from erstwhile ocean. For Alasdair Aston, who eschews hoe, rake, and regimen, everything, but everything, in the garden is lovely, and he can joyfully honour his garden's surrender to all of nature's wanton ways — time, pests, weeds, neglect. From such irony (though you cannot be certain these days) to the contemporary born-again ecologist is but a short step. And along the way is Michael Hamburger contemplating the weeds and forsaking chemicals and machines.

All debates about art and nature in the garden have tended to occur at times of intense gardenist change, like that heyday of gardenist revolutions between the restoration of the monarchy in 1660 to the death of 'Capability' Brown in 1783; poets were quick to weigh in and support or oppose new developments. Anne Finch records her husband's conversion of an old-fashioned mount into a new-fangled Italianate terrace; Pope mocks Timon's baroque taste and urges upon Lord Burlington a more classically derived style; William Mason and Anna Seward are caustic about fashionable extravagances in garden design, while Samuel Jackson Pratt and George Colman ridicule the filtering down of grand ideas to vernacular practitioners who miss their point with 'mimic ruins, kept in good repair'. What we also trace in responses to these declensions of garden design is a fresh, but slowly forged new identity between the private sensibility and a less coercive landscape architecture; imagery and meanings which once had been general and available became increasingly personal. One of the awkward moments of this shift can be discerned in those eighteenth-century poets who feel committed to a high poetic level of generalization, yet are forced into either elaborate footnotes (Gilbert West at Stowe) or bathetic specificities (Duck, Giles) in order to anchor their verses in the site they have opted to describe.

Cowley, who takes discussion of gardens seriously even if to the detriment of his poetry, is one of the first poets to be alert to historical perspectives: 'God the first garden made, and the first city, Cain.' Yet there were eventually need and opportunity in cities for all manner of gardens, from public parks to allotments to roof gardens. This need for 'garden' space within towns (*rus in urbe*) begins earlier than we sometimes realize, with the late-seventeenth-century opening of royal parks like St James's to a general populace who, as Rochester unblinkingly observes, managed to rediscover in public spaces the private garden's heady mixture of good and evil. 'Public gardens' is really something of a contradiction in terms, since gardens have traditionally been created as private retreats. 'Pleasure gardens', likewise, is redundant, unless we have a secret agenda of hortulan pain and disillusionment, or, more probably, we think there is little pleasure except in gardens. Both phrases, however, remind us both of the reinvention of gardenist ideas and forms to address new social needs and of the necessary flexibility of a garden's art of milieu within larger environments.

If these garden poems chart historical developments, they also can help us remark the continuities within those changing emphases, the enduring needs of gardeners in their gardens and poets in their poems. One recurring theme is how essentially ambiguous the garden can be: haven and safe retreat, a paradise, on the one hand; yet on the other and simultaneously a place of danger; a place of indulgence, even immorality, and a place of rectitude, a site of propriety; a triumphant creation, but also harbouring its own destruction—in Christian terms this is the serpent (a presence intimated even by serpentine paths!) The serpent's classical counterpart, which Stephen Hawes encounters in the form of a fountain (as visitors can still do at the Villa D'Este), is perhaps the dragon that Hercules slew to gain access to the golden apples in the Garden of the Hesperides.

But by far the richest and most obvious of recurring themes is the continual celebration of a garden's liberation of the five senses: smells and scents; taste—from that first forbidden apple onwards; sounds; the feel of loam or the texture of leaves; and the sight of all colours, but especially green. Another continuity, perhaps surprisingly, is the unchanging scope of the garden for providing props for poetic meditation. The medieval poet alerts us to a garden repertoire, confirmed by contemporary visual arts, of sites and designed items which orientate and structure his dreaming and thinking: fountains, knots, crossed alleys, turf seats, courtyards, flowery fields, 'pleasaunces', and 'herbers'. These continue to reappear, like the walled garden, though sometimes in new, fashionable disguise as gazebo or baroque waterworks: the small flowers in the green grass of *The Flower and the Leaf* become the 'flowery lawn' of the eighteenth-century Leasowes; Coleridge has his lime-tree bower; Kubla Khan facilitates a pleasure ground that, though its language may take advantage of a more recent vogue for grottoes and groves, is still recognizably the large medieval pleasaunce. The exotic, too, has always attached itself to gardens, and it continues to root itself in unexpected places, like a Cockney's backyard, Robert Druce's garden gnomes, or even in a college garden after snow.

The Song of Solomon announces, if we need to be told, that the garden is apt for metaphor. Though I have tended to exclude poems which do not privilege gardens as real and experienced places, it is the dullest and most horticulturally obsessed versifier who does not register that a garden offers myriad analogies with the world beyond its walls. As the seventeenth-century Japanese poet, Matsuo Basho, wrote,

> Many things of the past
> Are brought to my mind,
> As I stand in the garden
> Staring at a cherry tree.
> (trans. N. Yuasa)

Since, therefore, metaphors will creep into the mind in the garden anyway, and since the boundaries within all good metaphors, or within our expectations of their vehicle and tenor, can be so slippery, it seemed ungenerous to mount guard with a fiery sword to keep them all out. It is an eccentric poetic moment when D. J. Enright, secure in the knowledge of a strong metaphorical tradition of garden writing, dramatizes his inability to find meaning in a mass of Sunday flowers: 'I looked at them more closely: they were emblematic | Of something, I couldn't make out what.'

Some poems show us how people go about fashioning their gardens into metaphors, like the music-hall song about the cockney's expansive release in an 'instant' Sunday garden planted with the cabbages he did not sell from his barrow the day before. But there will be other poems which, while negotiating gardens through metaphor or tenaciously pursuing their own metaphoric career in gardens, still keep an eye on actual gardening practice, on how the garden has figured in human experience, or on real gardens (or at the very least, in the words of Marianne Moore, 'imaginary gardens with real toads in them'). And while a poet is 'Walking alone devising on the flowers', he or she can still alert us to the flower garden as much as to the device, conceit, or metaphor made of it. Shakespeare's comparison of responsible statecraft and garden maintenance, Beaumont's meditation upon lost Edens and hoped-for paradise, William Blake's intimation of how a building can distort the genius of a garden place, or Empson's discovery of rolling the lawn as religious penance—gardens endlessly yield their metaphors. Some gardens will be searched for what they suggest of large, political and cultural, concerns; others will be personal, solipsistic—sites of 'this treasure hunt | Of Selves', where, as in *The Romance of the Rose*, the garden visitor is confronted with a mirror.

Some garden metaphors are too evident or inert, like the perennial paradise. Yet maybe sometimes we miss the subtle shrub for the obvious shrubbery: when Chaucer writes of birds singing like angels, the dreamer wants us to realize that he is already 'in heaven'; when Brown asserts of his lovesome garden that 'God walks in mine', it is not so much the slack pantheism that should stick but the echo of Genesis 3: 8 when the Lord God walked in the garden in the cool of the day to seek fallen man and woman for the first but not the last time.

One metaphor that lurks within all garden experience and therefore subsumes all other metaphors in garden verse is that of the *theatrum mundi*, the garden as a theatre of the world. For Shakespeare, properly as a man of the theatre, all the world was a stage; for all gardenists, the garden provides an even more effective platform for that analogy.

To start with, before there were buildings designed specifically as theatres, gardens had incorporated stages for dramatic and musical performances; then it was not long before some gardens were wholly designed like theatrical amphitheatres, and the fossils of this tradition are still visible in such English gardens as Claremont or Rousham. And before there were buildings called museums, gardens were closely allied to cabinets of curiosity (as Mildmay Fane reveals by his praise of Summerly) or they functioned as locations to display collections of sculpture; hence the usage by which gardens are called 'theatres' in the sense of a whole collection or congeries of things (think of the title of John Parkinson's *Theatrum Botanicum* of 1640). And if gardens have been theatres and museums (as they continue to be during public fêtes in Tennyson's *The Princess*), it is even easier for them to be an out-of-doors equivalent to the whole house: what the bedroom, the study, the bathroom, or the sitting-room has witnessed, the garden recovers for its own repertoire.

Hints of all these versions of garden-theatres lurk throughout these poems. The effort at plenitude, already noticed, brings all the botanical world to parade upon the garden's stage in the older meaning of theatre as complete collection. In the more modern sense of a stage for the performance of many parts and the acting out of innumerable visions, garden scenery affords changeable, adaptable backdrops. The roles one may adopt, as poets by their very nature love to do, are played in gardens with as much fervour or insouciance as behind footlights. Children—'for the leaves were full of children, | Hidden excitedly, containing laughter'—can be the most creative actors in even the most unprepossessing garden; adults have preferred more elaborate stage-sets, like Pope's Timon at his villa, or the Bourbon monarchy at Caserta near Naples, where Richard Wilbur in some disillusion considers the metaphor afresh: 'The garden of the world, which no one sees, | Never had walls, is fugitive with lives.'

Four principles have guided this selection. The first is that the poetry must have some interest as verse. The second is that each piece chosen must, equally, offer some perspective upon garden-making, garden use (or abuse), or the idea of the garden. The third principle of selection is that extracts from longer works have been admitted when they were, to start with, more or less self-contained, and when they honoured the first two criteria. The fourth principle is that exceptions could prove any of the first three rules.

Poets write about gardens almost as readily as about falling in love, sometimes at one and the same time. The interaction of two arts makes demands upon both, and enhances both. However, what has particularly concerned me is to illustrate experiences of gardens that are central to our understanding of both the arts of poetry and garden design, yet which fail to be adequately registered by other writers, especially garden historians.

Though the academic study of gardens has been reluctant to leave élite examples for the vernacular, students of literature have recently been encouraged to read outside the canon of the great and the good. Accordingly there are some examples here of verse—ballads, popular songs,

music-hall lyrics, satirical squibs—that themselves often address equally
vernacular gardens, the undesigned, done-it-oneself contrivances that
have, of course, filled more garden hours of human experience than have
the likes of Versailles or Stowe.

A word about exclusions: a garden being such a capacious entity, it was
sometimes difficult to decide where to draw the line. To start with, there
seemed no place for poems about flowers *per se*—what Miles and John
Hadfield in their delightful *Gardens of Delight* (1964) called 'seed-
catalogue verses', the kind which Richard Barnfield's stanza may serve to
illustrate

> The pink, the primrose, cowslip, and daffadilly,
> The harebell blue, the crimson columbine,
> Sage, lettuce, parsley, and the milk-white lily,
> The rose, and speckled flower called sops-in-wine,
> Fine pretty kingcups, and the yellow boots
> That grow by rivers, and by shallow brooks . . .

Yet it was impossible to dèny a place to Herbert's 'The Flower', and its
implicit gardenist sensibility (watching green return after winter; plants
growing straight, then 'swelling through store') urged its inclusion; but
Waller's 'Go, lovely Rose', though clearly not about a flower *per se*, did not
in the last resort seem apt (unhappily). Other exclusions involve all but a
few examples of inscriptions, of which gardens have sometimes been full;
yet many could have been composed for just about any location. Out, too,
have gone many poems whose gardens were wholly metaphorical.
Metaphors, as we have seen, cling to gardens like bindweed; love-lyrics in
the sixteenth and seventeenth centuries resorted to the garden so readily
for their conceits that in practice we learn little about gardens. Campion's
'There is a garden in her face' is an unhappy consequence of this particu-
lar exclusiveness, though less rigour would have provided occasional mirth
for readers encountering metaphors that, unlike Campion's easy elegance,
somehow go awry:

> And would you see my mistress' face?
> It is a flowery garden place,
> Where knots of beauties have such grace,
> That all is work and nowhere space.

John Donne perhaps tells us little to nothing about Lucy, Countess of
Bedford's famous gardens at Twickenham Park; yet his poem recalls us
splendidly to the traditional role of gardens as places in which to meditate.

Finally, poems in or about fields, parkland, and especially about the
larger landscape were easy to exclude. However, during the heyday of the
so-called English landscape garden, when the garden's traditional sense of
limited enclosure was almost completely eroded, it was not always easy to
trace the line between garden and park. But some of the great landscape

gardens from this period—Chiswick, for example, Richmond Park, or the much-written-about Stowe—had to be represented if only for the efforts they elicited from the writers.

The decision to invoke extracts has been equally difficult. There are some striking garden experiences that seemed too fleeting to capture even in extract: the theatrical possibilities of gardens for the dramas of life are intimated in T. S. Eliot's 'La Figlia che Piange'—

> Lean on a garden urn—
> Weave, weave the sunlight in your hair—
> Clasp your flowers to you with a pained surprise—

or in 'Burnt Norton' the mysteries of space and time ('our first world', 'The unheard music hidden in the shrubbery') are suggested by moving through garden enclosures—'Along the empty alley, into the box circle, | To look down into the drained pool.' Yet these fragments—even if extractable—scarcely stand by themselves and had regretfully to be left out. So, too, did a poem like Carew's 'To Saxham', where the gardens register so fleetingly in the larger landscape, as they do in most country-house poems, that its inclusion seemed indulgent.

Otherwise the chance to detach a reasonably self-contained passage from its context has proved a boon: William Mason, among several others here, stretches one's tolerance for indifferent verse to its limits, yet he registered such crucial moments of garden history—the assault upon William Chambers's Chinese fantasies, the return of flowers and local subdivisions of space to the garden—that he cannot be omitted. The interests of garden history or the history of garden experience must account for all otherwise-dubious decisions, though not without the occasional wish that poets like Gilbert West had followed Pope's great achievement and made Stowe 'live in one distinguish'd line' rather than many.

The sequence of poems, with the exception of the first two passages and the last, follows the chronology of their writers' dates of birth and then the poem's date of book publication (with a few recent texts the date will refer to an appearance in a magazine); these latter are given at the end of each poem, with some occasional notice of other dates where these seem useful. Where authors or their dates are unknown, texts have been given an approximate place in that chronology. I have invented titles for some extracts, if this helped to orientate readers; a few pieces complete in themselves but without titles have equally been provided with them, also within square brackets. Spellings and some punctuation have been conservatively modernized, except, as in the case of Spenser, James I, or Clare, where dialect, vernacular usage, or archaic epigraphy was an integral part of poetic effect. Some footnotes, glossing usages or allusions in the texts, have been added; but wherever possible, notably with botanical references,

I have wanted to interpose as little as possible between readers and the poems.

It might have been desirable and possible to group poems by theme: but in practice too many poets respond in any one poem to so many of a garden's plenitudes that it would have been impossibly arbitrary or procrustean to have determined which section to confine them in. The chronological system at least allows poems by one author to be grouped together, just as it allows anyone with a historical imagination to search for developments or continuities in the arts of poetry or garden-making or both.

Finally, some acknowledgements. There has been, surprisingly, no Oxford Book of Garden Verse before this. But other anthologists have been in the garden before me, and to them I am indebted both for the odd poem that had escaped my trawls and for helping me to decide what I was not interested in: see especially Denis Wood, *Poets in the Garden* (London, 1978), Margaret Elphinstone, *A Treasury of Garden Verse* (Edinburgh, 1990), and Roy Strong, *A Celebration of Gardens* (London, 1991). In addition, two French anthologies also helped me to decide what aspects of gardens I wanted to register in poetry in English: Daniel Gelin (ed.), *Cent poetes côté jardin* (Paris, 1990) and Bernard and Renée Kayser, *L'Amour des jardins célébré par les écrivains* ([Paris], 1986).

More importantly, I have profited over the years from friends and colleagues who have kindly steered me towards material for this anthology, which has been in the making long before Oxford University Press invited me to edit it, or who have helped me track elusive references and notes. Therefore grateful thanks, alphabetically but by no means mechanically, to Stephen Bending, J. S. Bratton, Geoffrey C. Britton, Morny Davison, Robert Druce, Anne van Erp, Alistair Fowler, Warwick Gould, Linda Cabe Halperin (for drawing my attention to and transcribing the poem on Hartwell), Anthony Hecht, Linden Huddlestone, Michael Leslie, Derek Lucas, the late C. A. Patrides, Chris Ridgway, Nicholas Roskill, David Selwyn, and to Robert Williams; also to the staffs of the London Library and the Poetry Library in the South Bank Centre, to the National Trust and Clwyd County Record Office, and to Mrs Wendy Scott for some last-minute assistance with preparing texts of the earlier poetry.

The Oxford Book of
Garden Verse

King James Bible
1611

1   *Genesis 2: 8–10*

AND the Lord God planted a garden eastward in Eden; and there he put
the man whom he had formed.

And out of the ground made the Lord God to grow every tree that is
pleasant to the sight, and good for food; the tree of life also in the midst of
the garden, and the tree of knowledge of good and evil.

And a river went out of Eden to water the garden; and from thence it
was parted, and became into four heads.

2   *Song of Solomon 4: 12–16*

A GARDEN inclosed is my sister, my spouse; a spring shut up, a fountain
sealed.

Thy plants are an orchard of pomegranates, with pleasant fruits;
camphire, with spikenard,

Spikenard and saffron; calamus and cinnamon, with all trees of
frankincense: myrrh and aloes, with all the chief spices:

A fountain of gardens, a well of living waters, and streams from
Lebanon.

Awake, O north wind; and come, thou south; blow upon my garden, that
the spices thereof may flow out. Let my beloved come into his garden, and
eat his pleasant fruits.

Geoffrey Chaucer
*c.*1343–1400

3   from *The Parliament of Fowls*

WITH that mine hand in his he took anon,
Of which I comfort caught, and went in fast;
But, Lord, so I was glad and well begoon,

3 well begoon] in a happy situation

I

For overal where that I mine eyes cast
Were trees clad with leaves that aye shall last,
Each in his kind, of colour fresh and green
As emerald, that joye was to seen.

The builder oak, and eke the hardy ash,
The pillar elm, the coffin unto carain;
The boxtree piper, holm to whippes lash,
The sailing fir, the cypress, death to playne;
The shooter yew, the asp for shaftes plain,
The olive of peace, and eke the drunken vine,
The victor palm, the laurel to divine.

A garden saw I full of blosmy boughs
Upon a river, in a grene mead,
There as sweetness evermore enow is,
With flowers white, blue, yellow, and red,
And colde welle-streames, nothing dead,
That swimmen full of smale fishes light,
With finnes red, and scales silver bright.

On every bough the briddes heard I sing
With voice of angel in their harmony;
Some busied them their briddes forth to bring;
The little conies to their play gone hie,
And further all about I gan espy
The dredful roe, the buck, the hart, the hind,
Squirrels, and beastes small of gentle kind.

Of instruments of stringes in accord
Heard I so play a ravishing sweetness
That God, that maker is of all and lord,
Ne hearde never better, as I guess.
Therewith a wind, unnethe it might be less,
Made in the leaves green a noise soft
Accordant to the fowles song aloft.

Th'air of that place so attempre was
That never was grievance of hot nor cold;
There wax eke every wholesome spice and grass:
No man may there waxe sick nor old.

overal] everywhere	eke] also	coffin unto carain] coffin for corpses
death to playne] for mourning death	asp] aspen	enow] enough briddes]
birds dredful] fearful	unnethe] hardly	attempre] temperate

2

Yet was there joye more a thousandfold
Than man can tell; nor never would it night,
But aye clear day to any mannes sight.

Under a tree, beside a well, I sey
Cupid, our lord, his arrows forge and file;
And at his feet his bow all ready lay,
And Will, his daughter, tempered all this while
The hevedes in the well, and with her will
She couched them, after they should serve,
Some for to slay, and some to wound and carve.

(*c*.1380)

4   from *The Romance of the Rose*

THE garden was, by measuring,
Right even and square in compassing;
It as long was as it was large.
Of fruit had every tree his charge,
But it were any hideous tree
Of which there were two or three.
There were, and that wot I full well,
Of pomegranates a full great deal,
That is a fruit full well to like,
Namely to folk when they ben sick.
And trees there were, great foison
That bearen nuts in their season,
Such as men nutmegges call
That sweet of savour ben withall.
And alemandres great plenty,
Figs, and many a date-tree
There wexen, if men had need,
Through the garden in length and brede.
There was eke waxing many a spice,
As clowe-gelofre and licorice,
Gingevre and greyn de parys
Canell and setewale of price,
And many a spice delectable
To eaten when men rise from table.

sey] saw   hevedes] arrowheads

4 But] unless   Namely] especially   foison] plenty   withall]
indeed   alemandres] of almond trees   eke] also   brede]
breadth   clowe-gelofre] cloves   Gingevre] ginger   greyn de parys]
grains of paradise, i.e. cardamoms   Canell] cinnamon   setewale] zedoary, a spice

And many homely trees there were
That peaches, coynes, and apples bear;
Medlars, plums, pears, chesteynes,
Cherries, of which many one fain is;
Nuts, aleys, and bolas,
That for to see it was solace.
With many high laurels and pine
Was ranged clene all that gardeyn,
With cypress, and with oliveres,
Of which that nigh no plenty here is.
There were elmes great and strong,
Maples, ash, oak, asp, planes long,
Fine yew, poplar and lindens fair,
And other trees full many a pair.·

What should I tell you more of it?
There were so many trees yet.
That I should all encumbered be
Er I had reckoned every tree.

These trees were set, that I devise,
One from another, in assise,
Five fathom or six, I trowe so;
But they were high and great also,
And for to keep out well the sun,
The croppes were so thickly run,
And every branch in other knet,
And full of greene leaves set,
That sunne might there not descend,
Lest it the tender grasses shend.
There might men does and roes see,
And of squirrels full great plenty,
From bough to bough always leaping.
Conies there were also playing,
That comen out of their clapers,
Of sundry colours and manners,
And maden many a tourneying
Upon the freshe grass springing.

In places saw I welles there,
In whiche there no frogges were,
And fair in shadow was every well,
But I ne can the number tell

---

coynes] quinces   chesteynes] chestnuts   fain] pleased   aleys] service
(sorb) berries   bolas] wild plums   oliveres] olive trees   asp]
aspen   assise] position   croppes] foliage   knet] knotted, intertwined
shend] harm   clapers] warrens   welles] springs

4

Of streames small that by device
Mirth had done come through condys,
Of which the water, in running,
Gan make a noise full liking.
   About the brinkes of these wells,
And by the streames overal else
Sprang up the grass, as thicke set
And as soft as any velvet,
On which men might his lemman lay,
As on a featherbed to play,
For the earth was full soft and sweet.
Through moisture of the welle wet
Sprang up the sweete greene grass,
As fair, as thick, as myster was.
But much amended it the place,
That th'earthe was of such a grace
That it of flowers had plenty,
That both in summer and winter be.
   There sprang the violet all new,
And fresh pervinke, rich of hue,
And flowers yellow, white, and red—
Such plenty grew there never in mead.
Full gay was all the ground, and quaint,
And powdered, as men had it paint,
With many a fresh and sundry flower
That casten up full good savour.

                  (Trans. *c*.1360; pub. 1532)

John Lydgate
?1370–1449

5   from *The Complaint of the Black Knight*

AND by a river forth I gan costey
Of water clear as beryl or crystal,
Til at the last I found a little way

condys] conduits, pipes   overal] everywhere   lemman] lover   myster]
need   pervinke] periwinkle   quaint] pleasing
5 costey] walk along

Toward a park enclosed with a wall,
In compass round; and by a gate small,
Whoso that wolde, freely might goon
Into this parke walled with green stoon.

And in I went to hear the briddes' song,
Which on the branches, both in plain and vale,
So loude sang that all the wode rang,
Like as it should shiver in pieces small.
And, as me thoughte, that the nightingale
With so great might her voice gan out wrest,
Right as her heart for love would brest.

The soil was plain, smooth, and wonder soft,
All overspread with tapites that Nature
Had made herself, canopied eke aloft
With bowys green, the flowers for to cure,
That in their beauty they may long endure
From all assault of Phoebus' fervent fire
Which in his sphere so hot shone and clear

The air temperate, and the smothe wind
Of Zepherus among the blossoms white,
So wholesome was and nourishing by kind,
That smale buddes and round blomes lite,
In manner gan of her breath delight,
To give us hope that their fruit shall take
Against autumn, ready for to shake.

I saw there Daphne closed under rind,
Green laurel and the wholesome pine;
The myrrh also that weepeth ever of kind,
The cedar high, upright as a line,
The filbert eke, that lowe does incline
Her bowes green to the erthe down,
Unto her knight icalled Demophoun.

There saw I eke the fresshe hawethorne
In white motley that so sweet does smell,
Ash, fir, and oak with many a young acorn,
And many a tree more than I can tell.

wolde] would	briddes] birds	brest] break		tapites] tapestries
eke] also	bowys] boughs	cure] care for, protect		by kind] according to its
nature				

And me before, I saw a little well
That had his course (as I gan behold)
Under an hill with quick stremes cold.

The gravel gold, the water pure as glass,
The bankys round the well environing,
And soft as velvet the young grass,
That thereupon lustily came springing.
The suit of trees aboute compassing
Her shadow cast, closing the welle round
And all the herbes growing on the ground.

(early 15th cent.)

Anonymous

6   *I Have a New Garden*

I HAVE a new garden,
And new is begun;
Such another garden
Know I not under sun.

In the midst of my garden
Is a pear set,
And it will no pear bear
But a pear Jenet.

The fairest maid of this town
Prayed me
For to graften her a graft
Of my pear tree.

When I had them grafted,
All at her will,
The wine and the ale
She did in fill.

And I grafted her
Right up in her home,
And by that day twenty weeks
It was quick in her womb.

6 pear Jenet] an early pear   did in fill] i.e. filled me up with

7

That day twelve month
That maid I met;
She said it was a pear Robert
But not pear Jonet!

(early 15th cent.)

James I of Scotland
1394–1437

7

from *The King's Quair*

Now was there made fast by the touris wall
A garden fair, and in the corners set
An arbour green with wandis long and small
Railit about; and so with treis set
Was all the place, and hawthorn hedges knet,
That life was non walking there forby
That might within scarse ony wight aspy.

So thick the bewis and the leaves green
Beshaded all the alleys that there were.
And myddis every arbour might be seen
The sharpe greene sweete juniper,
Growing so fair with branches here and there,
That—as it semed to a life without—
The bewis spread the arbour all about.

And on the smalle greene twistis sat
The little sweete nightingale, and song
So loud and clear the ympnis consecrat
Of lufis use, now soft, now loud among,
That all the garden and the wallis rong
Right of their song, and of the copill next
Of their sweet harmony . . .

(*c.*1488)

---

pear Robert . . . pear Jonet] i.e. the baby's father is called Robert and not John, presumably the poet's name

7 touris] tower's	wandis] palings	life] living person	bewis] boughs
myddis] within	twistis] branches	ympnis] hymns	lufis] love's
copill] couplet			

John Gardner
mid-15th century

8

from *The Feat of Gardening*

How so well a gardener be,
Here he may both hear and see
Every time of the year and of the moon
And how the crafte shall be done,
In what manner he shall delve and set
Both in drought and in wet,
How he shall his seeds sow;
Of every month he must know
Both of wortes and of leek,
Onions and of garlic,
Parsley, clary and eke sage
And all other herbage.

In the calendars of Januar'
You shall trees both set and rear
To grafty there on apple and pear;
And what trees is kind them to bear
Apple and a apple-tree.
For there is kind is most to be
Of pear I mind yorne
To graft it upon a hawthorn.

(wr. 1440–1450; pub. 1894)

Anonymous

9

from *The Flower and the Leaf*

WHEREFORE I marvel greatly of myself
That I so long withouten sleepe lay,
And up I rose three houres after twelve,
About the springing of the day,
And on I put my gear and mine array
And to a pleasaunt grove I gan pass,
Long or the bright sun uprisen was;

8 wortes] cole (*Brassica oleracea*)   clary] (*Salvia sclarea*)   I mind yorne] I think it best
9 or] before

9

In which were oakes great, straight as a line,
Under the which the grass so fresh of hue
Was newly sprung; and an eight foot or nine
Every tree well from his fellow grew,
With branches broad, lade with leaves new,
That sprongen out ayen the sunne sheen,
Some very red and some a glad light green;

Which as me thought was right a pleasant sight,
And eke the briddes song for to hear
Would have rejoiced any earthly wight.
And I, that could not yet in no manner
Hear the nightingale of all the year,
Full busily harkened with heart and with ear
If I her voice perceive could anywhere.

And at the last a path of little breade
I found, that greatly had not used be,
For it forgrowen was with grass and weed
That well unneth a wight might it see.
Thought I, this path some whither goeth, pardee,
And so I followed, till it me brought
To right a pleasaunt arbour, well y-wrought,

That benched was, and with turfes new
Freshly turfed, whereof the greene grass,
So small, so thick, so short, so fresh of hue,
That most like unto green velvet it was.
The hedge also, that yede in compass
And closed in all the green arbour,
With sycamore was set and eglatere,

Wreathen in fere so well and cunningly
That every branch and leaf grew by measure,
Plain as a board, of an height, by and by—
I see never thing, I you ensure,
So well done; for he that took the cure
It to make, I trow, did all his pain
To make it pass all those that men have seen.

ayen the sunne] to greet the sun		briddes] birds'	breade] width
unneth] hardly	pardee] indeed	yede] went	eglatere] honeysuckle
in fere] together	cure] trouble		

And shapen was this arbour, roof and all,
As a pretty parlour, and also
The hedge as thicke as a castle wall,
That who that list without to stand or go,
Though he would all day prien to and fro,
He should not see if there were any wight
Within or no; but one within well might

Perceive all those that yeden there without
In the field, that was on every side
Covered with corn and grass, that, out of doubt,
Though one would seek all the world wide,
So rich a field could not be espied
On no coast, as of the quantity,
For of all good thing there was plenty.

(late 15th cent.)

Anonymous

10   from *The Assembly of Ladies*

In September, at falling of the leaf,
The fresh season was altogether done
And of the corn was gathered in the sheaf;
In a garden, about twain after noon,
There were ladies walking, as was their wone,
Four in number, as to my mind doth fall,
And I the fifth, simplest of all.

Of gentle women four there were also,
Disporting them everiche after their guise,
In cross alleys walking by two and two,
And some alone after their fantasies.
Thus occupied we were in divers wise,
And yet in truth we were not alone:
There were knights and squires many one ...

prien] peer
10 wone] habit   everiche] each one   guise] manner   fantasies] fancy,
inclination

So came I forth in to a strait passage,
Which brought me to an arbour fair and green
Made with benches full craftily and clean;

That, as me thought, might no creature
Devise a better by proportion.
Save it was closed well, I you ensure,
With masonry of compass environ
Full secretly, with staires going down.
In midst the place, a turning wheel, certayne,
And upon that a pot of margoleyne;

With margarites growing in ordinance
To show themselves as folk went to and fro,
That to behold it was a great pleasance;
And how they were accompanied with more,
Ne m'oublie-mies and sovenez also;
The poor pansies ne were not dislodged there—
No, no, Got wot, their place was everywhere.

The floor beneath was paved fair and smooth
With stones square of many divers hue,
So well joined that, for to say the truth,
All seemed one, who that none other knew.
And underneath the streames, new and new,
As silver new bright springing in such wise,
That whence it came you could it not devise.

(late 15th cent.)

Stephen Hawes
?1475–1511

11   from *The Pastime of Pleasure*

THEN in we went to the garden glorious
Like to a place of pleasure most solacious,

of compass environ] in a complete circuit   certayne] indeed   margoleyne]
marjoram   margarites] daisies   m'oublie-mies] forget-me-nots   sovenez]
remember me's (*Veronica chamoedrys*)   new and new] continually   devise]
tell, imagine

With Flora painted and wrought curiously
In divers knots of marvellous greateness.
Rampant lions stood up wonderously
Made all of herbs with dulcet swetenes,
With many dragons of marvellous likeness
Of divers flowers made full craftily
By Flora coloured with colours sundry.
Amidst the garden so much delectable
There was an arbour fair and quadrant
To paradise right well comparable,
Set all about with flowers fragrant,
And in the middle there was resplendysshaunt
A dulcet spring and marvellous fountain
Of gold and azure made all certain.

In wonderful and curious similitude
There stood a dragon of fine gold so pure
Upon his tail of mighty fortitude
Wreathed and scaled all with azure,
Having three heads diverse in figure,
Which in a bath of the silver grette
Spouted the water that was so dulcette.

(1509)

Nicholas Grimald
?1519–?1562

12   *The Garden*

THE issue of great Jove, draw near, you Muses nine;
Help us to praise the blissfull plot of garden ground so fine.
The garden gives good food, and aid for leaches' cure;
The garden, full of great delight, his master doth allure.
Sweet salad herbs be here, and herbs of every kind,
The ruddy grapes, the seemly fruits be here at hand to find.
Here pleasure wanteth not, to make a man full fain;
Here marvellous the mixture is of solace, and of gain.
To water sundry seeds, the furrow by the way
A running river, trilling down with liquor, can convey.

swetenes] sweetness   resplendysshaunt] resplendent
12 leaches'] doctors'   fain] glad, well-pleased

Behold, with lively hue, fair flowers that shine so bright,
With riches, like the orient gems, they paint the mold in sight.
Bees, humming with soft sound (their murmur is so small),
Of blooms and blossoms suck the tops, on dewed leaves they fall.
The creeping vine holds down her own bewedded elms,
And, wandering out with branches thick, reeds folded overwhelms.
Trees spread their coverts wide, with shadows fresh and gay,
Full well their branched boughs defend the fervent sun away.
Birds chatter, and some chirp, and some sweet tunes do yield;
All mirthful, with their songs so blithe, they make both air, and field.
The garden, it allures, it feeds, it glads the sprite;
From heavy hearts all doleful dumps the garden chaseth quite.
Strength it restores to limbs, draws, and fulfils the sight,
With cheer revives the senses all, and maketh labour light.
O, what delights to us the garden ground doth bring;
Seed, leaf, flower, fruit, herb, bee, and tree, and more than I may sing.

(1557)

Thomas Tusser
?1524–1580

13   from *A Hundred Good Points of Husbandry*

In March and April, from morning to night,
In sowing and setting, good housewives delight;
To have in a garden or other like plot,
To trim up their house, and to furnish their pot.

The nature of flowers, Dame Physic doth show;
She teacheth them all, to be known to a few.
To set or to sow, or else sown to remove,
How that should be practised, learn if ye love.

Land falling or lying full south or south-west,
For profit by tillage, is lightly the best:
So garden with orchard and hop-yard I find,
That want the like benefit, grow out of kind.

sprite] spirit

If field to bear corn, a good tillage doth crave,
What think ye of garden, what garden would have?
In field without cost, be assured of weeds;
In garden be sure, thou losest thy seeds.

At spring (for the summer) sow garden ye shall,
At harvest (for winter) or sow not at all.
Of digging, removing, and weeding, ye see,
Makes herb the more wholesome, and greater to be.

Time fair, to sow or to gather be bold,
But set or remove when the weather is cold.
Cut all thing or gather, the moon in the wane,
But sow in increasing, or give it his bane.

Now sets do ask watering, with pot or with dish,
New sown do not so, if ye do as I wish:
Through cunning with dibble, rake, mattock, and spade,
By line, and by level, trim garden is made.

Who soweth too lateward, hath seldom good seed,
Who soweth too soon, little better shall speed.
Apt time and the season, so diverse to hit,
Let air and layer, help practice and wit.

(1571)

George Gascoigne
1534–1577

14   *Gascoigne's Gardenings*
*whereof were written in one end of a close walk, which he has in
his garden, this discourse following*

THE figure of this world I can compare
To garden plots, and such like pleasant places.
The world breeds men of sundry shape and share,
As herbs in gardens grow of sundry graces;
Some good, some bad, some amiable faces,
Some foul, some gentle, some of froward mind,
Subject, like bloom, to blast of every wind.

14 close walk] a narrow, hedged walk   froward] refractory, ungovernable

And as you see the flowers most fresh of hue,
That they prove not always the wholesomest,
So fairest men are not always found true
But even as withered weeds fall from the rest,
So flatterers fall naked from their nest.
When truth hath tried, their painting 'ticing tale,
They lose their gloss and all their jests seem stale.

Yet some do present pleasure most esteem,
Till beams of bravery wither all their wealth;
And some again there be can rightly deem
Those herbs for best, which may maintain their health.
Considering well that age draws on by stealth,
And when the fairest flower is shrunk and gone,
A well grown root will stand and shift for one.

Then thus the restless life which men here lead
May be resembled to the tender plant;
In spring it sprouts, as babes in cradle breed,
Flourish in May, like youths that wisdom want,
In autumn ripes and roots, lest store wax scant,
In winter shrinks and shrouds from every blast,
Like crooked age when lusty youth is past.

And as the ground or grace whereon it grew
Was fat or lean, even so by it appears;
If barren soil, why then it changes hue,
It fadeth fast, it flits to fumbling years;
But if he gathered root amongst his fears,
And light on land that was well mucked in deed,
Then stands it still, or leaves increase of seed.

As for the rest, fall sundry ways (God wot);
Some faint like froth at every little puff,
Some smart by sword, like herbs that serve the pot,
And some be weeded from the finer stuff,
Some stand by props to maintain all their ruff.
And thus (under correction be it told)
Hath Gascoigne gathered in his garden mould.

(1573)

'ticing] enticing   ruff] i.e. collar or ruff of flowers supported by the props

16

15   *In a chair in the same garden was written this following*

IF thou sit here to view this pleasant garden place
Think thus: at last will come a frost, and all these flowers deface;
But if thou sit at ease to rest thy weary bones,
Remember death brings final rest to all our grievous groans.
So whether for delight, or here thou sit for ease,
Think still upon the latter day, so shalt thou God best please.

(1573)

Edmund Spenser
?1552–1599

from *The Faerie Queene*

16   [*The Bower of Bliss*]

THENCE passing forth, they shortly do arriue,
   Whereas the Bowre of *Blisse* was situate;
   A place pickt out by choice of best aliue,
   That natures worke by art can imitate:
   In which what euer in this worldly state
   Is sweet, and pleasing vnto liuing sense,
   Or that may dayntiest fantasie aggrate,
   Was poured forth with plentifull dispence,
And made there to abound with lauish affluence.

Goodly it was enclosed round about,
   Aswell their entred guestes to keepe within,
   As those vnruly beasts to hold without;
   Yet was the fence thereof but weake and thin;
   Nought feard their force, that fortilage to win,
   But wisedomes powre, and temperaunces might,
   By which the mightiest things efforced bin:
   And eke the gate was wrought of substaunce light,
Rather for pleasure, then for battery or fight.

16 fortilage] a small fort

17

Yt framed was of precious yuory,
   That seemd a worke of admirable wit;
   And therein all the famous history
   Of *Iason* and *Medaea* was ywrit;
   Her mighty charmes, her furious louing fit,
   His goodly conquest of the golden fleece,
   His falsed faith, and loue too lightly flit,
   The wondred *Argo*, which in venturous peece
First through the *Euxine* seas bore all the flowr of *Greece*. . . .

Thus being entred, they behold around
   A large and spacious plaine, on euery side
   Strowed with pleasauns, whose faire grassy ground
   Mantled with greene, and goodly beautifide
   With all the ornaments of *Floraes* pride,
   Wherewith her mother Art, as halfe in scorne
   Of niggard Nature, like a pompous bride
   Did decke her, and too lauishly adorne,
When forth from virgin bowre she comes in th'early morne.

Thereto the Heauens alwayes Iouiall,
   Lookt on them louely, still in stedfast state,
   Ne suffred storme nor frost on them to fall,
   Their tender buds or leaues to violate,
   Nor scorching heat, nor cold intemperate
   T'afflict the creatures, which therein did dwell,
   But the milde aire with season moderate
   Gently attempred, and disposd so well,
That still it breathed forth sweet spirit & holesome smell.

More sweet and holesome, then the pleasaunt hill
   Of *Rhodope*, on which the Nimphe, that bore
   A gyaunt babe, her selfe for griefe did kill;
   Or the Thessalian *Tempe*, where of yore
   Faire *Daphne Phœbus* hart with loue did gore;
   Or *Ida*, where the Gods lou'd to repaire,
   When euer they their heauenly bowres forlore;
   Or sweet *Parnasse*, the haunt of Muses faire;
Or *Eden* selfe, if ought with *Eden* mote compaire.

Much wondred *Guyon* at the faire aspect
   Of that sweet place, yet suffred no delight
   To sincke into his sence, nor mind affect,
   But passed forth, and lookt still forward right,

Bridling his will, and maistering his might:
Till that he came vnto another gate,
No gate, but like one, being goodly dight
With boughes and braunches, which did broad dilate
Their clasping armes, in wanton wreathings intricate.

So fashioned a Porch with rare deuice,
    Archt ouer head with an embracing vine,
    Whose bounches hanging downe, seemed to entice
    All passers by, to tast their lushious wine,
    And did themselues into their hands incline,
    As freely offering to be gathered:
    Some deepe empurpled as the *Hyacint*,
    Some as the Rubine, laughing sweetly red,
Some like faire Emeraudes, not yet well ripened.

And them amongst, some were of burnisht gold,
    So made by art, to beautifie the rest,
    Which did themselues emongst the leaues enfold,
    As lurking from the vew of couetous guest,
    That the weake bowes, with so rich load opprest,
    Did bow adowne, as ouer-burdened.
    Vnder that Porch a comely dame did rest,
    Clad in faire weedes, but fowle disordered,
And garments loose, that seemd vnmeet for womanhed.

In her left hand a Cup of gold she held,
    And with her right the riper fruit did reach,
    Whole sappy liquor, that with fulnesse sweld,
    Into her cup she scruzd, with daintie breach
    Of her fine fingers, without fowle empeach,
    That so faire wine-presse made the wine more sweet:
    Thereof she vsd to giue to drinke to each,
    Whom passing by she happened to meet:
It was her guise, all Straungers goodly so to greet.

So she to *Guyon* offred it to tast;
    Who taking it out of her tender hond,
    The cup to ground did violently cast,
    That all in peeces it was broken fond,
    And with the liquor stained all the lond:

scruzd] squeezed

19

Whereat *Excesse* exceedingly was wroth,
Yet no'te the same amend, ne yet withstond,
But suffered him to passe, all were she loth;
Who not regarding her displeasure forward goth.

There the most daintie Paradise on ground,
It selfe doth offer to his sober eye,
In which all pleasures plenteously abound,
And none does others happinesse enuye:
The painted flowres, the trees vpshooting hye,
The dales for shade, the hilles for breathing space,
The trembling groues, the Christall running by;
And that, which all faire workes doth most aggrace,
The art, which all that wrought, appeared in no place.

One would haue thought, (so cunningly, the rude
And scorned parts were mingled with the fine,)
That nature had for wantonesse ensude
Art, and that Art at nature did repine;
So striuing each th'other to vndermine,
Each did the others worke more beautifie;
So diff'ring both in willes, agreed in fine:
So all agreed through sweete diuersitie,
This Gardin to adorne with all varietie.

And in the midst of all, a fountaine stood,
Of richest substaunce, that on earth might bee,
So pure and shiny, that the siluer flood
Through euery channell running one might see;
Most goodly it with curious imageree
Was ouer-wrought, and shapes of naked boyes,
Of which some seemd with liuely iollitie,
To fly about, playing their wanton toyes,
Whilest others did them selues embay in liquid ioyes.

And ouer all, of purest gold was spred,
A trayle of yuie in his natiue hew:
For the rich mettall was so coloured,
That wight, who did not well auis'd it vew,
Would surely deeme it to be yuie trew:
Low his lasciuious armes adown did creepe,
That themselues dipping in the siluer dew,
Their fleecy flowres they tenderly did steepe,
Which drops of Christall seemd for wantones to weepe.

no'te] could not   yuie] ivy

Infinit streames continually did well
  Out of this fountaine, sweet and faire to see,
  The which into an ample lauer fell,
  And shortly grew to so great quantitie,
  That like a little lake it seemd to bee;
  Whose depth exceeded not three cubits hight,
  That through the waues one might the bottom see,
  All pau'd beneath with Iaspar shining bright,
That seemd the fountaine in that sea did sayle vpright.

And all the margent round about was set,
  With shady Laurell trees, thence to defend
  The sunny beames, which on the billowes bet,
  And those which therein bathed, mote offend.
  As *Guyon* hapned by the same to wend,
  Two naked Damzelles he therein espyde,
  Which therein bathing, seemed to contend,
  And wrestle wantonly, ne car'd to hyde,
Their dainty parts from vew of any, which them eyde.

(1590)

17   *[The Garden of Adonis]*

SHE brought her to her ioyous Paradize,
  Where most she wonnes, when she on earth does dwel.
  So faire a place, as Nature can deuize:
  Whether in *Paphos*, or *Cytheron* hill,
  Or it in *Gnidus* be, I wote not well;
  But well I wote by tryall, that this same
  All other pleasant places doth excell,
  And called is by her lost louers name,
The *Gardin* of *Adonis*, farre renowmd by fame.

In that same Gardin all the goodly flowres,
  Wherewith dame Nature doth her beautifie,
  And decks the girlonds of her paramoures,
  Are fetcht: there is the first seminarie
  Of all things, that are borne to liue and die,
  According to their kindes. Long worke it were,
  Here to account the endlesse progenie
  Of all the weedes, that bud and blossome there;
But so much as doth need, must needs be counted here.

17 wonnes] lives   *Paphos ... Gnidus*] all shrines of Venus

It sited was in fruitfull soyle of old,
　And girt in with two walles on either side;
　The one of yron, the other of bright gold,
　That none might thorough breake, nor ouer-stride:
　And double gates it had, which opened wide,
　By which both in and out men moten pas;
　Th'one faire and fresh, the other old and dride:
　Old *Genius* the porter of them was,
Old *Genius*, the which a double nature has.

He letteth in, he letteth out to wend,
　All that to come into the world desire;
　A thousand thousand naked babes attend
　About him day and night, which doe require,
　That he with fleshly weedes would them attire:
　Such as him list, such as eternall fate
　Ordained hath, he clothes with sinfull mire,
　And sendeth forth to liue in mortall state,
Till they againe returne backe by the hinder gate.

After that they againe returned beene,
　They in that Gardin planted be againe;
　And grow afresh, as they had neuer seene
　Fleshly corruption, nor mortall paine.
　Some thousand yeares so doen they there remaine;
　And then of him are clad with other hew,
　Or sent into the chaungefull world againe,
　Till thither they returne, where first they grew:
So like a wheele around they runne from old to new.

Ne needs there Gardiner to set, or sow,
　To plant or prune: for of their owne accord
　All things, as they created were, doe grow,
　And yet remember well the mightie word,
　Which first was spoken by th'Almightie lord,
　That bad them to increase and multiply:
　Ne doe they need with water of the ford,
　Or of the clouds to moysten their roots dry;
For in themselues eternall moisture they imply.

moten] must　　　　*Genius*] god of generation　　　　imply] contain

Infinite shapes of creatures there are bred,
  And vncouth formes, which none yet euer knew,
  And euery sort is in a sundry bed
  Set by it selfe, and ranckt in comely rew:
  Some fit for reasonable soules t'indew,
  Some made for beasts, some made for birds to weare,
  And all the fruitfull spawne of fishes hew
  In endlesse rancks along enraunged were,
That seem'd the *Ocean* could not containe them there.

Daily they grow, and daily forth are sent
  Into the world, it to replenish more;
  Yet is the stocke not lessened, nor spent,
  But still remaines in euerlasting store,
  As it at first created was of yore.
  For in the wide wombe of the world there lyes,
  In hatefull darkenesse and in deepe horrore,
  An huge eternall *Chaos*, which supplyes
The substances of natures fruitfull progenyes.

All things from thence doe their first being fetch,
  And borrow matter, whereof they are made,
  Which when as forme and feature it does ketch,
  Becomes a bodie, and doth then inuade
  The state of life, out of the griesly shade.
  That substance is eterne, and bideth so,
  Ne when the life decayes, and forme does fade,
  Doth it consume, and into nothing go,
But chaunged is, and often altred to and fro.

The substance is not chaunged, nor altered,
  But th'only forme and outward fashion;
  For euery substance is conditioned
  To change her hew, and sundry formes to don,
  Meet for her temper and complexion:
  For formes are variable and decay,
  By course of kind, and by occasion;
  And that faire flowre of beautie fades away,
As doth the lilly fresh before the sunny ray.

rew] row

Great enimy to it, and to all the rest,
 That in the *Gardin* of *Adonis* springs,
 Is wicked *Time*, who with his scyth addrest,
 Does mow the flowring herbes and goodly things,
 And all their glory to the ground downe flings,
 Where they doe wither, and are fowly mard:
 He flyes about, and with his flaggy wings
 Beates down both leaues and buds without regard,
Ne euer pittie may relent his malice hard.

Yet pittie often did the gods relent,
 To see so faire things mard, and spoyled quight:
 And their great mother *Venus* did lament
 The losse of her deare brood, her deare delight;
 Her hart was pierst with pittie at the sight,
 When walking through the Gardin, them she spyde,
 Yet no'te she find redresse for such despight.
 For all that liues, is subiect to that law:
All things decay in time, and to their end do draw.

But were it not, that *Time* their troubler is,
 All that in this delightfull Gardin growes,
 Should happie be, and haue immortall blis:
 For here all plentie, and all pleasure flowes,
 And sweet loue gentle fits emongst them throwes,
 Without fell rancor, or fond gealosie;
 Franckly each paramour his leman knowes,
 Each bird his mate, ne any does enuie
Their goodly meriment, and gay felicitie.

There is continuall spring, and haruest there
 Continuall, both meeting at one time:
 For both the boughes doe laughing blossomes beare,
 And with fresh colours decke the wanton Prime,
 And eke attonce the heauy trees they clime,
 Which seeme to labour vnder their fruits lode:
 The whiles the ioyous birdes make their pastime
 Emongst the shadie leaues, their sweet abode,
And their true loues without suspition tell abrode.

fowly mard] folly marred flaggy] drooping no'te] could not leman]
lover   attonce] together

Right in the middest of that Paradise,
   There stood a stately Mount, on whose round top
   A gloomy groue of mirtle trees did rise,
   Whose shadie boughes sharpe steele did neuer lop,
   Nor wicked beasts their tender buds did crop,
   But like a girlond compassed the hight,
   And from their fruitfull sides sweet gum did drop,
   That all the ground with precious deaw bedight,
Threw forth most dainty odours, & most sweet delight.

And in the thickest couert of that shade,
   There was a pleasant arbour, not by art,
   But of the trees owne inclination made,
   Which knitting their rancke braunches part to part,
   With wanton yuie twyne entrayld athwart,
   And Eglantine, and Caprifole emong,
   Fashiond aboue within their inmost part,
   That nether *Phœbus* beams could through them throng,
Nor *Aeolus* sharp blast could worke them any wrong.

And all about grew euery sort of flowre,
   To which sad louers were transformd of yore;
   Fresh *Hyacinthus*, *Phœbus* paramoure,
   Foolish *Narcisse*, that likes the watry shore,
   Sad *Amaranthus*, made a flowre but late,
   Sad *Amaranthus*, in whose purple gore
   Me seemes I see *Amintas* wretched fate,
To whom sweet Poets verse hath giuen endlesse date.

There wont faire *Venus* often to enioy
   Her deare *Adonis* ioyous company,
   And reape sweet pleasure of the wanton boy;
   There yet, some say, in secret he does ly,
   Lapped in flowres and pretious spycery,
   By her hid from the world, and from the skill
   Of *Stygian* Gods, which doe her loue enuy;
   But she her selfe, when euer that she will,
Possesseth him, and of his sweetnesse takes her fill.

(1590)

rancke] thick, dense   Caprifole] honeysuckle, woodbine   *Aeolus*] god of winds

Henry Constable
1562–1613

18   *Of his Mistress, upon Occasion of her Walking in a*
Garden

My lady's presence makes the roses red,
Because to see her lips they blush for shame:
The lily's leaves, for envy, pale became,
And her white hands in them this envy bred.
The marigold abroad her leaves doth spread,
Because the sun's and her power is the same;
The violet of purple colour came,
Dyed with the blood she made my heart to shed.
In brief, all flowers from her their virtue take:
From her sweet breath their sweet smells do proceed,
The living heat which her eye-beams do make
Warmeth the ground, and quickeneth the seed.
The rain wherewith she watereth these flowers
Falls from mine eyes, which she dissolves in showers.

(1594)

Josuah Sylvester
1563–1618

from *Du Bartas his Divine Weeks and Works*

19   *[Description of the beauties of the Garden of Eden]*

Thus, yet in league with heaven and earth he lives,
Enjoying all the goods the Almighty gives;
And yet not treading Sin's false mazy measures,
Sails on smooth surges of a sea of pleasures.
   Here underneath a fragrant hedge reposes,
Full of all kinds of sweet all-coloured roses,
Which (one would think) the angels daily dress
In true love-knots, triangles, lozenges.
   Anon he walketh in a level lane,
On either side beset with shady plane,
Whose archéd boughs, for freize and cornice bear
Thick groves, to shield from future change of air;

26

Then in a path impaled, in pleasant wise,
With sharp-sweet orange, lemon, citron trees,
Whose leafy twigs, that intricately tangle,
Seem painted walls whereon true fruits do dangle.

Now in a plenteous orchard planted rare
With un-graft trees, in checker round and square,
Whose goodly fruits so on his will do wait,
That plucking one, another's ready straight;
And having tasted all (with due satiety)
Finds all one goodness, but in taste variety.

Anon he stalketh with an easy stride,
By some clear river's lily-pavéd side,
Whose sand's pure gold, whose pebbles precious gems,
And liquid silver all the curling streams;
Whose chiding murmur, mazing in and out,
With crystal cisterns, moats a mead about.

And the artless bridges, over-thwart this torrent,
Are rocks self-archéd by the eating current;
Or loving palms, whose lusty females willing
Their marrow-boiling loves to be fulfilling,
(And reach their husband-trees on the other banks)
Bow their stiff backs, and serve the passing-planks.

Then in a goodly garden's alleys smooth,
Where prodig' Nature sets abroad her booth
Of richest beauties, where each bed and border
Is like pied posies divers dyes and order.

Now, far from noise, he creepeth covertly
Into a cave of kindly porphyry,
Which, rock-fall'n spouts, congealed by colder air,
Seem with smooth antics to have sealed fair:
There laid at ease, a cubit from the ground,
Upon a jasper fringed with ivy round,
Purfled with veins, thick thrummed with mossy beaver,
He falls asleep fast by a silent river;
Whose captive streams, through crooked pipes still rushing,
Makes sweeter music with their gentle gushing
Than now at Tivoli: the hydrantic brawl
Of rich Ferrara's stately cardinal;
Or Ctesibe's rare engines, framed there
Whereas they made of Ibis, Jupiter.

impaled] hedged in   antics] decorative grotesqueries (as in a grotto)   Purfled]
with a decorative border   thrummed] edged, trimmed   hydrantic] of waterworks
(with pun, perhaps, on water antics)   Ferrara's . . . cardinal] Ippolito d'Este, Cardinal of
Ferrara, whose gardens at the Villa D'Este, Tivoli, were famed for their waterworks
Ctesibe] Ctesibius, Alexandrian inventor (*fl.* 250 BC)

Musing, anon through crooked walks he wanders,
Round-winding rings, and intricate meanders,
False guiding paths, doubtful beguiling strays,
And right-wrong errors of an endless maze:
Not simply hedgèd with a single border
Of rosemary, cut-out with curious order,
In satyrs, centaurs, whales and half-men-horses,
And thousand other counterfeited corses;
But with true beasts, fast in the ground still sticking,
Feeding on grass, and the airy moisture licking:
Such as those Bonarets, in Scythia bred
Of slender seeds, and with green fodder fed;
Although their bodies, noses, mouths and eyes,
Of new-weaned lambs have full the form and guise,
And should be very lambs save that (for foot)
Within the ground they fix a living root,
Which at their navel grows and dies that day
That they have browsed the neighbour-grass away.
  O wondrous virtue of God only good!
The beast hath root, the plant hath flesh and blood:
The nimble plant can turn to and fro,
The numbèd beast can neither stir nor go;
The plant is leafless, branchless, void of fruit,
The beast is lustless, sexless, sireless, mute;
The plant with plants his hungry paunch doth feed,
The admired beast is sown a slender seed.
  Then up and down a forest thick he passeth,
Which selfly opening in his presence, 'baseth
Her trembling tresses never-vading spring,
For humble homage to her mighty king:
Where thousand trees, waving with gentle puffs
Their plumy tops, sweep the celestial roofs;
Yet envying all the massy Cerbas' fame,
Sith fifty passes can but clasp the same.

(1598)

Bonarets] corruption of baromertz, a fabulous plant also called the Scythian Lamb
Cerbas] tree of huge circumference reported in West Indies   Sith] since

20 *The Garden*

THE world's a garden; pleasures are the flowers,
 Of fairest hues, in form and number many:
 The lily, first, pure-whitest flower of any,
Rose sweetest rare, with pinkèd gilliflowers,
The violet, and double marigold,
 And pansy too: but after all mischances,
Death's winter comes and kills with sudden cold
 Rose, lily, violet, marigold, pink, pansies.

         (1621)

William Shakespeare
1564–1616

21   from *Richard II, III. iv.*

Gardener. Go, bind thou up young dangling apricots,
 Which like unruly children make their sire
 Stoop with oppression of their prodigal weight;
 Give some supportance to the bending twigs.
 Go thou, and like an executioner
 Cut off the heads of too fast growing sprays
 That look too lofty in our commonwealth:
 All must be even in our government.
 You thus employed, I will go root away
 The noisome weeds which without profit suck
 The soil's fertility from wholesome flowers.

Man. Why should we, in the compass of a pale,
 Keep law and form and due proportion,
 Showing, as in a model, our firm estate,
 When our sea-wallèd garden, the whole land,
 Is full of weeds, her fairest flowers choked up,
 Her fruit trees all unpruned, her hedges ruined,
 Her knots disordered, and her wholesome herbs
 Swarming with caterpillars?

21 pale] fenced enclosure   knots] garden planted in the form of a knot, a figure of
continuous interlacing bands

Gardener. Hold thy peace.
He that hath suffered this disordered spring
Hath now himself met with the fall of leaf:
The weeds which his broad spreading leaves did shelter,
That seemed in eating him to hold him up,
Are plucked up root and all by Bolingbroke—
I mean the Earl of Wiltshire, Bushy, Green.

Man. What, are they dead?

Gardener. They are; and Bolingbroke
Hath seized the wasteful King. O, what pity is it
That he had not so trimmed and dressed his land
As we this garden! We at time of year
Do wound the bark, the skin of our fruit trees,
Lest being overproud in sap and blood
With too much riches it confound itself;
Had he done so to great and growing men,
They might have lived to bear, and he to taste
Their fruits of duty. Superfluous branches
We lop away, that bearing boughs may live:
Had he done so, himself had borne the crown,
Which waste of idle hours hath quite thrown down.

(1597)

Aemilia Lanyer
?1569–1645

22   from *The Description of Cookham*

YET you (great lady) mistress of that place,
From whose desires did spring this work of grace;
Vouchsafe to think upon those pleasures past,
As fleeting worldly joys that could not last;
Or, as dim shadows of celestial pleasures,
Which are desired above all earthly treasures,
Oh how (me thought) against you thither came,
Each part did seem some new delight to frame!
The house received all ornaments to grace it,
And would endure no foulness to deface it.

dressed] tended
22 against] in preparation for

The walks put on their summer liveries,
And all things else did hold like similies:
The trees with leaves, with fruits, with flowers clad,
Embraced each other, seeming to be glad,
Turning themselves to beauteous canopies,
To shade the bright sun from your brighter eyes;
The crystal streams with silver spangles graced,
While by the glorious sun they were embraced;
The little birds in chirping notes did sing,
To entertain both you and that sweet spring.
And Philomela with her sundry lays,
Both you and that delightful place did praise.
Oh how me thought each plant, each flower, each tree
Set forth their beauties then to welcome thee!
The very hills right humbly did descend,
When you to tread upon them did intend.
And as you set your feet, they still did rise,
Glad that they could receive so rich a prize.
The gentle winds did take delight to be
Among those woods that were so graced by thee,
And in sad murmur uttered pleasing sound,
That pleasure in that place might more abound:
The swelling banks delivered all their pride
When such a phoenix once they had espied.
Each arbour, bank, each seat, each stately tree,
Thought themselves honoured in supporting thee.
The pretty birds would oft come to attend thee,
Yet flee away for fear they should offend thee;
The little creatures in the burrow by
Would come abroad to sport them in your eye,
Yet fearful of the bow in your fair hand
Would run away when you did make a stand.
Now let me come unto that stately tree,
Wherein such goodly prospects you did see;
That oak that did in height his fellows pass,
As much as lofty trees, low growing grass:
Much like a comely cedar straight and tall,
Whose beauteous stature far exceeded all.
How often did you visit this fair tree,
Which seeming joyful in receiving thee,
Would like a palm tree spread his arms abroad,
Desirous that you there should make abode;
Whose fair green leaves much like a comely veil,
Defended Phoebus when he would assail;

Whose pleasing boughs did yield a cool fresh air,
Joying his happiness when you were there.
Where being seated, you might plainly see
Hills, vales, and woods, as if on bended knee
They had appeared, your honour to salute,
Or to prefer some strange unlooked for suit;
All interlaced with brooks and crystal springs,
A prospect fit to please the eyes of kings;
And thirteen shires appeared all in your sight,
Europe could not afford much more delight.
What was there then but gave you all content,
While you the time in meditation spent,
Of their Creator's power, which there you saw
In all His creatures held a perfect law.

(1611)

John Donne
1572–1631

23   *Twicknam Garden*

BLASTED with sighs, and surrounded with tears,
    Hither I come to seek the spring,
    And at mine eyes, and at mine ears,
Receive such balms, as else cure everything;
    But O, self traitor, I do bring
The spider love, which transubstantiates all,
    And can convert manna to gall,
And that this place may thoroughly be thought
    True paradise, I have the serpent brought.

'Twere wholesomer for me, that winter did
    Benight the glory of this place,
    And that a grave frost did forbid
These trees to laugh, and mock me to my face;
    But that I may not this disgrace
Endure, nor yet leave loving, Love, let me
    Some senseless piece of this place be;
Make me a mandrake, so I may groan here,
    Or a stone fountain weeping out my year.

prefer] submit
23 Blasted] withered or shrivelled (by a disease-bearing wind)

Hither with crystal vials, lovers come,
   And take my tears, which are love's wine,
And try your mistress' tears at home,
For all are false, that taste not just like mine;
   Alas, hearts do not in eyes shine,
Nor can you more judge woman's thoughts by tears,
   Than by her shadow, what she wears.
O perverse sex, where none is true but she,
   Who's therefore true, because her truth kills me.

                  (wr. ?1607–8 pub. 1633)

Richard Barnfield
1574–1627

24   **from *The Affectionate Shepherd***

OR if thou dar'st to climb the highest trees
For apples, cherries, medlars, pears, or plums,
Nuts, walnuts, filberts, chestnuts, services,
The hoary peach, when snowy winter comes;
   I have fine orchards full of mellowed fruit,
   Which I will give thee to obtain my suit.

Not proud Alcinous himself can vaunt
Of goodlier orchards, or of braver trees
Than I have planted; yet thou will not grant
My simple suit, but like the honey bees
   Thou sucks the flower till all the sweet be gone,
   And lov'st me for my coin till I have none.

Leave Gwendolyn (sweet-heart) though she be fair
Yet she is light; not light in virtue shining,
But light in her behaviour, to impair
Her honour in her chastities declining;
   Trust not her tears, for they can wantonize,
   When tears in pearl are trickling from her eyes.

24 services] fruit of the service or sorb tree   Alcinous] king of the Phaeacians with a famous garden in Homer's *Odyssey* (see no. 49)

If thou will come and dwell with me at home,
My sheep-cote shall be strewed with new green rushes;
We'll hunt the trembling prickets as they roam
About the fields, along the hawthorn bushes.
    I have a piebald curre to hunt the hare:
    So we will live with dainty forest fare.

Nay more than this, I have a garden plot,
Wherein there wants nor herbs, nor roots, nor flowers
(Flowers to smell, roots to eat, herbs for the pot),
And dainty shelters when the welkin lours;
    Sweet smelling beds of lilies and of roses,
    Which rosemary banks and lavender encloses.

There grows the gilliflower, the mint, the daisy
(Both red and white), the blue-veined violet,
The purple hyacinth, the spike to please thee,
The scarlet-dyed carnation bleeding yet;
    The sage, the savory, and sweet marjoram,
    Hyssop, thyme, and eye-bright, good for the blind and dumb.

The pink, the primrose, cowslip, and daffodilly,
The hare-bell blue, the crimson columbine,
Sage, lettuce, parsley, and the milk-white lily,
The rose, and speckled flower called sops-in-wine;
    Fine pretty king-cups, and the yellow boots
    That grows by rivers, and by shallow brooks.

And many thousand more (I cannot name)
Of herbs and flowers that in gardens grow,
I have for thee; and conies that be tame,
Young rabbits, white as swan, and black as crow,
    Some speckled here and there with dainty spots;
    And more I have two mylch and milk-white goats.

All these, and more, I'll give thee for thy love,
If these, and more, may 'tice thy love away:
I have a pigeon-house, in it a dove,
Which I love more than mortal tongue can say;
    And last of all, I'll give thee a little lamb
    To play withall, new weaned from her dam.

(1594)

prickets] young bucks   curre] dog   welkin] sky   spike] spikenard
boots] marsh marigold   mylch] milk-giving

George Herbert
1593–1633

The Flower

How fresh, O Lord, how sweet and clean
Are thy returns! ev'n as the flowers in spring;
To which, besides their own demean,
The late-past frosts tributes of pleasure bring.
    Grief melts away
    Like snow in May,
As if there were no such cold thing.

Who would have thought my shrivelled heart
Could have recovered greennesse? It was gone
Quite under ground; as flowers depart
To see their mother-root, when they have blown;
    Where they together
    All the hard weather,
Dead to the world, keep house unknown.

These are thy wonders, Lord of power,
Killing and quickning, bringing down to hell
And up to heaven in an hour;
Making a chiming of a passing-bell.
    We say amiss,
    This or that is:
Thy word is all, if we could spell.

O that I once past changing were,
Fast in thy Paradise, where no flower can wither!
Many a spring I shoot up fair,
Offring at heav'n, growing and groaning thither:
    Nor doth my flower
    Want a spring-shower,
My sins and I joining together.

But while I grow in a straight line,
Still upwards bent, as if heav'n were mine own,
Thy anger comes, and I decline:
What frost to that? what pole is not the zone,

demean] bearing or demeanour, punning perhaps on estate or demesne   offring]
aiming at

Where all things burn,
When thou dost turn,
And the least frown of thine is shown?

And now in age I bud again,
After so many deaths I live and write;
I once more smell the dew and rain,
And relish versing: O my only light,
It cannot be
That I am he
On whom thy tempests fell all night.

These are thy wonders, Lord of love,
To make us see we are but flowers that glide:
Which when we once can find and prove,
Thou hast a garden for us, where to bide.
Who would be more,
Swelling through store,
Forfeit their Paradise by their pride.

(1633)

Thomas Randolph
1603–1635

26   *On a Maid of Honour Seen by a Scholar in Somerset Garden*

As once in black I disrespected walked,
Where glittering courtiers in their tissues stalked,
I cast by chance my melancholy eye
Upon a woman (as I thought) passed by.
But when I viewed her muff, and beaver reared
As if Priapus-like she would have feared
The ravenous Harpies from the clustered grape,
Then I began much to mistrust her shape;
When viewing curiously, away she slipped,
And in a fount her whited hand she dipped,

26 beaver] kind of fur hat   Priapus] Roman god of gardens and fertility (phallic
statues were placed in gardens to frighten away birds or thieves)   feared] scared or
frightened away

The angry water as if wronged thereby,
Ran murmuring thence a second touch to fly,
At which away she stalks, and as she goes
She views the situation of each rose;
And having higher raised her gown, she gazed
Upon her crimson stocking which, amazed,
Blushed at her open impudence, and sent
Reflection to her cheek, for punishment.
As thus I stood the gardener chanced to pass,
'My friend' (quoth I) 'what is this stately lass?'
'A maid of honour, Sir,' said he, and goes
Leaving a riddle, was enough to pose
The crafty Oedipus, for I could see
Nor maid, nor honour, sure no honesty.

(1638)

James Shirley
1596–1666

27   *The Garden*

THIS garden does not take my eyes,
Though here you show how art of men
Can purchase nature at a price
Would stock old paradise again.

These glories while you dote upon,
I envy not your spring nor pride,
Nay boast the summer all your own,
My thoughts with less are satisfied.

Give me a little plot of ground,
Where might I with the sun agree,
Though every day he walk the round,
My garden he should seldom see.

Those tulips that such wealth display,
To court my eye, shall lose their name,
Though now they listen, as if they
Expected I should praise their flame.

But I would see my self appear
Within the violet's drooping head,
On which a melancholy tear
The discontented morn hath shed.

Within their buds let roses sleep,
And virgin lilies on their stem,
Till sighs from lovers glide, and creep
Into their leaves to open them.

I'the centre of my ground compose
Of bays and yew my summer room,
Which may so oft as I repose,
Present my arbour, and my tomb.

No woman here shall find me out,
Or if a chance do bring one hither,
I'll be secure, for round about
I'll moat it with my eyes' foul weather.

No bird shall live within my pale,
To charm me with their shames of art,
Unless some wandering nightingale
Come here to sing, and break her heart.

Upon whose death I'll try to write
An epitaph in some funeral stone,
So sad, and true, it may invite
My self to die, and prove my own.

(1646)

Mildmay Fane, Earl of Westmorland
1602–1666

28   *To Sir John Wentworth, Upon his Curiosities and Courteous Entertainment at Summerly in Lovingland*

WHEN thou the choice of Nature's wealth hast scanned,
And brought it to compare with Lovingland;
Know that thou may'st as well make wonder less,
By fancying of two timbering phoenixes
At the same time, and dream two suns to rise
At once, to cast fire 'midst those spiceries:
   (Pregnant she is) yet that must not deny
   The purest gold to come from Barbary,
   Diamonds and pearl from th'Indies, to confer
   On every clime some thing peculiar,
   (For so she hath:) And like a sum to all
   That curious is, seems here most liberal,
   Affording in epitome at least,
   What e'er the world can boast of, or call best.
Now as contracted virtue doth excell
In power and force, this seems a miracle,
Wherein all travellers may truly say,
They never saw so much in little way;
And thence conclude their folly, that did steer
To seek for that abroad, at home was near
In more perfection: Wouldst thou Phoebe meet,
Apollo, or the Muses? not in Crete
And Greece, but here, at Summerly, those are
Removed to dwell, under a patron's care,
Who can as much civility express,
As Candie lies, or Grecia barbarousness:
Wouldst thou be sheltered under Daphne's groves,
Or choose to live in Tempe, or make loves
To any place where shepherds wont to lie
Upon the hills, piping security
Unto their flocks? here the sweet park contains
More evenness than the Arcadian plains:
Nor yet enchanted by those shadowed rings,
Some say the fairies print with revellings,

---

timbering] building (the phoenix burnt itself to death in a nest it had built)
Candie] Candia, i.e. Crete   Tempe] plain at the foot of Mount Olympus

But's all in one dye clad, and doth appear
Like the spring's favourite throughout the year.
The useful ash, and sturdy oak are set
At distance, and obey; the brambles met
Embracing twine int'arbours, to conceal
And harbour such as stock this common-weal;
Until their master please they should delight
His, or his friends' desire and appetite:
All tales of satyrs banished are from hence,
And fabled goblins that delude the fence;
'Tis real ven'son and abroad, in paste
Alike may satisfy both eye and taste,
The nobler plants, as fir deal, and the pine
Weeping out rezin, bleeding turpentine,
Like the life-guard, upon the hall attend
At nearer distance; where the gods descend
To keep their courts, and either globe's devised,
To grasp the elements epitomized.
   The sun-beams' steady fire, with the air
   Of the inconstant winds indialled are:
   So whilst the one, the hour doth infer,
   The other points a rule for the mariner:
   Earth here's embroidered into walks, some straight,
   Others like serpents are, or worms to bait
   Occasion's hook till every humour come,
   And feed here fat as in Elysium.
   Nor is there water wanting in this wood,
   Clear as if running, calm as if it stood,
   And so contrived by Nature's helper Art,
   There's no appearance from the whole or part,
   That any sullen sluice to malice bent
   Can open to impair that element;
   Nor yet th'ambition of a spring's o'er-flow,
   Cause it t'exceed, or limits overthrow.
Thus like a gold chain linked, or bracelet strung,
From carcanet pleasures on pleasures hung,
And such delightful objects did descry
Pursuing of each other, that the eye
Astonished at such wonder, did crave rest,
For fear of forfeiting its interest
In so great bliss, for over-dazzled it grew,
And dim of sight made by each object new.

carcanet] necklace with pendant jewels

So there's a parley granted, and some space
To gather strength 'twixt this and t'other place,
But very short, not half a mile at most.
We landed were again, and made a coast;
Where if all ancient poets were to write,
They'd need no other fountain to indite
Story of all kinds with, but dip their pen,
Then swear the Muses more than nine, were ten;
For here dwelt one whose magic could infuse
A fluency beyond all other Muse,
And court the soil, with so much art applied,
That all the world seems barbarous beside.
    Here fish and fowl inhabit with such state,
    As lords and ladies wont when served in plate,
    Rich arras, or the like, bill, breed, and swim
    In all delightful solace to the brim.
Decoyed by so much rapture, on we pass
Unto a castle that enchanted was
By the magic spell of music; till there set
We found a cod like to Euterpe's net,
To catch all passengers: the Lesbian lute,
O'ercome in harmony became there mute;
Whilst as for table to the song-books served
The crystal fountain: so have I observed,
When walking near a stream, the heavens to be
Beneath my feet, to ease astronomy;
There tell the gamut of the stars, and crack
Of all their motions even with Tycho Brahe.
    The fablers of old, I guess, might find
    Some objects t'help invention, but the mind
    Was sure prophetic, for whatever is
    Described for rare by them, t'was meant by this.
And yet this falls short too, when he whom
The cost and care owes tributes, there to sum
Up all with such humanity, and press
Of crowded favours, and heaped courtesies,
    As friendship were a jeweller the while,
    His welcome seemed the diamond, those the soil.

                       (1648)

cod] bag at end of a trawl-net   Euterpe] the muse of music   gamut] scale
Tycho Brahe] Danish nobleman, *virtuoso*, astrologer, amateur architect, and garden designer
(1546–1601)

Edmund Waller
1606–1687

At Penshurst

HAD Dorothea lived when mortals made
Choice of their deities, this sacred shade
Had held an altar to her power, that gave
The peace, and glory, which these alleys have:
Embroidered so with flowers where she stood,
That it became a garden of a wood.
Her presence has such more than human grace,
That it can civilize the rudest place:
And beauty too, and order can impart,
Where nature ne'er intended it, nor art.
The plants acknowledge this, and her admire,
No less than those of old did Orpheus' lyre:
If she sit down, with tops all towards her bowed,
They round about her into arbours crowd:
Or if she walk, in even ranks they stand,
Like some well marshalled and obsequious band.
Amphion so made stones and timber leap
Into fair figures, from a confused heap:
And in the symmetry of her parts is found
A power like that of harmony in sound.
    Ye lofty beeches, tell this matchless dame,
That if together ye fed all one flame,
It could not equalise the hundredth part,
Of what her eyes have kindled in my heart!—
Go, boy, and carve this passion on the bark
Of yonder tree; which stands the sacred mark
Of noble Sidney's birth; when such benign,
Such more than mortal-making stars did shine;
That there they cannot but forever prove
The monument, and pledge, of humble love;
His humble love, whose hope shall never rise higher,
Than for a pardon that he dares admire.

(1645)

Amphion] harper whose music made the stone of Thebes's city-walls fall into place
Sidney] the poet Sir Philip Sidney (1554–86) whose family home was Penshurst

30   from *On St James's Park, as Lately Improved by His
Majesty*

OF the first Paradise there's nothing found;
Plants set by Heaven are vanished, and the ground;
Yet the description lasts; who knows the fate
Of lines that shall this paradise relate?
    Instead of rivers rolling by the side
Of Eden's garden, here flows in the tide;
The sea, which always served his empire, now
Pays tribute to our Prince's pleasure too.
Of famous cities we the founders know;
But rivers, old as seas, to which they go,
Are nature's bounty; 'tis of more renown
To make a river, than to build a town.
    For future shade, young trees upon the banks
Of the new stream appear in even ranks;
The voice of Orpheus, or Amphion's hand,
In better order could not make them stand;
May they increase as fast, and spread their boughs,
As the high fame of their great owner grows!
May he live long enough to see them all
Dark shadows cast, and as his palace tall!
Methinks I see the love that shall be made,
The lovers walking in that amorous shade;
The gallants dancing by the river's side;
They bathe in summer, and in winter slide.
Methinks I hear the music in the boats,
And the loud echo which returns the notes;
While overhead a flock of new-sprung fowl
Hangs in the air, and does the sun control,
Darkening the sky; they hover o'er, and shroud
The wanton sailors with a feathered cloud.
Beneath, a shoal of silver fishes glides,
And plays about the gilded barges' sides;
The ladies, angling in the crystal lake,
Feast on the waters with the prey they take;
At once victorious with their lines, and eyes,
They make the fishes, and the men, their prize.
A thousand Cupids on the billows ride,
And sea-nymphs enter with the swelling tide;
From Thetis sent as spies, to make report,
And tell the wonders of her sovereign's court.

Orpheus] his singing was said to move trees and rocks   Amphion] see note to
previous poem   Thetis] mythological sea nymph, mother of Achilles

All that can, living, feed the greedy eye,
Or dead, the palate, here you may descry;
The choicest things that furnished Noah's ark,
Or Peter's sheet, inhabiting this park;
All with a border of rich fruit-trees crowned,
Whose loaded branches hide the lofty mound.
Such various ways the spacious alleys lead,
My doubtful Muse knows not what path to tread.
Yonder, the harvest of cold months laid up,
Gives a fresh coolness to the royal cup;
There ice, like crystal firm, and never lost,
Tempers hot July with December's frost;
Winter's dark prison, whence he cannot fly
Though the warm spring, his enemy, draws nigh.
Strange! that extremes should thus preserve the snow,
High on the Alps, or in deep caves below.

Here, a well-polished mall gives us the joy
To see our Prince his matchless force employ;
His manly posture, and his graceful mien,
Vigour and youth, in all his motions seen;
His shape so lovely, and his limbs so strong,
Confirm our hopes we shall obey him long.
No sooner has he touched the flying ball,
But 'tis already more than half the mall;
And such a fury from his arm has got,
As from a smoking culverin 'twere shot.

Near this my Muse, what most delights her, sees
A living gallery of aged trees;
Bold sons of earth, that thrust their arms so high,
As if once more they would invade the sky.
In such green palaces the first kings reigned,
Slept in their shades, and angels entertained;
With such old counsellors they did advise,
And, by frequenting sacred groves, grew wise.
Free from the impediments of light and noise,
Man, thus retired, his nobler thoughts employs.

(1661; text of 1664)

Peter's sheet] see Acts 10: 9–17   mall] alley in which the game 'pall-mell' was played
culverin] a kind of hand-gun

John Milton
1608–1674

from *Paradise Lost*

31

[*Satan's first view of the Garden of Eden*]

BENEATH him with new wonder now he views
To all delight of human sense exposed
In narrow room nature's whole wealth, yea more,
A heaven on earth, for blissful Paradise
Of God the garden was, by him in the east
Of Eden planted; Eden stretched her line
From Auran eastward to the royal towers
Of great Seleucia, built by Grecian kings,
Or where the sons of Eden long before
Dwelt in Telassar: in this pleasant soil
His far more pleasant garden God ordained;
Out of the fertile ground he caused to grow
All trees of noblest kind for sight, smell, taste;
And all amid them stood the tree of life,
High eminent, blooming ambrosial fruit
Of vegetable gold; and next to life
Our death the tree of knowledge grew fast by,
Knowledge of good bought dear by knowing ill.
Southward through Eden went a river large,
Nor changed his course, but through the shaggy hill
Passed underneath ingulfed, for God had thrown
That mountain as his garden mould high raised
Upon the rapid current, which through veins
Of porous earth with kindly thirst up drawn,
Rose a fresh fountain, and with many a rill
Watered the garden; thence united fell
Down the steep glade, and met the nether flood,
Which from his darksome passage now appears,
And now divided into four main streams,
Runs diverse, wandering many a famous realm
And country whereof here needs no account,
But rather to tell how, if art could tell,
How from that sapphire fount the crispèd brooks,
Rolling on orient pearl and sands of gold,
With mazy error under pendant shades
Ran nectar, visiting each plant, and fed

JOHN MILTON

Flowers worthy of Paradise which not nice art
In beds and curious knots, but nature boon
Poured forth profuse on hill and dale and plain,
Both where the morning sun first warmly smote
The open field, and where the unpierced shade
Embrowned the noontide bowers: thus was this place,
A happy rural seat of various view;
Groves whose rich trees wept odorous gums and balm,
Others whose fruit burnished with golden rind
Hung amiable, Hesperian fables true,
If true, here only, and of delicious taste:
Betwixt them lawns, or level downs, and flocks
Grazing the tender herb, were interposed,
Or palmy hillock, or the flowery lap
Of some irriguous valley spread her store,
Flowers of all hue, and without thorn the rose:
Another side, umbrageous grots and caves
Of cool recess, o'er which the mantling vine
Lays forth her purple grape, and gently creeps
Luxuriant; meanwhile murmuring waters fall
Down the slope hills, dispersed, or in a lake,
That to the fringèd bank with myrtle crowned,
Her crystal mirror holds, unite their streams.
The birds their choir apply; airs, vernal airs,
Breathing the smell of field and grove, attune
The trembling leaves, while universal Pan
Knit with the Graces and the Hours in dance
Led on the eternal spring.

32   *[Satan stalks Eve in the Garden before the Fall]*

Thus saying, from her husband's hand her hand
Soft she withdrew, and like a wood-nymph light
Oread or dryad, or of Delia's train,
Betook her to the groves, but Delia's self
In gait surpassed and goddess-like deport,
Though not as she with bow and quiver armed,
But with such gardening tools as art yet rude,
Guiltless of fire had formed, or angels brought.

Hesperian fables] fables about the legendary Gardens of the Hesperides
32 Delia] Greek goddess Artemis (cf. Roman Diana), reputedly born on Delos

46

To Pales, or Pomona thus adorned,
Likeliest she seemed, Pomona when she fled
Vertumnus, or to Ceres in her prime,
Yet virgin of Proserpina from Jove.
Her long with ardent look his eye pursued
Delighted, but desiring more her stay.
Oft he to her his charge of quick return
Repeated, she to him as oft engaged
To be returned by noon amid the bower,
And all things in best order to invite
Noontide repast, or afternoon's repose.
O much deceived, much failing, hapless Eve,
Of thy presumed return! Event perverse!
Thou never from that hour in Paradise
Found'st either sweet repast, or sound repose;
Such ambush hid among sweet flowers and shades
Waited with hellish rancour imminent
To intercept thy way, or send thee back
Despoiled of innocence, of faith, of bliss.
For now, and since first break of dawn the fiend,
Mere serpent in appearance, forth was come,
And on his quest, where likeliest he might find
The only two of mankind, but in them
The whole included race, his purposed prey.
In bower and field he sought, where any tuft
Of grove or garden-plot more pleasant lay,
Their tendance or plantation for delight,
By fountain or by shady rivulet
He sought them both, but wished his hap might find
Eve separate, he wished, but not with hope
Of what so seldom chanced, when to his wish,
Beyond his hope, Eve separate he spies,
Veiled in a cloud of fragrance, where she stood,
Half spied, so thick the roses bushing round
About her glowed, oft stooping to support
Each flower of slender stalk, whose head though gay
Carnation, purple, azure, or specked with gold,
Hung drooping unsustained, them she upstays
Gently with myrtle band, mindless the while,
Her self, though fairest unsupported flower,
From her best prop so far, and storm so nigh.
Nearer he drew, and many a walk traversed

Pales] Roman god of pastures and of flocks   Pomona] Roman goddess of fruits,
married to Vertumnus after first refusing him   Vertumnus] Roman god of fruits

Of stateliest covert, cedar, pine, or palm,
Then voluble and bold, now hid, now seen
Among thick-woven arborets and flowers
Embordered on each bank, the hand of Eve:
Spot more delicious than those gardens feigned
Or of revived Adonis, or renowned
Alcinous, host of old Laertes' son,
Or that, not mystic, where the sapient king
Held dalliance with his fair Egyptian spouse.
Much he the place admired, the person more.
As one who long in populous city pent,
Where houses thick and sewers annoy the air,
Forth issuing on a summer's morn to breathe
Among the pleasant villages and farms
Adjoined, from each thing met conceives delight,
The smell of grain, or tedded grass, or kine,
Or dairy, each rural sight, each rural sound;
If chance with nymph-like step fair virgin pass,
What pleasing seemed, for her now pleases more,
She most, and in her look sums all delight.

(1667)

Joseph Beaumont
1616–1699

33   *The Garden*

THE garden's quit with me: as yesterday
I walked in that, today that walks in me;
   Through all my memory
It sweetly wanders, and has found a way
   To make me honestly possess
     What still another's is.

Yet this gain's dainty sense doth gall my mind
With the remembrance of a bitter loss.
   Alas, how odd and cross
Are earth's delights, in which the soul can find
   No honey, but withal some sting
     To check the pleasing thing!

Alcinous] king of the Phaeacians in Homer's *Odyssey*, renowned for his gardens (see no. 49)
tedded] spread out to dry

48

For now I'm haunted with the thought of that
Heav'n-planted garden, where felicity
    Flourish'd on every tree.
Lost, lost it is; for at the guarded gate
  A flaming sword forbiddeth sin
    (That's I) to enter in.

O paradise! when I was turned out
Hadst thou but kept the serpent still within,
    My banishment had been
Less sad and dangerous: but round about
  This wide world runneth raging he
    To banish me from me:

I feel that through my soul he death hath shot;
And thou, alas, hast locked up life's tree.
    O miserable me,
What help were left, had Jesus's pity not
  Showed me another tree, which can
    Enliven dying man.

That tree, made fertile by his own dear blood;
And by his death with quick'ning virtue fraught.
    I now dread not the thought
Of barracado'd Eden, since as good
  A paradise I planted see
    On open Calvary.

                     (pub. 1914 from MS of 1645)

Abraham Cowley
1618–1667

34   *The Garden*

    HAPPY art thou, whom God does bless
  With the full choice of thine own happiness;
    And happier yet, because thou'rt blest
    With prudence, how to choose the best.

34 thou] the ode is addressed to John Evelyn (1620–1706), diarist and gardenist

In books and gardens thou hast placed aright
    (Things which thou well dost understand,
And both dost make with thy laborious hand)
    Thy noble, innocent delight,
And in thy virtuous wife, where thou again dost meet
    Both pleasures more refined and sweet,
    The fairest garden in her looks,
    And in her mind the wisest books.
Oh, who would change these soft, yet solid joys,
    For empty shows and senseless noise,
    And all which rank ambition breeds,
Which seem such beauteous flowers, and are such poisonous
    weeds?

When God did Man to His own likeness make,
As much as clay, though of the purest kind,
    By the great Potter's art refined,
    Could the divine impression take;
    He thought it fit to place him where
A kind of heaven too did appear,
As far as earth could such a likeness bear,
    That man no happiness might want,
Which earth to her first Master could afford;
    He did a garden for him plant
By the quick hand of His omnipotent word.
As the chief help and joy of human life,
He gave him the first gift; first, ev'n before a wife.

For God, the universal architect,
    'T had been as easy to erect
A Louvre or Escurial, or a tower
That might with Heaven communication hold,
As Babel vainly thought to do of old:
    He wanted not the skill or power,
    In the world's fabric those were shown,
    And the materials were all his own.
But well he knew what place would best agree
With innocence and with felicity:
And we elsewhere still seek for them in vain,
If any part of either yet remain;
If any part of either we expect,
This may our judgement in the search direct;
God the first garden made, and the first city, Cain.

Escurial] the Escorial palace near Madrid

Oh blessed shades! O gentle cool retreat
   From all the immoderate heat,
In which the frantic world does burn and sweat!
This does the Lion-Star, ambition's rage,
This avarice, the Dogstar's thirst assuage.
Everywhere else their fatal power we see,
They make and rule Man's wretched destiny:
   They neither set, nor disappear,
   But tyrannize o're all the year,
Whilst we ne're feel their flame or influence here.
   The birds that dance from bough to bough
   And sing above in every tree,
   Are not from fears and cares more free,
Than we who lie, or sit, or walk below,
   And should by right be singers too.
What prince's quire of music can excel
   That which within this shade does dwell
   To which we nothing pay or give?
   They like all other poets live
Without reward, or thanks, for their obliging pains;
   'Tis well if they become not prey.
The whistling winds add their less artful strains,
And a grave base the murmuring fountains play.
Nature does all this harmony bestow,
   But to our plants, arts, music too,
The pipe, theorbo, and guitar we owe;
   The lute itself, which once was green and mute,
   When Orpheus struck the inspired lute,
   The trees danced round, and understood
   By sympathy the voice of wood.

These are the spells that to kind sleep invite,
And nothing does within resistance make,
   Which yet we moderately take.
   Who would not choose to be awake,
While he's encompassed round with such delight,
To the ear, the nose, the touch, the taste and sight?
When Venus would her dear Ascanius keep
A prisoner in the downy bands of sleep,

Lion-Star] the constellation Leo   Dogstar] Sirius, which when in ascendancy was supposed to cause excess   theorbo] kind of lute   Ascanius] the son of Aeneas, but perhaps Cowley's mistake for Adonis whom Venus (according to Spenser, see no. 17) kept hidden in a garden

She odorous herbs and flowers beneath him spread
    As the most soft and sweetest bed;
Not her own lap would more have charmed his head.
Who, that has reason, and his smell,
Would not among roses and jasmine dwell,
    Rather than all his spirits choke
With exhalations of dirt and smoke?
    And all the uncleanness which does drown
In pestilential clouds a populous town?
The earth itself breathes better perfumes here,
Than all the female men or women there,
Not without cause, about them bear.

When Epicurus to the world had taught,
    That pleasure was the chiefest good,
(And was perhaps i'the right, if rightly understood)
    His life he to his doctrine brought,
And in a garden shade that sovereign pleasure sought:
Whoever a true epicure would be,
May there find cheap and virtuous luxury.
Vitellius his table, which did hold
As many creatures as the Ark of old;
That fiscal table, to which every day
All countries did a constant tribute pay,
Could nothing more delicious afford
    Than Nature's liberality,
Helped with a little art and industry,
Allows the meanest gardener's board.
The wanton taste no fish or fowl can choose,
For which the grape or melon she would lose,
Though all the inhabitants of sea and air
Be listed in the glutton's bill of fare;
    Yet still the fruits of earth we see
Placed the third storey high in all her luxury.

But with no sense the garden does comply,
None courts, or flatters, as it does the eye.
When the great Hebrew King did almost strain
The wondrous treasures of his wealth and brain,
His royal southern guest to entertain;
    Though she on silver floors did tread,
With bright Assyrian carpets on them spread,
    To hide the metal's poverty.

Vitellius] Roman emperor notorious for gluttony   great Hebrew king] Solomon,
entertaining the Queen of Sheba

Though she looked up to roofs of gold,
And nought around her could behold
But silk and rich embroidery,
And Babylonian tapestry,
And wealthy Hiram's princely dye;
Though Ophir's starry stones met everywhere her eye,
Though she herself, and her gay host were dressed
With all the shining glories of the east;
When lavish Art her costly work had done,
The honour and the prize of bravery
Was by the garden from the palace won;
And every rose and lily there did stand
Better attired by Nature's hand.
The case thus judged against the King we see,
By one that would not be so rich, though wiser far than he.

Nor does this happy place only dispense
Such various pleasures to the sense;
Here health itself does live,
That salt of life, which does to all a relish give,
Its standing pleasure, and intrinsic wealth,
The body's virtue, and the soul's good fortune health.
The Tree of Life, when it in Eden stood,
Did its immortal head to heaven rear,
It lasted a tall cedar till the Flood,
Now a small thorny shrub it does appear.
Nor will it thrive too everywhere,
It always here is freshest seen;
'Tis only here an evergreen.
If through the strong and beauteous fence
Of temperance and innocence,
And wholesome labours, and a quiet mind,
Any diseases passage find,
They must not think here to assail
A land unarmed, or without a guard;
They must fight for it, and dispute it hard,
Before they can prevail.
Scarce any plant is growing here
Which against Death some weapon does not bear.
Let cities boast that they provide,
For life, the ornaments of pride;
But 'tis the country and the field
That furnish it with staff and shield.

Where does the wisdom and the power divine
In a more bright and sweet reflection shine?
Where do we finer strokes and colours see
Of the Creator's real poetry,
    Than when we with attention look
Upon the third day's volume of the Book?
If we could open and intend our eye,
    We all like Moses should espy
Ev'n in a bush the radiant Deity.
But we despise these his inferior ways
(Though no less full of miracle and praise)
    Upon the flowers of heaven we gaze;
The stars of earth no wonder in us raise,
    Though these perhaps do more than they,
      The life of mankind sway.
Although no part of mighty Nature be
More stored with beauty, power, and mystery;
Yet to encourage human industry,
God has so ordered, that no other part
Such space, and such dominion leaves for Art.

We nowhere Art do so triumphant see,
    As when it grass or buds the tree.
In other things we count it to excel,
If it a docile scholar can appear
To Nature, and but imitate her well,
It over-rules, and is her master here.
It imitates her Maker's power divine,
And changes her sometimes, and sometimes does refine;
It does, like Grace, the fallen tree restore
To its blest state of Paradise before.
Who would not joy to see his conquering hand
Over all the vegetable world command,
And the wild giants of the wood receive
    What law he's pleased to give?
He bids the ill-natured crab produce
The gentler apples winey juice,
    The golden fruit that worthy is
    Of Galatea's purple kiss;
    He does the savage hawthorn teach
    To bear the medlar and the pear,
    He bids the rustic plum to rear
    A noble trunk, and be a peach.

Galatea] Greek sea nymph

Even Daphne's coyness he does mock,
And weds the cherry to her stock,
Though she refused Apollo's suit;
Even she, that chaste and virgin tree,
Now wonders at herself, to see
That she's a mother made, and blushes in her fruit.

Methinks I see great Diocletian walk
In the Salonian Garden's noble shade,
Which by his own imperial hands was made.
I see him smile (methinks) as he does talk
With the ambassadors, who come in vain,
    To entice him to a throne again.
If I, my friends (said he) should to you show
All the delights, which in these gardens grow,
'Tis likelier much, that you should with me stay,
Than 'tis that you should carry me away.
And trust me not, my friends, if every day
    I walk not here with more delight,
Than ever after the most happy fight,
In triumph, to the Capitol, I rode
To thank the gods, and to be thought myself almost a god.

(1667)

Andrew Marvell
1621–1678

35   *The Garden*

How vainly men themselves amaze
To win the palm, the oak, or bays,
And their uncessant labours see
Crowned from some single herb or tree,
Whose short and narrow vergèd shade
Does prudently their toils upbraid,
While all flowers and all trees do close
To weave the garlands of repose.

Diocletian] Roman emperor who spent the years after his abdication in 305 in his palace at
Salona

Fair Quiet, have I found thee here,
And Innocence, thy sister dear!
Mistaken long, I sought you then
In busy companies of men.
Your sacred plants, if here below,
Only among the plants will grow.
Society is all but rude,
To this delicious solitude.

No white nor red was ever seen
So am'rous as this lovely green.
Fond lovers, cruel as their flame,
Cut in these trees their mistress' name.
Little, alas, they know, or heed,
How far these beauties hers exceed!
Fair trees! wheres'e'er your barks I wound,
No name shall but your own be found.

When we have run our passion's heat,
Love hither makes his best retreat.
The gods, that mortal beauty chase,
Still in a tree did end their race.
Apollo hunted Daphne so,
Only that she might laurel grow.
And Pan did after Syrinx speed,
Not as a nymph, but for a reed.

What wondrous life is this I lead!
Ripe apples drop about my head;
The luscious clusters of the vine
Upon my mouth do crush their wine;
The nectarene, and curious peach,
Into my hands themselves do reach;
Stumbling on melons, as I pass,
Ensnared with flowers, I fall on grass.

Meanwhile the mind, from pleasures less,
Withdraws into its happiness:
The mind, that ocean where each kind
Does straight its own resemblance find,
Yet it creates, transcending these,
Far other worlds, and other seas,
Annihilating all that's made
To a green thought in a green shade.

Still] always

56

Here at the fountain's sliding foot,
Or at some fruit-tree's mossy root,
Casting the body's vest aside,
My soul into the boughs does glide:
There like a bird it sits, and sings,
Then whets, and combs its silver wings;
And, till prepared for longer flight,
Waves in its plumes the various light.

Such was that happy garden-state,
While man there walked without a mate:
After a place so pure, and sweet,
What other help could yet be meet!
But 'twas beyond a mortal's share
To wander solitary there:
Two paradises 'twere in one
To live in paradise alone.

How well the skilful gardener drew
Of flowers and herbs this dial new,
Where from above the milder sun
Does through a fragrant zodiac run;
And, as it works, the industrious bee
Computes its time as well as we.
How could such sweet and wholesome hours
Be reckoned but with herbs and flowers!

(1681)

36 *The Mower Against Gardens*

LUXURIOUS man, to bring his vice in use,
Did after him the world seduce,
And from the fields the flowers and plants allure,
Where nature was most plain and pure.
He first enclosed within the gardens square
A dead and standing pool of air,
And a more luscious earth for them did knead,
Which stupified them while it fed.
The pink grew then as double as his mind;
The nutriment did change the kind.

dial] some form of sundial, perhaps showing the time by the plants that were open at different hours

With strange perfumes he did the roses taint,
   And flowers themselves were taught to paint.
The tulip, white, did for complexion seek,
   And learned to interline its cheek:
Its onion root they then so high did hold,
   That one was for a meadow sold.
Another world was searched, through oceans new,
   To find the *Marvel of Peru.*
And yet these rarities might be allowed
   To man, that sovereign thing and proud,
Had he not dealt between the bark and tree,
   Forbidden mixtures there to see.
No plant now knew the stock from which it came;
   He grafts upon the wild the tame:
That th' uncertain and adulterate fruit
   Might put the palate in dispute.
His green seraglio has its eunuchs too,
   Lest any tyrant him outdo.
And in the cherry he does nature vex,
   To procreate without a sex.
'Tis all enforced, the fountain and the grot,
   While the sweet fields do lie forgot:
Where willing nature does to all dispense
   A wild and fragrant innocence:
And fauns and fairies do the meadows till,
   More by their presence than their skill.
Their statues, polished by some ancient hand,
   May to adorn the gardens stand:
But howsoe'er the figures do excel,
   The gods themselves with us do dwell.

                      (1681)

37   from *Upon Appleton House, to my Lord Fairfax*

FROM that blest bed the hero came,
Whom France and Poland yet does fame:
Who, when retirèd here to peace,
His warlike studies could not cease;
But laid these gardens out in sport
In the just figure of a fort;
And with five bastions it did fence,
As aiming one for every sense.

Marvel of Peru] a tropical American plant (*mirabilis jalapa*)

58

ANDREW MARVELL

When in the east the morning ray
Hangs out the colours of the day,
The bee through these known alleys hums,
Beating the *dian* with its drums.
Then flowers their drowsy eyelids raise,
Their silken ensigns each displays,
And dries its pan yet dank with dew,
And fills its flask with odours new.

These, as their Governor goes by,
In fragrant volleys they let fly;
And to salute their Governess
Again as great a charge they press:
None for the virgin Nymph; for she
Seems with the flowers a flower to be.
And think so still! though not compare
With breath so sweet, or cheek so fair.

Well shot, ye firemen! Oh how sweet,
And round your equal fires do meet,
Whose shrill report no ear can tell,
But echoes to the eye and smell.
See how the flowers, as at parade,
Under their colours stand displayed:
Each regiment in order grows,
That of the tulip, pink, and rose.

But when the vigilant patrol
Of stars walks round about the Pole,
Their leaves, that to the stalks are curled,
Seem to their staves the ensigns furled.
Then in some flower's belovèd hut
Each bee as sentinel is shut,
And sleeps so too: but, if once stirred,
She runs you through, nor asks the word.

Oh thou, that dear and happy isle
The garden of the world ere while,
Thou paradise of foúr seas,
Which heaven planted us to please,
But, to exclude the world, did guard
With watery if not flaming sword;

dian] reveille   pan] part of musket holding the priming   flask] gunpowder
flask   word] password

59

What luckless apple did we taste,
To make us mortal, and thee waste?

Unhappy! shall we never more
That sweet militía restore,
When gardens only had their towers,
And all the garrisons were flowers,
When roses only arms might bear,
And men did rosy garlands wear?
Tulips, in several colours barred,
Were then the Switzers of our Guard.

The gardener had the soldier's place,
And his more gentle forts did trace.
The nursery of all things green
Was then the only magazine.
The winter quarters were the stoves,
Where he the tender plants removes.
But war all this doth overgrow;
We ordnance plant and powder sow.

And yet there walks one on the sod
Who, had it pleasèd him and God,
Might once have made our gardens spring
Fresh as his own and flourishing.
But he preferred to the Cinque Ports
These five imaginary forts,
And, in those half-dry trenches, spanned
Power which the ocean might command.

For he did, with his utmost skill,
Ambition weed, but conscience till—
Conscience, that heaven-nursèd plant,
Which most our earthy gardens want.
A prickling leaf it bears, and such
As that which shrinks at every touch;
But flowers eternal, and divine,
That in the crowns of saints do shine.

The sight does from these bastions ply,
The invisible artillery;
And at proud Cawood Castle seems
To point the battery of its beams.

Cawood Castle] seat of Archbishop of York, two miles from Nun Appleton

As if it quarrelled in the seat
The ambition of its prelate great.
But o'er the meads below it plays,
Or innocently seems to graze.

(1681; wr. ?1650s)

Nicholas Hookes
1628–1712

38   *To Amanda walking in the Garden*

AND now what monarch would not gardener be,
My fair Amanda's stately gait to see;
How her feet tempt! How soft and light she treads,
Fearing to wake the flowers from their beds!
Yet from their sweet green pillows every where,
They start and gaze about to see my fair;
Look at yon flower yonder, how it grows
Sensibly! How it opens its leaves and blows,
Puts its best Easter clothes on, neat and gay!
Amanda's presence makes it holy-day:
Look how on tip-toe that fair lily stands
To look on thee, and court thy whiter hands
To gather it! I saw in yonder crowd
That tulip-bed, of which Dame Flora's proud,
A short dwarf flower did enlarge its stalk,
And shoot an inch to see Amanda walk;
Nay, look, my fairest, look how fast they grow!
Into a scaffold method spring! As though
Riding to Parliament were to be seen
In pomp and state some royal amorous queen:
The gravelled walks, though even as a die,
Lest some loose pebble should offensive lie,
Quilt themselves over with downy moss for thee,
The walls are hanged with blossomed tapestry;
To hide her nakedness when looked upon,
The maiden fig-tree puts Eve's apron on;
The broad-leaved sycamore, and every tree
Shakes like the trembling aspe, and bends to thee,

38 scaffold method] system of viewing-stands for processions   die] dice, proverbial
expression   aspe] aspen

And each leaf proudly strives with fresher air,
To fan the curled tresses of thy hair;
Nay, and the bee too, with his wealthy thigh,
Mistakes his hive, and to thy lips doth fly;
Willing to treasure up his honey there,
Where honey-combs so sweet and plenty are:
Look how that pretty modest columbine
Hangs down its head to view those feet of thine.
See the fond motion of the strawberry,
Creeping on the earth to go along with thee!
The lovely violet makes after too,
Unwilling yet, my dear, to part with you;
The knot-grass and the daisies catch thy toes
To kiss my fair one's feet before she goes;
All court and wish me lay Amanda down,
And give my dear a new green flowered gown.
      Come let me kiss thee falling, kiss at rise,
      Thou in the garden, I in paradise.

(1653)

Charles Cotton
1630–1687

from *The Wonders of the Peak*

39   [*Chatsworth*]

SOUTHWARD from hence ten miles, where Derwent laves
His broken shores with never clearing waves,
There stands a stately and stupendous pile
Like the proud Regent of the British Isle,
Shedding her beams over the barren vale,
Which else bleak winds and nipping frosts assail
With such perpetual war, there would appear
Nothing but winter ten months of the year.

      This palace, with wild prospects girded round,
Stands in the middle of a falling ground,
At a black mountain's foot, whose craggy brow
Secures from eastern tempests all below,

39 laves] washes

Under whose shelter trees and flowers grow,
With early blossom, maugre native snow;
Which elsewhere round a tyranny maintains,
And binds cramped Nature long in crystal chains.
The fabric's noble front faces the west,
Turning her fair broad shoulders to the east,
On the south side the stately gardens lie,
Where the scorned peak rivals proud Italy,
And on the north sev'ral inferior plots
For servile use scattered to lie in spots.

The outward gate stands near enough, to look
Her oval front in the objected brook;
But that she has better reflection
From a large mirror nearer of her own,
For a fair lake, from wash of floods unmixed,
Before it lies, an area spread betwixt.
Over this pond, opposite to the gate,
A bridge of a quaint structure, strength, and state,
Invites you to pass over it, where dry
You trample may on shoals of wanton fry,
With which those breeding waters do abound,
And better carps are nowhere to be found.
A tower of antique model the bridge foot
From the peak-rabble does securely shut,
Which, by stone stairs delivers you below
Into the sweetest walks the world can show.
There wood and water, sun and shade contend,
Which shall the most delight, and most befriend;
There grass and gravel in one path you meet,
For ladies tend'rer, and men's harder feet.
Here into open lakes the sun may pry,
A privilege the closer groves deny,
Or if confed'rate winds do make them yield,
He then but chequers what he cannot gild.
The ponds, which here in double order shine,
Are some of them so large, and all so fine,
That Neptune in his progress once did please
To frolic in these artificial seas,
Of which a noble monument we find,
His royal chariot left, it seems, behind,

maugre] in spite of

Whose wheels and body moored up with a chain,
Like Drake's old hulk at Deptford, still remain.
No place on earth was e'er discovered yet,
For contemplation, or delight so fit.
The groves, whose curled brows shade every lake,
Do everywhere such waving landskips make,
As painters' baffled art is far above,
Who waves, and leaves could never yet make move.
Hither the warbling people of the air
From their remoter colonies repair,
And in these shades, now setting up their rests,
Like Caesar's Swiss, burn their old native nests.
The Muses too perch on the bending sprays
And in these thickets chant their charming lays;
No wonder then if the heroic song
That here took birth and voice, do flourish long.

To view from hence the glittering pile above
(Which must at once wonder create, and love)
Environed round with Nature's shames, and ills,
Black heaths, wild rocks, bleak crags, and naked hills,
And the whole prospect so inform, and rude,
Who is it, but must presently conclude?
That this is Paradise, which seated stands
In midst of deserts, and of barren sands.
So a bright diamond would look, if set
In a vile socket of ignoble jet,
And such a face the new-born Nature took,
When out of Chaos by the fiat struck.
Doubtless, if anywhere, there never yet
So brave a structure on such ground was set,
Which sure the Foundress built, to reconcile
This to the other members of the Isle,
And would therein, first her own grandeur show,
And then what Art could, spite of Nature, do.

But let me lead you in, 'tis worth the pains
T'examine what this princely house contains,
Which, if without so glorious to be seen,
The glazier's work before substantial was
I must confess, thrice as much lead as glass,

landskips] painted representations of landscape   inform] formless   fiat] 'Let
there be . . .'   Foundress] Bess of Hardwick, Countess of Shrewsbury (c.1527–1608),
or possibly Nature herself

Which in the sun's meridian, cast a light,
As it had been within an hour of night.
The windows now look like so many suns,
Illustrating the noble room at once;
The primitive casements modelled were no doubt
By that through which the pigeon was thrust out,
Where now whole sashes are but one great eye,
T'examine, and admire thy beauties by.
And, if we hence look out, we shall see there
The gardens too i' the reformation share.
Upon a terrace, as most houses high,
Though from this prospect humble to your eye,
A stately plot, both regular, and vast
Suiting the rest, was by the Foundress cast,
In those incurious times, under the rose
Designed, as one may saucily suppose,
For lilies, peonies, daffodils, and roses
To garnish chimneys, and make Sunday posies,
Where gooseberries, as good as ever grew,
'Tis like were set; for winter-greens the yew,
Holly, and box: for then these things were new
With oh! the honest rosemary and bays,
So much esteemed in those good wassail days.

Now in the middle of this great parterre,
A fountain darts her streams into the air
Twenty foot high, till by the winds depressed,
Unable longer upward to contest,
They fall again in tears for grief and ire,
They cannot reach the place they did aspire.
As if the sun melted the waxen wings
Of these Icarian temerarious springs,
For braving thus his generative ray,
When their true motion lies another way
Th'ambitious element repulsed so
Rallies, and saves her routed waves below,
In a large basin of diameter
Such as old Rome's expensive lakes did bear,
Where pacific sea expanded lies,
A liquid theatre for Naumachies;
And where in case of such a pageant war,
Romans in statue still spectators are.

Naumachies] staged sea-fights, sometimes enacted in Renaissance gardens as well as evoked by sculpture and fountains

Where the ground swells nearer the hill above
And where once stood a crag and cherry grove,
(Which of renown then shared a mighty part)
Instead of such a barbarous piece of art,
Such poor contrived, dwarfish and ragged shades,
'Tis now adorned with fountains and cascades,
Terrace on terrace with their stair-cases
Of brave, and great contrivance, and to these
Statues, walks, grass-plots, and a grove indeed
Where silent lovers may lie down and bleed.
And though all things were, for that age, before
In truth so great, that nothing could be more,
Yet now they with much greater lustre stand,
Touched up, and finished by a better hand.

But that which crowns all this, and does impart
A lustre far beyond the power of art,
Is the great owner, he, whose noble mind
For such a fortune only was designed,
Whose bounties as the ocean's bosom wide,
Flow in a constant, unexhausted tide
Of hospitality and free access,
Liberal condescension, cheerfulness,
Honour and truth, as every of them strove
At once to captivate respect and love;
And all with such order performed, and grace
As rivet wonder to the stately place.

(1681)

John Wilmot, Earl of Rochester
1647–1680

40   from *A Ramble in St James's Park*

EACH imitative branch does twine
In some loved fold of Aretine,
And nightly now beneath their shade
Are buggeries, rapes, and incests made.

40 Aretine] Pietro Aretino (1492–1556), here as author of erotic poems

Unto this all-sin-sheltering grove
Whores of the bulk and the alcove,
Great ladies, chambermaids, and drudges,
The ragpicker, and heiress trudges.
Carmen, divines, great lords, and tailors,
Prentices, poets, pimps, and jailers,
Footmen, fine fops do here arrive,
And here promiscuously they swive . . .

(1680; wr. early 1670s)

John Evelyn, The Younger
1655–1699

from *Of Gardens* by René Rapin (1666)

41   *[On waterworks]*

WHEN in your gardens entrance you provide,
The waters, there united, to divide:
First, in the middle a large fountain make,
Which from a narrow pipe its rise may take,
And to the air those waves, by which 'tis fed,
Remit again; about it raise a bed
Of moss, or grass, or if you think this base,
With well-wrought marble circle in the place.
Statues of various shapes may be disposed
About the tube; sometimes it is inclosed
By dubious Scylla, or with sea-calves graced,
Or by a brazen Triton 'tis embraced.
A Triton thus at Luxembourg presides,
And from the dolphin, which he proudly rides,
Spouts out the streams: this place, though beautified
With marble round, though from Arcueil supplied;
Yet to Saint Cloud must yield in this out-shined,
That there the Hostel d'Orleans we find.
The little town, the groves before scarce known,
Enabled thus, will now give place to none.
So great an owner any seat improves;
One whom the king, one whom the people loves.

bulk] hull of ship   swive] copulate

41 Luxembourg] gardens of the Luxembourg Palace, Paris   Arcueil] Roman
aqueduct at

This garden, as a pattern, may be shown
To those who would add beauty to their own.
All other fountains this so far transcends,
That none in France besides with it contends,
None so much plenty yields; none flows so high,
A gulf i' th' middle of the pond does lie,
In which a swollen tunnel opens wide;
Through hissing chinks the waters freely slide,
And in their passage like a whirlwind move,
With rapid force into the air above,
As if a watery dart were upward thrown,
But when these haughty waves do once fall down,
Resounding loud, they on each other beat,
And with a dewy shower the basin wet . . .

Hence spouting streams in verdant groves we see.
And pains, the waves into subjection brings,
And still survives in monumental springs.
All this he did, while he, not Lewis reigned,
And Atlas-like the tott'ring state sustained.
Here variously disposed the fountains run,
First head-long fall, then rise where they begun.
Receive all forms, and move on every side;
With horrid noise, Chimera gaping wide,
Out of her open mouth the water throws.
For from her mouth a rapid torrent flows,
From her wide throat, as waves in circles spout,
A serpent turning sprinkles all the rout.
A brazen hunter watchfully attends;
And threatening death the crooked tunnel bends.
Instead of shot, thence pearly drops proceed;
Drops not so fatal as if made of lead.
This soon the laughter of the vulgar moves,
Whose acclamation the deceit approves.

But why should I repeat how many ways
In the deep caves art with water plays?
The place grows moist with artificial rain,
And hissing springs, which here burst out amain.
Rebounding high, streams everywhere sweat through,
And with great drops the banging stones bedew.
They who the grots and fountains oversee,
May as they please the streams diversify.

Lewis] Louis XIV

Though the kind Naiades comply with those,
Who when they grots of pebble do compose,
And springs bring in, still beautify the cells,
With eastern stones, or Erythraean shells.
Others of hollow pumice may be made,
And well placed shells may on the top be laid.
But all these arts, which modern ages own,
Were to our happy ancestors unknown,
These sights must be exposed to the people's view,
Whose greedy eyes such novelties pursue ...

Rivers diffused a thousand ways may pass,
With hastening waves through the divided grass.
Like sudden torrents, which the rain gives head,
Through precipices some may swiftly spread;
And in the pebbles a soft noise excite.
Some on the surface with a tim'rous flight,
May steal; if anything its speed retard,
Then its shrill murmurs through the fields are heard.
Enraged it leaps up high, and with weak strokes
The pebbles, which it overflows, provokes.
Threatening the bank it beats against the shore,
And roots of trees which froth all sprinkles o'er.
That slender brook, from whence hoarse noises came,
Which as it had no substance, had no name;
When other riv'lets from the vales come in,
Th' ignoble current then will soon begin
To gather strength; for bridges may be fit,
And by degrees great vessels will admit,
Sometimes by grassy banks the river goes;
Sometimes with joy it skips upon green moss;
Sometimes it murmurs in exalted groves,
And with its threats the narrow path reproves.
When 'tis dispersed, then let the meads be drowned,
Let slimy mud enrich the barren ground.
If it runs deep, with dams its force restrain;
And from the meadows noxious water drain.
Where from their fountains rivers do break loose,
And the moist spring the valleys overflows;
When on the meads black showers do descend,
With mounds of earth the groves from clouds defend.

Erythraean] part of ocean on the Arabian coast

As different figures best with streams agree,
So on the sides let there some difference be.
Still with variety the borders grace,
There either grass, or fragrant flowers place;
Or with a wharf of stone the bank secure;
But troubled fens let their own reeds obscure:
Or weeds, where croaking frogs and moorhens lie;
Nothing but grass your banks must beautify,
Where silver springs afford transparent waves,
And glistering sand the even bottom paves,
On which green elms their leaves in autumn sheed.
Thus rivers both our care and culture need.
While in their channels they run headlong down,
We must take heed, as they haste, no stone
Fallen from the hanging brink, may keep them back,
And through the vales their course uneasy make.

Ye springs and fountains in the woods resound,
And with your noise the silent groves confound.
Frequent their windings, all their avenues,
And into the dry roots new life infuse.

While pleasant streams invite your thoughts and eyes,
And with resistless charms your sense surprise;
Of human life you then may meditate,
Obnoxious to the violence of fate,
Life unperceived, like rivers, steals away.
And though we court it, yet it will not stay.
Then may you think of its uncertainty,
Constant in nothing but inconstancy.
See what rude waves disturb the things below,
And through what stormy voyages we go.
So Hypanis, you'll say, and Peneus so,
Simois, and Volsoian Amasenus flow;
Naupactian Achelous, Inachus,
With slow Melanthus, swift Parthenius,
Thus ran along, and so Dyraspes went,
Whose current Borysthenian streams augment.

Besides the fountains, which to art we owe,
That falls of water also can bestow
Such, as on rugged Jura we descry,
On rocks; and on the Alps which touch the sky.

sheed] shed   Hypanis . . . Dyraspes] all rivers in classical literature

Where from steep precipices it descends,
And where America itself extends
To the rude north; exposed to Hurus blast:
On Canada's bold shore the ocean passed.
There among groves of fir trees evergreen,
Streams falling headlong from the cliffs are seen.
The cataracts resound along the shore;
Struck with the noise, the woods and valleys roar.
These wonders which by nature here are shown,
Ruellian Naiads have by art out-done,
Into the air a rock with lofty head
Aspires, the hasty waters thence proceed.
Dashed against rugged places they descend,
And broken thus themselves in foam they spend.
They sound, as when some torrent uncontrolled,
With mighty force is from a mountain rolled.
The earth with horrid noise affrighted groans,
Flints which lie underneath, and moistened stones,
Are beat with waves; th' untrodden paths resound,
And groves and woods do loudly echo round.

(1673)

Samuel Gilbert
d. ?1692

42   from *The Florist's Vade-Mecum*

WERE I employ'd a garden to contrive,
Wherein to plant each beauteous vegetive;
First then my wall so fashioned should be,
Each side and part the sun each day should see:
So that the fruits within, or outside set
An equal share of's ripening beams should get.
A fountain in the midst should so be plac'd,
By which the plot should not be only grac'd,
But that one spring should force the water out
In seeming showers of rain, each part about
Farther or shorter distance, more or less,
Water to big, or smaller drops shall press,

Hurus] wind coming from Lake Huron

As the inclosed plants or flowers require;
Gentle or fiercer rain, to your desire.
Invented shades to keep out Sol's south flames,
And apt reflections to inforce his beams,
As nature of each plant shall want his aid,
Or those that by his heat may be dismayed,
Assisting nature by industrious art;
To perfect every plant in every part,
But not like some, whose crimes do rise so high
Boldly to pull down heaven's deity.
I hate that so sordid ign'rance doth dispence
With making nature God, slight providence,
But let each vegetive best ordered prove
Such letters, so may spell the God above,
That men may read him thence, and make each clod
Speak God of nature, make not nature God:
But blaz'ner of's wise providence and power,
First made, then so preserves each plant and flower . . .

Here may we sit, and each his time purloin,
And see our Art, with Madam Nature join;
And how the jewels that adorn the skies,
Or what shines brighter, ladies' beauteous eyes
Can't be compared to Flora's mantle, that
She throws on earth, and mortals wonder at;
Embroidered Tellus doth her glory sing
As well as birds at the approach of spring,
And we with ravished eyes, see Flora smile,
Whilst chirping music doth our ears beguile:
Feel softest down, in tender buds of roses,
Arabian smells in her perfumed posies.
To exercise our taste, Pomona she
Sends us the juicy off-springs of each tree:
But when this sensual banquet we have done,
On winged thoughts soar higher than the sun;
And then contemplate how the three in one
All mortal actions view from his bright throne.
And thence resolve, ourselves as gardens keep;
Pluck up the weeds of sin, soon as they peep.
His graces be our flowers; for watering pots
Our eye, oft letting fall repentent drops;
That cause those flowers' increase, and give occasion
For our removal to a new plantation.

Tellus] Roman earth-goddess   Pomona] Roman goddess of fruits

Each day concluding, with account made even,
To have no walks, but those that lead to heaven;
Such as in gardens innocence employ,
That virtues raise, so vices must destroy.
Then gard'ner of universe, his powers
Pluck not as weeds, but take us up as flowers.

(1682)

Anne Finch, Countess of Winchilsea
1661–1720

43   *Upon my Lord Winchilsea's Converting the Mount in*
his Garden to a Terrace,
And other alterations and improvements, in his house,
park, and gardens

IF we those generous sons deservedly praise
Who o'er their predecessors marble raise,
And by inscriptions on their deeds, and name,
To late posterity, convey their fame,
What with more admiration shall we write
On him, who takes their errors from our sight?
And lest their judgement be in question brought,
Removes a mountain, to remove a fault
Which long had stood (though threatened oft in vain),
Concealing all the beauties of the plain.
Heedless when young, cautious in their decline,
None gone before pursued the vast design,
Till ripened judgement, joined with youthful flame,
At last but came, and saw, and overcame.
And as old Rome refined what e'er was rude,
And civilized, as fast as she subdued,
So lies this hill, hewn from its rugged height,
Now levelled to a scene of smooth delight,
Where on a terrace of its spoils we walk,
And of the task, and the performer talk,
From whose unwearied genius men expect
All that can further polish or protect;
To see a sheltering grove the prospect bound,
Just rising from the same prolific ground,

Where late it stood, the glory of the seat,
Repelled the winter blasts, and screened the summer's heat;
So praised, so loved, that when untimely fate
Sadly prescribed it a too early date,
The heavy tidings cause a general grief,
And all combine to bring a swift relief.
Some plead, some pray, some counsel, some dispute,
Alas in vain, where power is absolute.
Those whom paternal awe forbids to speak,
Their sorrows, in their secret whispers break,
Sigh as they pass beneath the sentenced trees,
Which seem to answer in a mournful breeze.
The very clowns (hired by his daily pay),
Refuse to strike, nor will their lord obey,
Till to his speech he adds a leading stroke,
And by example does their rage provoke.
Then in a moment, every arm is reared,
And the robbed palace sees, what most she feared,
Her lofty grove, her ornamental shield,
Turned to a desert, and forsaken field.
So fell Persepolis, bewailed of all
But him, whose rash resolve procured her fall.
No longer now, we such destructions fear,
No longer the resounding axe we hear,
But in exchange, behold the fabric stand,
Built, and adorned by a supporting hand;
Complete in all its late unequal frame,
No loam and lath does now the building shame,
But graceful symmetry without is seen,
And use, with beauty, are improved within.
And though our ancestors did gravely plot,
As if one element they valued not,
Nor yet the pleasure of the noblest scene,
'Gainst light and air to raise a strong defence;
Their wiser offspring does those gifts renew,
And now we breathe and now the eager view
Through the enlarged windows takes her way,
Does beauteous fields, and scattered woods survey,
Flies o'er the extended land, and sinks but in the sea.
Or when contented with an easier flight,
The new wrought gardens give a new delight,
Where every fault, that in the old was found,
Is mended, in the well disposèd ground.

clowns] labourers   plot] plan

Such are the effects when wine, nor loose delight,
Devour the day, nor waste the thoughtless nights,
But generous arts, the studious hours engage,
To bless the present, and succeeding age.
Oh! may Eastwell still with their aid increase,
Plenty surround her, and within be peace.
Still may her temperate air his health maintain,
From whom she does such strength and beauty gain.
Flourish her trees, and may the verdant grass
Again prevail, where late the plough did pass.
Still may she boast a kind and fruitful soil,
And still now pleasure give to crown his toil.
And may someone, with admiration filled,
In just applause, and in numbers skilled,
Not with more zeal, but more poetic heat,
Thoroughly adorn what barely we relate.
Then, should the Elysian groves no more be named,
Nor Tempe's Vale be any longer famed,
She should the theme to every verse afford,
Until the Muse, when to advantage soared,
Should take a nobler aim, and dare describe her lord.

(?1702)

Jonathan Swift
1667–1745

44   from *My Lady's Lamentation and Complaint*
against the Dean

How proudly he talks
Of zigzags and walks;
And all the day raves
Of cradles and caves;
And boasts of his feats,
His grottos and seats;
Shews all his gew-gaws,
And gapes for applause?
A fine occupation
For one of his station!

Tempe's Vale] plain at the foot of Mount Olympus

A hole where a rabbit
Would scorn to inhabit,
Dug out in an hour
He calls it a bow'r.

(1728)

John Clerk of Penicuik
1676–1755

from *The Country Seat*

['*Precepts and advices*']

45

COME now ye rural deities and show
What forms will beautify the neighb'ring plains.
The verdant banks, and meads, that so they may
With never-fading charms allure our eyes.
Stretch out the lines of every avenue
With spreading trees in many stately rows;
Display the parterres and the shady walks,
The sloping greens, the ponds and water-works.
The fruitful orchard and the mazy grove
Where billing birds may meet in fond caress;
Where every goddess and their train
A clear and secret bathing place may find.
Where Flora with a knot of gaudy flowers
May dress her lovely head, and in the shades
Vertumnus and Pomona breathe their loves.
And thus unseen, may all the heavenly powers
Adorn the solitude of rural bowers.

That avenue will most delight the sight
That on some beauteous object shapes its way.
Such is a temple, whose high towering spire
Divides the hovering clouds, and seems to be
A lofty pillar to support the heavens.
This lovely prospect may your busy mind
With useful speculations entertain;
Consider first, that all you do enjoy
Is owing to the god, whose awful shrine

45 Vertumnus and Pomona] Roman god and goddess of fruits, husband and wife

These sacred walks enclose, and where
With thankful heart you often should resort.
And if that here your fathers lie entombed,
Your stately house and pleasant fields at last,
With other charms of life you must forego,
And this way travel to the shades below.

Another noble prospect may be deemed
That of the great metropolis or town;
Where noise and tumult you delight to shun.
Her gilded spires reflect the beamy ray
On each surrounding field, and with a glance
Try to recall the fled inhabitants.
Far from all churlish habits she returns
With usury the favours she receives,
And to the active patriot always gives.
Her loud harmonious bells a warning give
To shun such powerful draughts of rural joy
As may intoxicate the lazy mind.
She calls as Cincinnatus left his plough,
So we our chief delights should not pursue
But for our country's sake our cares renew.

Around the fabric spread the wide parterre
Like to a verdant mantle edged with gold,
Or an embroidered carpet all perfumed
With Indian sweets, here with a mystic mien
Let Nature in the pride of blooming flowers
Triumphant sit, and all the gardener's toils
Direct with matchless grace, here let her show
How wild and shapeless fields may be adorned
With easy labour and without constraint.
How each neglected corner, each defect
May by a little art converted be
To beauties, that may please the nicest eye.
Forbear then all these trifling mazy knots
Of shrubs and flowers that crowd the flagrant scene.
Nature enjoins all cost and toil to spare
Which mar the prospect or obstruct the air.

Gardens must always some proportion bear
To every kind of structure which they grace.
For though no rule is fixed, the man of taste

Cincinnatus] Roman hero called from his plough to rule the state in 485 BC

May cause each discord slide in harmony.
What though a royal garden should contain
In every single plot a spacious field,
Yet more confined dimensions may content
The master of a humble edifice.
Likewise a due proportion must be kept
Between the charge of laying out your grounds
In pompous order and their due repairs.
A small neat garden claims to be preferred
To those of larger size with shabby mien,
Where nothing but disorder can be seen.

Variety is what we next admire
In every garden; hence the various forms
Of gravelly terraces and verdant slopes,
Fountains and statues, cataracts and grots,
The airy, open, and the covered walks,
With other objects rising to our view
Which for their multitude seem always new.

But every beauty ceases when compared
With what we in the fragrant orchard find.
Here vegetable life displays her charms
In radiant colours, and in sprightly dress
The summer's queen unfolds her juicy stores
In such ambrosial fruits, all covered o'er
With spangled rinds of purple and of gold.
Would you with double pleasure taste the bliss,
Which fair Pomona courteously bestows,
Then learn with skill to use the pruning hook,
The spade and rake with other garden tools
To make the ground submissive to your will.
With your own hands insert the fruitful bud,
And by the knife let every tree be taught
Its proper order, where to shoot or spread,
Or in what shape to raise its beauteous head.

Thus have the greatest monarchs of the world
Employed their time, and seemed alike to prize
The royal sceptre and the humble spade.
Thus mighty Cyrus with a gardener's care
Bestowed his peaceful intervals of war.
Soon as the world itself a being had
To Man the great all-seeing Power enjoined

With a laborious hand to dress the ground.
Now of all grounds the orchard claims the praise
As most resembling paradise.

Next may some little plots be laid aside
To be the parents of all reptile fruits,
The milky herb and every wholesome root:
'Tis here the virtuous and the wise may know,
How health and vigour best may be preserved,
By moderate labour free from anxious cares.
How mortals in the Golden Age were fed,
Till they like savage beasts began to stray,
And on their fellow creatures learned to prey.

Whether in orchard, or in kitchen grounds,
Nature requires the gardener's helping hand,
Yet never force her with unkindly art.
She with a mother's tender care bestows
On every region all such fruits and herbs
As most are fitted for the inhabitants.
But philosophic gardeners still may try
How far the golden orange or the vine,
Will bear the British soil and humid air.
The curious botanist may likewise raise
With artificial warmth exotic plants.
But those who are on true improvements bent
Must with our natural products be content.

Let copious streams from all the neighb'ring hills
In tubes or channels roll their lucid streams
Through all your garden plots and valley grounds.
Those with perpetual verdure crown the spring,
Enliven every plant and every tree,
Charming in various shapes the wandering eye.
Some streams by sportive jets are thrown aloft
And mixed in air; some with united force
Like thundering torrents from the highest rocks
Rush headlong down and fill the beauteous lakes.
You who take pleasure in aquatic schemes,
Avoid canals or ponds of any form,
Where living fountains never show their heads,
But stagnant lie from latent sources fed.
Such with their baleful steams infect the air

reptile] creeping

79

And are but awkward ornaments at best.
But if low fields or silent brooks deny
Their friendly aid to deck the limpid plain,
What Nature gives, receive; Diana's self
With her fair nymphs may bathe their snowy limbs,
In silver lakes, for want of crystal springs.

Proportion every fountain to the stream
Which gives it life. 'Tis monstrous to behold
A vast large basin, which no water fills
But what a little paltry jet bestows.
The fountain's margin should not much extend
Beyond what may the falling drops contain.
And the chief beauty of a fountain is
When gushing waters flow in plenteous streams.
But where the same are wanting, we must try
If groups of sculpture can defects supply.

Whether with stony wall, or thorny hedge
You fence your garden round, be always sure
To keep each lovely object still in sight:
But shun the artless practice to expose
Your fields at once to any single view.
At every step new objects must arise
And all your fields and garden plots be such
As may not only please our wandering eyes
But feed luxuriant fancy with surprise.

Distinguish well what suits a foreign clime,
And what to British air and soil belongs.
In this our Isle some fruits perfection owe
To walls of brick, but others more inured
To blustering winds and rains, on standards grow.
Nor multiply your walks, nor scrupulous be
To rear up some in every proper place.
These garden plots can never fail to please
Which most abound with sweet and fragrant flowers,
Where all the fountains are with torrents fed,
And all the walls with painted fruits are clad.

Whatever charms in rural life are known,
These most conspicuous are in woods and groves,
Where solitude no bold intruder finds.
Then through the bushy trees and lonesome shades,

Nature in all her several windings trace;
Search out the beauties which unfinished lie
And let assisting Art complete the scene.
If from a neighb'ring rock a spring descends
There let a fountain grace a shady grove:
And where uncommon moisture steeps the ground
Convert the place into a lake or pond.
If any opening gives a prospect round
Of distant fields; there place a seat or bower
Which may defend from heat and sudden rain.
And heighten into transports all your views.
If spacious plains shall intersect a wood
Let there your flocks and nimble deer be fed,
The milky kine, or beeves, or generous steeds;
Thus while we wander through the mazy ground
Surprising objects will regale our view,
And rural bliss in full perfection show.

(1731)

George Sewell
1680–1726

46   *Soliloquy*

WHY, Damon, with the forward day
Dost thou thy little spot survey,
From tree to tree, with doubtful cheer,
Observe the progress of the year,
What winds arise, what rains descend,
When thou before that year shalt end?

What do thy noonday walks avail,
To clear the leaf, and pick the snail?
Then wantonly to death decree
An insect usefuller than thee?
Thou and the worm are brother-kind,
As low, as earthy, and as blind.

Vain wretch; canst thou expect to see
The downy peach make court to thee?

Or that thy sense shall ever meet
The bean-flower's deep-embosom'd sweet?
Exhaling with an evening's blast;
Thy evenings then will all be past!

Thy narrow pride, thy fancied green
(For vanity's in little seen),
All must be left when Death appears
In spite of wishes, groans, and tears
Nor one of all thy plants that grow
But Rosemary will with thee go.

(1728)

John Ozell
d. 1743

47   from [Boileau's] *Epistle to my Gardener*

THOU as laborious, as thy master kind,
Who seems, to bless thy toil, by heaven designed.
Thou daily dost thy grateful task renew,
To guide the woodbine and the ruder yew.
Thou ruler of my garden, who so well,
The secrets of the sylvan art can'st tell;
Who at Auteuil, with such success has wrought,
And know'st as much as Quintinie has taught.
Oh, that my reason would to culture yield,
As to thy hand, this fair obedient field.
Why o'er my faults can't I as well succeed,
And root up every thorn and every weed?
  But tell me, Anthony, let's argue; say,
When from the rise to the decline of day,
Thou the sharp spade or watering pot dost use,
Making the most unwilling soil produce;
As to thy laws, thou dost my garden bend,
And on thy charge with happy care attend;
What think'st thou, when thou seest thy master muse,
When fixt, he heaven and earth alternate views;

47 Auteuil] Boileau's country estate   Quintinie] Jean de la Quintinie (1626–88),
leading French gardener

When with odd gestures to himself he talks,
And launching out by starts, alone he walks;
The birds, which in his alleys perch, he frights;
Then, Anthony, what think'st thou of his wits?
Art thou not apt to fancy he's possest,
As Maugis was, with fifty fiends at least;
Whose wond'rous story thou so oft has read,
And that some conjuring's always in his head.
No, no, thy master, thou has surely heard,
To be the Royal Chronicler's preferred:
In writing to set down the mighty deeds
Of a great king, whose prowess far exceeds
What e'er old tales are dinning in our ears,
Of Charlemagne, and his six pair of peers,
And whose high wisdom's greater still than theirs.
This in the village thou'st been told, and when
Thou seest me muse, believ'st 'tis for the pen.
That as I walk along this wall, at once
I'm routing the allies, and taking Mons.
  What would'st thou say, if thou should'st hear it said
He has quite other matters in his head?
That he, who's to record for future times,
The conqueror's fame, is busy now on rhymes:
And racking of his working brain to find
Such as may give an image of his mind,
And that the draught is for thyself designed.
Thou'st cry, 'My master is a doctor deemed,
And as a man of topping parts esteemed.
He sometimes better than a preacher speaks;
But to what purpose these fantastic freaks?
He would not with his tales the tuneful thrush
Disturb, nor drive him from his peaceful bush,
Were he to exercise like me, to shear,
To dig to plant, to gather, and to rear;
To fill one pot as soon as t'other's out,
To quench the sand's immeasurable drought;
To prune, to pale, and with incessant toil,
Supply the wants of the deficient soil.'
  I find thou thinkst, of us two, Anthony,
That thou hast more employment here than I,
And that my labour's lighter here than thine;
But sure you wouldst not change thy work for mine.

Maugis] sorcerer in the *chanson de geste*, *Quatre Fils Aymon*

Couldst thou a day or two, from gardening free,
Try how my work would with thy head agree;
Couldst thou become a poet, and a wit,
And stand to polish what in heat was writ;
To give the meanest things a noble air,
To make the roughest smooth, the rudest fair;
And pinks and roses out of thistles raise,
Make panegyric blame, and satire praise;
To grace with elegance the poorest themes,
Keep in due bounds, avoiding all extremes:
In short, to give a finished work such charms,
As may a d'Aguesseau content, or Termes.
A work that will, when it appears, with these,
In town and court, the nicest judges please.
Soon weary of this labour, pale and thin,
And tanned as if thou had'st exposed thy skin,
To twenty vernal winds, again thou'st take
Thy pot, thy spade, thy shovel, and thy rake,
And cry 'Before I'd this fatigue endure,
These hands a hundred acres shou'dst manure.
Ere with such visions I would vex my mind,
Be always searching what I seldom find;
To join discording words together strive,
And in the clouds in search of shadows live:
I'd rather in this garden spend my time
In digging, than be forced to pump for rhyme.'
    Come you, who think'st 'tis such a toil to dig,
I'll show thee what is pain and what fatigue:
And lazy as I am, will let thee see,
How short in working hard thou com'st of me.
Man ne'er on earth is free from pain and care,
He flies to rest, and finds fatigue is there
Condemned to labour in repose. In vain,
Fond hopes of ease possess the poet's brain.
The soothing sisters in some soft retreat,
Promise that quiet which he'll never meet.
Beneath the shade, and by the drowsy stream,
He'll soon perceive the rest he seeks, a dream.
Though planted for his sake, these peaceful woods;
Though sweet, the murmurs of the silver floods,

---

d'Aguesseau] Henri-François d'Aguesseau (1668–1751), appointed advocate-general in his
twenties   Termes] Roger de Saint-Lary et de Termes, Duke of Bellegarde (1563–
1646), supposed author of *Histoire des Amours du Grand Alcandre*

Yet there no ease is by the poet found;
Rhyme, cesure, cadence, and harmonious sound,
With flowing numbers, rich expectations fill
His head with care, and labour with him still.
Full of their charms impatient to enjoy,
Fast he pursues them, and they faster fly.
The nimble fairies leave him far behind,
And soon the wearied poet's out of wind.
He can't, howev'r, from this fatigue refrain,
Pleasing himself with trouble and with pain.
While thus tormented, he is still amused,
And courting is not vexed when he's refused . . .

'Tis time for me to end, besides, I see,
Yon melons, with impatience, wait for thee.
The flowers, methinks, to one another say,
Where's Anthony, that he's not here today?
Is it the wake? or for some new-made saint,
Do we our drink so long, though thirsty, want?
Something's fallen out, or, why has he forgot
To handle, as he's wont, the watering pot?

(1711)

Aaron Hill
1685–1750

48   *The Garden Window*

HERE, Amanda, gently bending,
    Sweetly pensive, loves to lean,
O'er the groves, her sight extending,
    Through the walks that shoot between;

Plac'd, says she, within this window,
    Screen'd, I distant charms survey,
Taught, by poor deceiv'd Olino,
    Nothing's safe, that looks too gay.

Here I view in soften'd shadings
    Am'rous flower to flower incline,
Too remote, to mourn their fadings,
    When with hanging heads they pine.

Here I smell the fragrant breezes,
    Safe from ev'ning's chilly blast;
Here the noonday sun-shine pleases,
    Fearless, when 'twill overcast.

Hence, I hear the tempest rising,
    See the grovy greatness shake,
Every distant ill despising,
    While I every good partake.

So commanding life's gay garden,
    Let me thornless wear the rose;
Choice like mine let fashion pardon,
    Tasting charms, but shunning woes.

(1753)

Alexander Pope
1688–1744

from Homer's *Odyssey*, Book VII
[*The Gardens of Alcinous*]

49

CLOSE to the gates a spacious garden lies,
From storms defended, and inclement skies:
Four acres was th' allotted space of ground,
Fenced with a green enclosure all around.
Tall thriving trees confessed the fruitful mold;
The red'ning apple ripens here to gold,
Here the blue fig with luscious juice o'erflows,
With deeper red the full pomegranate glows,
The branch here bends beneath the weighty pear,
And verdant olives flourish round the year.
The balmy spirit of the western gale
Eternal breathes on fruits untaught to fail:
Each dropping pear a following pear supplies,
On apples apples, figs on figs arise:
The same mild season gives the blooms to blow,
The buds to harden, and the fruits to grow.
  Here ordered vines in equal ranks appear
With all th' united labours of the year,

Some to unload the fertile branches run,
Some dry the black'ning clusters in the sun,
Others to tread the liquid harvest join,
The groaning presses foam with floods of wine.
Here are the vines in early flow'r descried,
Here grapes discoloured on the sunny side,
And there in autumn's richest purple dyed.
  Beds of all various herbs, for ever green,
In beauteous order terminate the scene.
Two plenteous fountains the whole prospect crowned;
This thro' the gardens leads its streams around,
Visits each plant, and waters all the ground:
While that in pipes beneath the palace flows,
And thence its current on the town bestows;
To various use their various streams they bring,
The People one, and one supplies the King.

(1713)

50 *To Mr Gay, Who wrote him a Congratulatory Letter On the Finishing his House*

AH, friend! 'tis true—this truth you lovers know—
In vain my structures rise, my gardens grow;
In vain fair Thames reflects the double scenes
Of hanging mountains and of sloping greens:
Joy lives not here; to happier seats it flies,
And only dwells where Wortley casts her eyes.
What are the gay parterre, the chequered shade,
The morning bower, the ev'ning colonnade,
But soft recesses of uneasy minds,
To sigh unheard in to the passing winds?
So the struck deer in some sequestered part
Lies down to die, the arrow at his heart;
There, stretched unseen in coverts hid from day,
Bleeds drop by drop, and pants his life away.

(Wr. ?1722)

50 Wortley] Lady Mary Wortley Montagu (1689–1762)

51   ## from *Epistle to Lord Burlington*

OFT have you hinted to your brother peer,
A certain truth, which many buy too dear:
Something there is, more needful than expense,
And something previous ev'n to taste—'tis sense:
Good sense, which only is the gift of Heav'n,
And tho' no science, fairly worth the seven:
A light, which in yourself you must perceive;
Jones and Le Nôtre have it not to give.

To build, to plant, whatever you intend,
To rear the column, or the arch to bend,
To swell the terrace, or to sink the grot;
In all, let Nature never be forgot.
But treat the goddess like a modest fair,
Nor over-dress, nor leave her wholly bare;
Let not each beauty ev'ry where be spied,
Where half the skill is decently to hide.
He gains all points, who pleasingly confounds,
Surprizes, varies, and conceals the bounds.

Consult the genius of the place in all;
That tells the waters or to rise, or fall,
Or helps th' ambitious hill the heav'ns to scale,
Or scoops in circling theatres the vale;
Calls in the country, catches op'ning glades,
Joins willing woods, and varies shades from shades;
Now breaks, or now directs, th' intending lines,
Paints as you plant, and as you work, designs.

Still follow sense, of ev'ry art the soul,
Parts answ'ring parts shall slide into a whole,
Spontaneous beauties all around advance,
Start ev'n from difficulty, strike from chance;
Nature shall join you; time shall make it grow
A work to wonder at—perhaps a STOWE.

Without it, proud Versailles! thy glory falls,
And Nero's terraces desert their walls:
The vast parterres a thousand hands shall make,
Lo! COBHAM comes, and floats them with a lake:
Or cut wide views thro' mountains to the plain,
You'll wish your hill or sheltered seat again.

Jones . . . Le Nôtre] Inigo Jones (1573–1652), British architect, and André Le Nôtre (1613–1700), French garden designer   COBHAM] Sir Richard Temple, Lord Cobham (1675–1749), creator of the gardens at Stowe

Ev'n in an ornament its place remark,
Nor in an hermitage set Dr Clarke.

  Behold Villario's ten-years toil complete;
His arbours darken, his espaliers meet;
The wood supports the plain, the parts unite,
And strength of shade contends with strength of light:
A waving glow the bloomy beds display,
Blushing in bright diversities of day,
With silver-quiv'ring rills meandered o'er—
Enjoy them, you! Villario can no more;
Tired of the scene parterres and fountains yield,
He finds at last he better likes a field.

  Thro' his young woods how pleased Sabinus strayed
Or sat delighted in the thick'ning shade,
With annual joy the red'ning shoots to greet,
Or see the stretching branches long to meet.
His son's fine taste an op'ner vista loves,
Foe to the dryads of his father's groves,
One boundless green, or flourished carpet views,
With all the mournful family of yews;
The thriving plants ignoble broomsticks made,
Now sweep those alleys they were born to shade.

  At Timon's villa let us pass a day,
Where all cry out, 'What sums are thrown away!'
So proud, so grand, of that stupendous air,
Soft and agreeable come never there.
Greatness, with Timon, dwells in such a draught
As brings all Brobdignag before your thought.
To compass this, his building is a town,
His pond an ocean, his parterre a down:
Who but must laugh, the master when he sees?
A puny insect, shiv'ring at a breeze.
Lo! what huge heaps of littleness around!
The whole, a laboured quarry above ground.
Two cupids squirt before: a lake behind
Improves the keenness of the northern wind.
His gardens next your admiration call,
On ev'ry side you look, behold the wall!
No pleasing intricacies intervene,
No artful wildness to perplex the scene;

Dr Clarke] one of the notables whose bust was placed in the Hermitage in Richmond Park
(see notes to nos. 59 and 61)   Villario] a satiric creation of Pope's, clearly a landscapist,
perhaps Richard Child, Earl Tylney of Castlemaine, who owned Wanstead House, Essex; but
more likely a synthetic figure

Grove nods at grove, each alley has a brother,
And half the platform just reflects the other.
The suff'ring eye inverted nature sees,
Trees cut to statues, statues thick as trees,
With here a fountain, never to be played,
And there a summer-house, that knows no shade.
Here Amphitrite sails thro' myrtle bow'rs;
There gladiators fight, or die, in flow'rs;
Unwatered see the drooping sea-horse mourn,
And swallows roost in Nilus' dusty urn.

(1728)

52   *The Garden* (after Cowley)

FAIN would my muse the flow'ry treasures sing,
And humble glories of the youthful spring;
Where opening roses breathing sweets diffuse,
And soft carnations show'r their balmy dews;
Where lilies smile in virgin robes of white,
The thin undress of superficial light,
And vary'd tulips show so dazzling gay,
Blushing in bright diversities of day.
Each painted flouret in the lake below
Surveys its beauties, whence its beauties grow;
And pale Narcissus on the bank, in vain
Transformed, gazes on himself again.
Here aged trees cathedral walks compose,
And mount the hill in venerable rows:
There the green infants in their beds are laid,
The garden's hope, and its expected shade.
Here orange-trees with blooms and pendants shine,
And vernal honours to their autumn join;
Exceed their promise in the ripened store,
Yet in the rising blossom promise more.
There in bright drops the crystal fountains play,
By laurels shielded from the piercing day:
Where Daphne, now a tree as once a maid,
Still from Apollo vindicates her shade,
Still turns her beauties from th' invading beam,
Nor seeks in vain for succour to the stream.
The stream at once preserves her virgin leaves,
At once a shelter from her boughs receives,

Where summer's beauty midst of winter stays,
And winter's coolness spite of summer's rays.

(1736)

Philip Stanhope, Earl of Chesterfield
1694–1773

53   *On Lord Ila's Improvements, near Hounslow Heath*

OLD Ila, to show his fine delicate taste
In improving his gardens purloined from the waste,
Bid his gard'ner one day to open his views,
By cutting a couple of grand avenues.
No particular prospect his Lordship intended,
But left it to chance how his walks should be ended,
With transports of joy he beheld at one view-end
His favourite prospect, a church that was ruined.
But, alas! what a sight did the next view exhibit
At the end of the walk hung a rogue on a gibbet.
He beheld it and wept, for it caused him to muse on
Full many a Campbell that died with his shoes on.
All amazed and aghast at the ominous scene
· He ordered it quick to be closed up again
With a clump of Scotch firs by way of a screen.

(1778)

Anne Ingram, Lady Irwin
c.1696–1764

54   from *Castle Howard, the Seat of the Rt. Hon. Charles,*
Earl of Carlisle

FROM every place you cast your wandering eyes,
You view gay landscapes, and new prospects rise,
There a green lawn bounded with shady wood,
Here downy swans sport in a lucid flood.
Buildings the proper points of view adorn,
Of Grecian, Roman and Egyptian form.

53 Ila] Archibald Campbell, Earl of Islay, later 3rd Duke of Argyll (1682–1761)

These interspersed with woods and verdant plains,
Such as possessed of old the Arcadian swains.
Hills rise on hills; and to complete the scenes,
Like one continued wood the horizon seems.
This in the main describes the points of view,
But something more is to some places due ...

Lead through the park, where lines of trees unite,
And verdurous lawns the bounding deer delight:
By gentle falls the docile ground descends,
Forms a fair plain, then by degrees ascends.
These inequalities delight the eye,
For Nature charms most in variety.
Whenever her general law by Art's effaced,
It shows a skill, but proves a want of taste:
O'er all designs Nature should still preside;
She is the cheapest and most perfect guide.

Far in the park there lies a spacious vale,
Formed to inspire a soft poetic tale.
On every side with shady wood 'tis bound,
A maiden verdure covers all the ground.
Hither Saint Hubert secretly repairs,
And hears the eager hunters vows and prayers.
The flying deer by sad experience feels,
The cruel hounds, close at his trembling heels,
In silent tears his last distress he shows,
Then falls Actaeon-like to bloody foes.

Here other woods and lawns demand a place,
Which well an abler poet's theme would grace:
But such unnumbered beauties bless this seat,
'Twere endless on each different charm to treat.
Hippocrates has somewhere justly said,
That arts are long, and nature's debt soon paid.
Could we the certain apophthegm reverse,
Were arts soon learned, and distant was the hearse,
Then would unrivalled Carlisle's genius shine,
Who has so early formed this great design:
But fate has fixed the limits of our stay,
And while I write, time gently glides away.

Saint Hubert] patron-saint of hunters   Actaeon] mythical hunter killed by his own
hounds

East from the house a beauteous down there lies,
Where Art with Nature emulating vies:
Not smoother surface boast the Tempean plains,
Though sung by poets in immortal strains;
Not finer verdure can young Flora bring,
Though she commands an ever-blooming spring.
Upon this plain a monument appears,
Sacred to piety and filial tears.
Here to his sire did grateful Carlisle raise,
A certain record a more lasting praise,
Than volumes writ in honour to his name;
Those often die, being made the sport of fame:
The moth, the worm, and envy, them annoy,
But time can only pyramids destroy.

Beyond this down a building rears its head
Sacred to the immortal virtuous dead.
The name of Carias's noted king it bears,
Made famous by his faithful consort's tears.
Nor was the structure Artemisia raised,
With greater justice more deservedly praised.
Though that a wonder was by ancients deemed,
This by the moderns is not less esteemed.
More difficult to please, and more perverse,
Judging more rashly, though they know much less.
Here Carlisle will thy sacred manes repose,
This solemn place thy ashes will enclose.
How it will please thy gentle shade to view,
Some ages hence, oh, may my prophecy prove true!
Descending from thy line a generous race,
Fit to adorn the camp, or court to grace:
Who, after having gained deserved applause,
For having bravely served their country's cause,
Shall to ambition rural joys prefer,
And fix their happiness and pleasure here.
So when the Trojan Prince, with glad surprise,
Surveyed the heroes who should from him rise,
All dangers and all labours he despised,
So much his noble progeny he prized;

Tempean plains] Vale of Tempe, below Mount Olympus   monument] the Pyramid,
a family tomb   building] the Mausoleum   Carias's noted king] Mausolus, whose
tomb was one of the Seven Wonders of the World   Artemisia] sister and wife of
Mausolus, whose tomb she erected   manes] Roman spirits of the dead   Trojan
Prince] Aeneas

Only to future prospects could attend,
Since from his line the Caesars should descend.

The garden now demands my humble lays,
Which merits a more worthy pen should praise.
So far extended, and so great the space,
Magnificence in every part we trace.
Before the house you view a large parterre,
Not crowded with the trifles brought from far;
No borders, alleys, edgings spoil the scene,
'Tis one unvaried piece of pleasing green;
No starved exotics here lament their fate,
Fettered and bound like prisoners of state;
Or as Diogenes in tub confined,
Wishing like him the enlivening sun to find.
'Tis ornamented by the sculptor's hand,
Here statues, obelisks, and vases stand.
Beyond 'tis circled by a pleasant grove,
Raised from the family of constant love:
No boisterous storms, nor an inclement sky,
Which tender leaves, and springing buds destroy,
Affect the sombre shade you here enjoy;
Perpetual verdure all the trees disclose,
Which like true love no change of seasons knows.

Nothing this happy climate can produce
Is wanting here for pleasure or for use.
The kitchen ground all kinds of fruit afford,
Which crown with luxury the tempting board.
Here blooming Flora and Pomona reign,
Vertumnus, too, who helps the labouring swain,
Have all agreed to show their watchful care
That Aeolus should this young Eden spare.
Let these kind deities their charge defend,
While I attempt the promised land to ascend.

A noble terrace lies before the front,
By which into a paradise you mount.
Not greater beauty boasts the Idalian grove,
Though that is sacred to the Queen of Love.
Such stately trees encircle every view,
As never in Dodona's forest grew.

Pomona ... Vertumnus] Roman goddess and god of fruits   Aeolus] god of winds
paradise] Ray or Wray Wood   Dodona] shrine which contained an oak sacred to Zeus

Here the smooth beech and reverend oak entwine,
And form a temple for the powers divine;
So ages past from ancient bards we've heard,
When men the deity in groves revered.
A towering wood superior in its kind
Was to the worship of the gods assigned;
While plebian trees, which lowly shade produce,
Were held unworthy of this sacred use.
Here broad meander walks, each way surprise;
And if variety's a charm we prize,
That charm this grove can in perfection boast
As Art in copying Nature pleases most.
Gardens of different forms delight the eye,
From whence a beauteous country we descry;
And sure, if any place deserves to claim,
This wood with justice Belvedere we name.
Statues at proper views enrich the scene,
Here chaste Diana and the Paphian Queen,
Though opposites in fame, though rivals made,
Contented stand under one common shade.
Such harmony of soul this place inspires,
All furious passions, and all fierce desires
Are here becalmed, and gentleness succeeds,
The certain parent whence content proceeds.
Who would not then prefer this pleasing bower,
Since life is fleeting, and the present hour
Is all that fate has put into our power,
To riches, grandeur, fame, ambition's pleas,
Since peace of mind gives greater joy than these?

(1732)

Paphian Queen] Venus, traditionally born at Paphos, Cyprus

James Thomson
1700–1748

from *The Seasons* (Autumn)

55

[*Stowe*]

OR is this gloom too much? Then lead, ye powers
That o'er the garden and the rural seat
Preside, which, shining through the cheerful land
In countless numbers, blest Britannia sees—
Oh! lead me to the wide extended walks,
The fair majestic paradise of Stowe!
Not Persian Cyrus on Ionia's shore
E'er saw such sylvan scenes, such various art
By genius fired, such ardent genius tamed
By cool judicious art, that in the strife
All-beauteous Nature fears to be outdone.
And there, O Pitt! thy country's early boast,
There let me sit beneath the sheltered slopes,
Or in that Temple where, in future times,
Thou well shalt merit a distinguished name,
And, with thy converse blest, catch the last smiles
Of Autumn beaming o'er the yellow woods.
While there with thee the enchanted round I walk,
The regulated wild, gay fancy then
Will tread in thought the groves of Attic land;
Will from thy standard taste refine her own,
Correct her pencil to the purest truth
Of Nature, or, the unimpassioned shades
Forsaking, raise it to the human mind.
Oh, if hereafter she with juster hand
Shall draw the tragic scene, instruct her thou
To mark the varied movements of the heart,
What every decent character requires,
And every passion speaks! Oh, through her strain
Breathe thy pathetic eloquence, that moulds
The attentive senate, charms, persuades, exalts,
Of honest zeal the indignant lightning throws,

Pitt] William Pitt the Elder (1708–78)   Temple] probably the Temple of Friendship,
designed by Gibbs and completed in 1739, which contained a bust of Pitt; Thomson's own
note points to 'The Temple of Virtue', perhaps meaning the Temple of British Worthies

And shakes corruption on her venal throne!
While thus we talk, and through Elysian Vales
Delighted rove, perhaps a sigh escapes—
What pity, Cobham! thou thy verdant files
Of ordered trees shouldst here inglorious range,
Instead of squadrons flaming o'er the field,
And long-embattled hosts! when the proud foe,
The faithless vain disturber of mankind,
Insulting Gaul, has roused the world to war;
When keen, once more, within their bounds to press
Those polished robbers, those ambitious slaves,
The British youth would hail thy wise command,
Thy tempered ardour and thy veteran skill.

(1744)

from *The Seasons* (Spring)

56
[*Garden flower piece*]

AT length the finished garden to the view
Its vistas open, and its alleys green.
Snatched through the verdant maze, the hurried eye
Distracted wanders; now the bowery walk
Of covert close, where scarce a speck of day
Falls on the lengthened gloom, protracted sweeps:
Now meets the bending sky; the river now
Dimpling along, the breezy ruffled lake,
The forest darkening round, the glittering spire,
Th' ethereal mountain, and the distant main.
But why so far excursive? when at hand,
Along these blushing borders, bright with dew,
And in yon mingled wilderness of flowers,
Fair-handed Spring unbosoms every grace;
Throws out the snow-drop and the crocus first;
The daisy, primrose, violet darkly blue,
And polyanthus of unnumbered dyes;
The yellow wall-flower, stained with iron brown;
And lavish stock, that scents the garden round:
From the soft wing of vernal breezes shed,
Anemonies; auriculas, enriched
With shining meal o'er all their velvet leaves;

Elysian Vales] the Elysian Fields   Cobham] Sir Richard Temple, afterwards
Viscount Cobham (1675–1749) creator of the gardens at Stowe after being dismissed from the
army

And full ranunculus, of glowing red.
Then comes the tulip race, where Beauty plays
Her idle freaks; from family diffused
To family, as flies the father-dust,
The varied colours run; and, while they break
On the charmed eye, th' exulting florist marks,
With secret pride, the wonders of his hand.
No gradual bloom is wanting; from the bud,
First-born of Spring, to Summer's musky tribes:
Nor hyacinths, of purest virgin white,
Low bent, and blushing inward; nor jonquils,
Of potent fragrance; nor Narcissus fair,
As o'er the fabled fountain hanging still;
Nor broad carnations, nor gay-spotted pinks;
Nor, showered from every bush, the damask-rose.
Infinite numbers, delicacies, smells,
With hues on hues expression cannot paint,
The breath of Nature, and her endless bloom.

(1746)

Gilbert West
1703–1756

57   from *Stowe, the Gardens of the Rt. Hon. Richard Lord
Viscount Cobham*

HENCE thro' the windings of the mazy wood
Descending, lo! the Octagon's clear flood,
And rustic Obelisk's aerial height,
Burst in one sudden view upon the sight.
Batavian poplars here in ranks ascend;
Like some high temple's arching Isles extend
The taper trunks, a living colonnade;
Eternal murmur animates the shade.
Above, two Doric edifices grace
An elevated platform's utmost space;
From whence, beyond the brook that creeps below,
Along yon beauteous hill's green sloping brow,

57 Doric edifices] twin pavilions by the Octagonal Lake designed by Sir John Vanbrugh

The garden's destin'd boundaries extend,
Where Cobham's pleasing toils, tho' late, shall end;
Beneath the far-stretched lake's capacious bed,
Receives the loud, precipitate cascade;
And tufted groves along the verdant side,
Cast their deep shadows o'er the silver tide:
The silver tide (where yonder high-rais'd mound
Forms the wide-floating lake's extremest bound)
In secret channels thro' the swelling hill,
Gives force and motion to th' impulsive wheel;
Whose constant whirl, the spouting jets supplies,
And bids aloft th' unwilling waters rise.
Fair on the brow, a spacious building stands,
Th' applauded work of Kent's judicious hands:
The spreading wings in arched circles bend,
And rustic domes each arched circle end.
Thence back returning, thro' the narrow glade,
See, where the ruin lifts its mould'ring head!
Within, close-shelter'd from the peering day,
Satyrs and fauns their wanton frolics play.
While sad Malbecco in the secret cell,
Hears each rude monster 'ring his matins bell'.
   Where yon high firs display their darksome green,
And mournful yews compose a solemn scene,
Around thy building, Gibbs, a sacred band
Of princes, patriots, bards, and sages stand:
Men, who by merit purchased lasting praise,
Worthy each British poet's noblest lays:
Or bold in arms for liberty they stood,
And greatly perished for their country's good:
Or nobly warmed with more than mortal fire,
Equalled to Rome and Greece the British lyre:
Or human life by useful arts refined,
Acknowledged benefactors of mankind.

(1732)

spacious building] the Temple of Venus designed by William Kent   ruin] The
Hermitage, also designed by Kent   building, Gibbs] Gibbs' Building, or Belvedere,
designed by James Gibbs (1682–1754)

Nathaniel Cotton
1705–1788

58   *On Lord Cobham's Garden*

It puzzles much the sages' brains,
    Where Eden stood of yore;
Some place it in Arabia's plains
    Some say it is no more.

But Cobham can these tales confute,
    As all the curious know;
For he hath proved, beyond dispute,
    That Paradise is Stowe.

                  (1791)

Stephen Duck
1705–1756

59   from *On Richmond Park*

Now to a softer theme descends my muse;
Through artful walks her pleasing path pursues;
Where lofty elms, and conic lindens rise,
Or where the extensive terrace charms her eyes;
Where elegance and noble grandeur meet,
As the ideas of its mistress, great,
Magnificently fair, majestically sweet.
See, on its margin, fields of waving corn,
These bearded crops, and flowerets this, adorn;
Ceres and Flora lovingly embrace,
And gay varieties the landscape grace.

Hence lead me, muses, through yon arched grove,
Adorned with sand below, and leaves above,
Or let me o'er the spacious oval trace,
Where verdant carpets spread the lovely place,
Where trees in regular confusion stand,
And sylvan beauties rise on every hand;

Or bear me, nymphs, to the sequestered cell,
Where Boyle and Newton, mighty sages, dwell,
Whose fame shall live, although the grot decay,
Long as those sacred truths their works display.

How sweetly pleasing is this cool retreat,
When Phoebus blazes with meridian heat!
In vain the fervid beams around it play,
The rocky roof repels the scorching ray;
Securely guarded with a sylvan scene,
In Nature's livery dressed, forever green.
To visit this, the curious stranger roves,
With grateful travel, through a wild of groves;
And though directed, oft mistakes his way,
Unknowing where the winding mazes stray;
Yet still his feet the magic paths pursue,
Charmed, though bewildered, with the pleasing view.

Not so attractive lately shone the plain,
A gloomy waste, not worth the muses' strain,
Where thorny brakes the traveller repelled,
And weeds and thistles overspread the field;
Till royal George and heavenly Caroline,
Bid Nature in harmonious lustre shine;
The sacred fiat through the chaos rung,
And symmetry from wild disorder sprung.

(1731)

A. M[errick, of Aylesbury]
(dates unknown)

60   *Hartwell Gardens*

WHETHER it is from Eden's sacred plan
Where the first scene of human life began
That this propensity has thus remained
And love to groves and gardens been retained,
Certain it is that first created shade
On human nature such impression made

---

sequestered cell ... Newton] William Kent's Hermitage, decorated inside with busts of
Boyle and Newton among others (see no. 61)

That the lost race an early fondness showed
For soft retreats and for the gloomy wood.
These with religion's mystic rites they graced,
In them their heroes and their gods were placed,
Each thicket did some deity disclose
And fragrant incense from their altars rose;
Nor were they for the muses less renowned,
Here ancient bards their inspiration found
Beneath the spreading beech the Mantuan sung
And Horace in the groves his lyre strung.

A scene like theirs, Sir, now invites the muse
And rapt'rous thoughts into my breast infuse;
'Tis Hartwell's pleasing shades inspire my lays,
Of her fair groves I would attempt the praise
Could I with justness the description show
In numbers such as his who sung famed Stowe.
Though others with more grandeur may surprise
Their temples and their statues thicker rise,
Walks more extensive measure out the ground,
And with variety of art abound
Magnificence and state that much amaze,
Yet more our wonder than our pleasure raise;
Nor proper ornament are wanting here
Of taste polite, and well designed appear
Structures that nicest rules of art express
And statues that the sculptor's skill confess.

On a delightful eminence is seen
A temple named from the Paphian Queen
The hindmost part all shaded by a wood
Whose opening front surveys a crystal flood
Where silver cygnets cut their liquid way
And sportive wild ducks on the surface play.
A stately terrace the canal surrounds
That yields a prospect o'er the neighb'ring grounds,
Whose fertile pastures with rich herbage rise
And golden plenty thence salutes our eyes.

Next o'er a spacious area we tread
With walks of grass and yellow sand bespread;

the Mantuan] Virgil   his ... Stowe] either Alexander Pope (see no. 51) or Gilbert
West (see no. 57)   Paphian Queen] Venus, traditionally born at Paphos

There distant on fair pedestals are seen
The dreaded thunderer and his jealous queen;
Fronting the dome a verdant court extends
Where on each side an easy slope descends;
A well-formed basin ornaments the plain
Whose ample verge does a full tide contain.
Here the smooth turf invites our skill to try,
While without rubs the missive bowls they fly
To seek the mistress on the sportive field,
And both at once doth health and pleasure yield.

If more delights the shady walk or grove,
Scenes that the muses and the virgins love,
Where sylvan beauties are displayed around
And warbling birds their notes melodious sound:
Such now ascending near at hand we trace
Where living walls of trees divide each space,
Which with such order and such art are ranged
That still our pleasure with our walk is changed.
Nor could those vistas more exact appear
Had Orpheus or Amphion's harp been there;
But if you rather choose the closer glade
For contemplation and for silence made,
A solemn gloom invites the loved retreat
Excluding both at once the light and heat.
Here sacred solitude in quiet reigns;
No sounds are heard but Philomela's strains
Who soon as night has closed the busy day
Wakes her sweet voice and tunes her mournful lay.

What next most pleasing to the muse she sees
A lofty shade and formed by aged trees,
With tow'ring heads and arms aspiring high
That almost threaten to invade the sky.
In such green palaces the first kings reigned
Slept in their shades and angels entertained;
Nor a more fit receptacle could find
Were those high guests to visit earth inclined,

thunderer . . . queen] Roman deities Jupiter and his sister/wife Juno   Amphion] who
playing made the stones of Thebes city-walls fall into place   Philomela] daughter of
legendary king of Athens, transformed into a nightingale (according to Roman myth) after
being raped by her brother-in-law and having her tongue cut out; here the nightingale

A. M[ERRICK, OF AYLESBURY]

If well formed statues ornamental prove
Or beauty add to th' venerable grove,
You'll see Alcides resting from his toil,
The satyr bound enraged at his foil;
If to the other side you turn your eyes,
A temple there does on fair columns rise
O' th' Tuscan order forming an alcove —
Such sacred were of old to Latian Jove.

Turning from hence we turn a mazy way
And a well planted wilderness survey,
Where as we through the young meanders rove
Behold the beauties of the rising grove;
When on a sudden from the labyrinth freed
Do in some new, some pleasing, tract proceed.

But stop! I see a lofty column rise
On which a statue fair attracts my eyes —
Exalted as it ought above the rest
Where great Nassau is with great art expressed;
What ornament could more adorn this place
Or than the hero yield an ampler grace;
What, sir, to you afford a juster fame
Or more your love of liberty proclaim;
This your respect to the great memory shows,
Your bosom with the patriot's passion glows;
The sons of freedom own with just applause
This noble ardour for the glorious cause.

Now whither shall the muse direct her view
Or what fair subject of her theme pursue?
That arch triumphal or that tower explore?
Or the rotunda may delight her more,
Or o'er again the verdant carpets tread
And to those walls of ever green be led,
Supinely there to rest me on those seats,
While arched shades repel meridian heats,
Where half encompassed with the circling yew
See the fair prospect opening to my view
Of nature clothed in art's improving dress,
That charms in great variety express.

Alcides] Hercules   his foil] being tricked   Nassau] William III

There fleecy herds rove o'er yon distant field,
Where lowing kine their milky tribute yield;
Here feathered choristers chant in the groves,
And zephyrs wanton round the cool alcoves.
Happy retreat! who would not but be made
The joyful tenant of so blest a shade?
Who higher could their fond ambition trace
Than in the enjoyment of so sweet a place?
Here undisturbed within these shades to rove,
Nor envy gods their famed Idalian Grove.
Though I could wish such pleasure to possess,
Repine not, sir, at this your happiness,
By whose improvement these fair walks appeared
And from a wilderness this Eden reared;
You with such judgement have rude nature changed,
And her wild product into order ranged
Shows that you well deserve the gifts of heaven,
Thus to improve, and thus enjoy what's given.

Be 't late e'er time the comely form removes
Or e'er rude hands invade these peaceful groves
E'er on these paths the wounding share is seen
Or trampling hoofs deface their cheerful green;
But in your worthy race may flourish long
And be the subject of some future song.

(1737)

Anonymous

61
from *Richmond Gardens: A Poem*

HAIL! Richmond, hail! thy matchless beauties'
Attractive charms, as uncontrolled as love.
Soon as thy fame had spread the country round,
Eager I bid adieu to native ground;
With curious haste from distant plains I rove
To tread the verdure of thy shady grove.
Soon as I enter the capacious bower,
A fragrant smell deduced from every flower
Greets my approach; while straight before my eyes
Aspiring elms at equal distance rise—

Idalian] connected with either the Cretan or the Phrygian Mount Ida   share]
ploughshare

Sublime in air, the prospect charms my sight,
And strikes my soul with wonder and delight.
Around the walls hang, tempting to the view,
The luscious peach and scarlet currant, too.
Of humbler growth the circling beds display
Ten thousand herbs produced by grateful May.
Edged with two lonely walks, meandering plays
A smooth canal; the sun's meridian rays
Glisten successive with a twinkling light,
Glance o'er the wat'ry gleam and dim the sight.
Beneath the surface, with impetuous sway,
To fond embrace the restless branches play,
With painful swing attempt a distant blow
At skies that seem ten thousand leagues below.

Forward advancing, but by slow degrees,
Straight I'm conveyed between the thickening trees.
Encompassed round, I dart my eyes on high,
But scarce can trace a passage to the sky.
The sylvan scene with more than nature dressed,
Involves the thoughts of her admiring guest.
In ranks confused, yet ranged in order too
Ten thousand towering storiars greet my view.
The winding circles of the mystic maze
Wrap me in wonder, while intent I gaze.
The treacherous paths in cross-confusion stray,
In little couples steer th' elaborate way;
Uncircumscribed, they aim at distant space,
But, faithless, wander to their destined place,
Attract the labouring eye a giddy round,
Then wind their courses to the centred ground,
Roving at random in one circle meet,
And disappoint the curious wand'rer's feet.
Here the new tenants of the grove appear,
Dressed in majestic state; for many a year
Indulged in native soil, vulgar, obscure,
In rural plains, from pomp and grandeur pure,
Stocked by some labouring bard, transplanted now
They wave their state upon her graceful brow.
In fett'red ranks proud of indulgent chance,
Sport of the wind their spiring branches dance;

storiars] neologism or even perhaps error for 'storials', i.e. old, pertaining to history

Fraught with contempt, their reverend summits bend,
Pleased to survey the little tenants blend
Their despicable heads to mean embrace,
Ambitious of the honours of the place.

Next to my view the Hermitage appears,
In ragged plight, the spoils of ancient years,
Like some discoloured remnant fixed on shore,
Or useless lumber of an ancient floor,
Some shattered fragment of a craggy rock,
Shivered by thundering Jove's avenging stroke.
Without, old hedges, spoils of ancient time,
As if reduced from a once glorious prime,
The cell enclosed with thick surrounding earth,
As if her parent womb was giving birth
To some prodigious monster . . .

Just like a shallow cave by nature made,
Each side surrounded with a silent shade.
The mouldy front, edged with surrounding trees,
Whose waving boughs convey the gentle breeze,
The spacious banks with humble moss o'erspread,
Produce of time, soft as a downy bed.
High o'er the lowly roof thin osiers twine,
Ivy and grateful brambles all combine,
To grasp with painful cling the solemn grot,
Resolved to guard secure the favourite spot.
Within on curious marble carved complete,
Majestic Boyle claims a superior seat,
Newton and Locke, Clarke, Wollaston appear,
Dressed with the native robes they used to wear.
Immortal bards, and as divine their name,
Dear to their country and as dear to fame,
Intrinsic worth! could I with Newton soar
And scan the plains no mortal scanned before,
On Milton's wings I'd dare a flight sublime,
And drop the fetters of indulgent rhyme;
In boundless strains I'd stretch my tuneful voice,
To aid my flight Urania should rejoice.
The sylvan grot in lively colours shown,
I'd mount the skies on pinions of my own . . .

Hermitage] designed by William Kent   Majestic Boyle . . . Newton . . . Wollaston]
eminent thinkers whose busts were placed inside the Hermitage by Queen Caroline

Swift from the humble grot, my favourite place,
The roving muse must aim at distant space;
To Merlin's Cave impartial she retreats,
And her delightful toils afresh repeats.
Thatched with old straw and bound by rural bard,
Like a large barn that fronts the farmer's yard,
The homely roof erects its lowly head,
And scarce appears to sight; but just surveyed
Between the opening boughs, aloft in air,
The thick'ning spires of rev'rend elms appear,
Promiscuous clash, mild zephyrs sportive play,
From bough to bough the rustling leaves convey
The murm'ring sound, from branch to branch on high,
Till in the wide expanse the feeble zephyrs die.
Just o'er the cave with unambitious state,
Weak willows rise but of a modern date;
With painful nod the little twigs extend
Around the roof; each side propitious blend
Their leafy members, glory of the place,
Then wave reluctant from the loved embrace.
In artless fold the twisting wreaths combine,
To screen the cave from sol's exuberant shine.
Silence perpetual sits on ev'ry side,
And the low cot stands dressed with gloomy pride;
The solemn breeze and cool refreshing air,
And hovering shades keep constant sentry there.
The op'ning valves admit her curious guest,
Impatient to behold the wond'rous scene undressed.
Entering the cave, the rich apartment smiles,
Replete with all the muse's grateful toils;
The noblest authors, great Apollo's race,
Sons of immortal fame, and sons of grace,
Blended in beauteous order ranged complete,
With more than native beauty grace the seat.
Merlin sits anxious o'er his glassy globe,
The reverend senior smiles, and plain his robe,
With honest beauty circling in his face;
His secretary smiles with lovely grace,
With pen in hand he seems intent to write,
And thoughtful waits with half-erected sight
His rev'rend master's nod, anxious to hear
The sage instructor dictate to his ear.

(1738)

Merlin's Cave] a second edifice erected to designs of William Kent

Philip Doddridge
1702–1751

Meditations on the Sepulchre in the Garden

John 19:41

THE sepulchres, how thick they stand
Through all the road on either hand!
And burst upon the startling sight
In ev'ry garden of delight!

Thither the winding alleys tend;
There all the flow'ry borders end;
And forms, that charmed the eyes before,
Fragrance and music are no more.

Deep in that damp and silent cell
My fathers and my brethren dwell;
Beneath its broad and gloomy shade
My kindred and my friends are laid.

But, while I tread the solemn way,
My faith that Saviour would survey,
Who deigned to sojourn in the tomb,
And left behind a rich perfume.

My thoughts with ecstasy unknown,
While from his grave they view his throne,
Through mine own sepulchre can see
A paradise reserved for me.

Samuel Boyse
1708–1749

from *The Triumphs of Nature*

[*In the Elysian Fields of Stowe*]

NEXT to the fair ascent our steps we traced
Whence shines afar the bold Rotunda placed;
The artful dome Ionic columns bear
Light as the fabric swells in ambient air,
Beneath unshrined the Tuscan Venus stands,
And beauty's queen the beauteous scene commands:
The fond beholder sees with sweet surprise,
Streams glitter, lawns appear, and forests rise—
Here thro' thick shades alternate buildings break
There thro' its borders steals the silver lake;
A soft variety delights the soul,
And harmony resulting crowns the whole!
   Now by the long canal we gently turn,
Whose verdant sides romantic scenes adorn;
As objects thro' the broken ground we see,
And there a statue rises, there a tree!
Here in an amphitheatre of green,
With slopes set off which form a rural scene,
On four Ionic pillars raised to sight,
Beams Carolina Britain's late delight!
Here the bright queen her heav'nly form displays,
Eternal subject of the Muse's praise;
But faint all praise her merit to impart,
Whose mem'ry lives in every British heart!
   Now leave we, devious, the declining plain,
A while to wander thro' the woodland scene;
Here where six centring walks united meet,
Morpheus invites us to his still retreat;
And while the tide of life uncertain flows,
'Bids you indulge your self, and taste repose!'
   But stop my muse—I feel a conscious fear,
As if concealed divinity was near!
What do I see?—what solemn views arise!
What wonders open to my thoughtful eyes!

Carolina] Queen Caroline, wife of George II   Morpheus] god of sleep, referring to
the Cave of Sleep

Midst purling streams in awful beauty drest,
The shrine of Ancient Virtue stands confessed;
A Doric pile! by studious Cobham placed,
To shew the world the worth of ages past;
When innocence—when truth still found regard,
And cherished merit had its due reward!
    Within four graceful statues honoured stand,
Inspire attention, and esteem command;
'Epaminondas first in arms renowned,
Whose glorious aim his country's freedom crowned
Born in each social virtue to excell,
With whom the Theban glory rose—and fell!'
'Lycurgus next, in steady virtue great,
Who for duration formed the Spartan state;
And wealth expelling, with her baneful train,
Left a republic worth the name of men!'
'There Socrates, th' Athenian wise and good,
With more than mortal sanctity endued;
Who freed philosophy from useless art,
And showed true science was to mend the heart.'
'Last stands the prince of bards, whose deathless lay
Does virtue in exalted verse convey;
Sets every passion in its native light,
And fills the soul with terror and delight!'
'These point, the way to reach immortal praise,
Is life on public Virtue's base to raise!
And shew that goodness and our country's love
Exalt us to the blissful seats above;
Where bards repose, and godlike patriots smile,
And glorious heroes rest from earthly toil!
While, like the ruin placed in view beneath,
The tyrant and oppressor rot in death;
All born of vice devoted to decay,
And hastening like the gliding brook away!'
    Now leaving with regret the solemn wood,
We by the winding stream our course pursued;
Where stands the lonesome grotto sweetly placed,
With all the art of sportive nature graced:
Two neighb'ring domes on spiral columns rise,
With shells and min'rals spangled to the eyes.

purling streams] the stream, later called the River Styx, that runs through the Elysian Fields
at Stowe   Ancient Virtue] the Temple of Ancient Virtue designed by William Kent
Epaminondas] the great Theban commander in the wars between Athens and Sparta
Lycurgus] legendary Spartan law-giver   prince of bards] Homer

Whence, still directed by the winding stream,
Amused, we to the three-arched building came.
Hence west the church adorns the opening height,
Eastward the spacious pond relieves the sight:
In which of form Chinese a structure lies,
Where all her wild grotesques displayed surprise;
Within Japan her glittering treasure yields,
And ships of amber sail on golden fields!
In radiant clouds are silver turrets found,
And mimic glories glitter all around.

(1742)

John Armstrong
1709–1779

64   from *The Art of Preserving Health*

BUT if through genuine tenderness of heart,
Or secret want of relish for the game,
You shun the glories of the chase, nor care
To haunt the peopled stream; the garden yields
A soft amusement, a humane delight.
To raise the insipid nature of the ground;
Or tame its savage genius to the grace
Of careless sweet rusticity, that seems
The amiable result of happy chance,
Is to create; and gives a god-like joy,
Which every year improves. Nor thou disdain
To check the lawless riot of the trees,
To plant the grove, or turn the barren mould.
O happy he! whom, when his years decline,
(His fortune and his fame by worthy means
Attained, and equal to his moderate mind;
His life approved by all the wise and good,
Even envied by the vain) the peaceful groves
Of Epicurus, from this stormy world,
Receive to rest; of all ungrateful cares
Absolved, and sacred from the selfish crowd.
Happiest of men! if the same soil invites
A chosen few, companions of his youth,
Once fellow rakes perhaps, now rural friends;

With whom in easy commerce to pursue
Nature's free charms, and vie for sylvan fame:
A fair ambition; void of strife or guile,
Or jealousy, or pain to be outdone.
Who plans the enchanted garden, who directs
The vista best, and best conducts the stream;
Whose groves the fastest thicken and ascend;
Whom first the welcome spring salutes; who shows
The earliest bloom, the sweetest proudest charms
Of Flora; who best gives Pomona's juice
To match the sprightly genius of champaign.
Thrice happy days! in rural business past . . .

(1744)

Richard Jago
1715–1781

from *Edge-Hill*

65   [*Instructions on landscaping*]

WOULD ye, with faultless judgement, learn to plan
The rural seat? To copy, as ye rove,
The well-formed picture, and correct design?
First shun the false extremes of high, and low.
With watery vapours this your fretted walls
Will soon deface; and that, with rough assault,
And frequent tempests shake your tottering roof.
Me most the gentle eminence delights
Of healthy champaign, to the sunny south
Fair-opening, and with woods, and circling hills,
Nor too remote, nor with too close embrace,
Stopping the buxom air, behind enclosed.
But if your lot hath fallen in fields less fair,
Consult their genius and, with due regard
To Nature's clear directions, shape your plan.
The site too lofty shelter, and the low
With sunny lawns, and open areas cheer.
The marsh drain and, with capacious urns,
And well-conducted streams refresh the dry.

Pomona] Roman goddess of fruits

So shall your lawns with healthful verdure smile,
While others, sickening at the sultry blaze,
A russet wild display, or the rank blade,
And matted tufts the careless owner shame.
Seek not, with fruitless cost, the level plain
To raise aloft, nor sink the rising hill.
Each has its charms though different, each in kind
Improve, not alter. Art with art conceal.
Let no straight terraced lines your slopes deform.
No barbarous walls restrain the bounded sight.
With better skill your chaste designs display;
And to the distant fields the closer scene
Connect. The spacious lawn with scattered trees
Irregular, in beauteous negligence,
Clothe bountiful. Your unimprisoned eye,
With pleasing freedom, through the lofty maze
Shall rove, and find no dull satiety.
The winding stream with stiffened line avoid
To torture, nor prefer the long canal,
Or laboured fount to Nature's easy flow,
And artless fall. Your gravelly winding paths
Now to the freshening breeze, or sunny gleam
Directed, now with high embowering trees,
Or fragrant shrubs concealed, with frequent seat,
And rural structure deck. Their pleasing form
To fancy's eye suggests inhabitants
Of more than mortal make, and their cool shade,
And friendly shelter to refreshment sweet,
And wholesome meditation shall invite.
To every structure give its proper site.
Nor, on the dreary heath, the gay alcove,
Nor the lone hermit's cell, or mournful urn
Build on the sprightly lawn. The grassy slope
And sheltered border for the cool arcade,
Or Tuscan porch reserve. To the chaste dome,
And fair rotunda give the swelling mount
Of freshest green. If to the Gothic scene
Your taste incline, in the well-watered vale,
With lofty pines embrowned, the mimic fane,
And mouldering abbey's fretted windows place.
The craggy rock, or precipitous hill,
Shall well become the castle's massy walls.
In royal villas the Palladian arch,
And Grecian portico, with dignity,

Their pride display: ill suits their lofty rank
The simpler scene. If chance historic deeds
Your fields distinguish, count them doubly fair,
And studious aid, with monumental stone,
And faithful comment, fancy's fond review.

(1767)

William Whitehead
1715–1785

66   *On the Late Improvements at Nuneham, the Seat
of the Earl of Harcourt*

DAME Nature, the goddess, one very bright day,
In strolling through Nuneham, met Brown in her way:
'And bless me', she said, with an insolent sneer,
'I wonder that fellow will dare to come here.
What more than I *did* has your impudence planned?
The lawn, wood, and water, are all of my hand;
In my very best manner, with Themis's scales,
I lifted the hills, and I scooped out the vales;
With Sylvan's own umbrage I graced ev'ry brow,
And poured the rich Thames through the meadows below.'
    'I grant it', he cried; 'to your sov'reign command
I bow, as I ought—Gentle lady, your hand;
The weather's inviting, so let us move on;
You know what you *did*, and now see what I've done.
I, with gratitude, own you have reason to plead,
That to these happy scenes you were bounteous indeed:
My lovely materials were many and great!
(For sometimes, you know, I'm obliged to create)
But say in return, my adorable dame,
To all you see here, can you lay a just claim?
Were there no slighter parts which you finished in haste,
Or left, like a friend, to give scope to my taste?
Who drew o'er the surface, did you, or did I,
The smooth-flowing outline, that steals from the eye,
The soft undulations, both distant and near,
That heave from the lawns, and yet scarcely appear?

66 Brown] Lancelot 'Capability' Brown, landscape gardener (1716–83)   Themis]
Greek goddess of justice and wisdom

(So bends the ripe harvest the breezes beneath,
As if Earth was in slumber and gently took breath)
Who thinned, and who grouped, and who scattered those trees,
Who bade the slopes fall with that delicate ease,
Who cast them in shade, and who placed them in light,
Who bade them divide, and who bade them unite?
The ridges are melted, the boundaries gone:
Observe all these changes, and candidly own
I have clothed you when naked, and, when overdrest,
I have stripped you again to your bodice and vest;
Concealed every blemish, each beauty displayed,
As Reynolds would picture some exquisite maid,
Each spirited feature would happily place,
And shed o'er the whole inexpressible grace.
  'One question remains. Up the green of yon steep,
Who threw the bold walk with that elegant sweep?
—There is little to see, till the summit we gain;
Nay, never draw back, you may climb without pain,
And, I hope, will perceive how each object is caught,
And is lost, in exactly the point where it ought.
That ground of your moulding is certainly fine,
But the swell of that knoll and those openings are mine.
The prospect, wherever beheld, must be good,
But has ten times its charms, when you burst from this wood,
A wood of my planting.'—The goddess cried, 'Hold!
'Tis grown very hot, and 'tis grown very cold':
She fanned and she shuddered, she coughed and she sneezed,
Inclined to be angry, inclined to be pleased,
Half smiled, and half pouted—then turned from the view,
And dropped him a curtsy, and blushing withdrew.
  Yet soon recollecting her thoughts, as she passed,
'I may have my revenge on this fellow at last:
For a lucky conjecture comes into my head,
That, whate'er he has done, and whate'er he has said,
The world's little malice will balk his design:
Each fault they call his, and each excellence mine.'

(1788)

Reynolds] Sir Joshua Reynolds (1723–92)

Thomas Gray
1716–1771

67 *On Lord Holland's Seat near Margate, Kent*

OLD, and abandoned by each venal friend,
 Here Holland took the pious resolution
To smuggle some few years, and strive to mend
 A broken character and constitution.

On this congenial spot he fixed his choice,
 Earl Goodwin trembled for his neighbouring sand;
Here seagulls scream and cormorants rejoice,
 And mariners, though shipwrecked, dread to land.

Here reign the blustering North and blighting East,
 No tree is heard to whisper, bird to sing.
Yet Nature cannot furnish out the feast;
 Art he invokes new horrors still to bring.

Now mouldering fanes and battlements arise,
 Arches and turrets nodding to their fall,
Unpeopled palaces delude his eyes,
 And mimic desolation covers all.

'Ah!' said the sighing peer, 'had Bute been true,
 Nor Shelburne's, Rigby's, Calcraft's friendship vain,
Far other scenes than these had blessed our view,
 And realized the ruins that we feign.

'Purged by the sword and beautified by fire,
 Then had we seen proud London's hated walls:
Owls might have hooted in St Peter's choir,
 And foxes stunk and littered in St Paul's.'

           (1769)

Goodwin] treacherous sandbanks   Bute . . . Calcraft] 3rd Earl of Bute, in whose
Cabinet Holland had served, and political colleagues of Holland's who had proved disloyal

Mark Akenside

1721–1770

68   *Inscription for a Grotto*

To me, whom, in their lays, the shepherds call
Actaea, daughter of the neighbouring stream,
This cave belongs. The fig-tree and the vine,
Which o'er the rocky entrance downward shoot,
Were placed by Glycon. He, with cowslips pale,
Primrose, and purple lychnis, decked the green
Before my threshold, and my shelving walls
With honeysuckle covered. Here, at noon,
Lulled by the murmur of my rising fount,
I slumber: here my clustering fruits I tend;
Or from the humid flowers at break of day,
Fresh garlands weave, and chase from all my bounds
Each thing impure or noxious. Enter in,
O stranger, undismayed. Nor bat, nor toad
Here lurks: and, if thy breast of blameless thoughts
Approve thee, not unwelcome shalt thou tread
My quiet mansion: chiefly, if thy name
Wise Pallas and the immortal Muses own.

(1772)

Henry Jones

1721–1770

69   *On a Fine Crop of Peas being Spoiled by a Storm*

WHEN Morrice views his prostrate peas,
    By raging whirlwinds spread,
He wrings his hands, and in amaze
    He sadly shakes his head.

'Is this the fruit of my fond toil,
    My joy, my pride, my cheer!
Shall one tempestuous hour thus spoil
    The labours of a year!

Oh! what avails, that day to day
    I nursed the thriving crop,
And settled with my foot the clay,
    And reared the social prop!

Ambition's pride had spurred me on
    All gard'ners to excell.
I often called them one by one,
    And boastingly would tell,

How I prepared the furrowed ground
    And how the grain did sow,
Then challenged all the country round
    For such an early blow.

How did their bloom my wishes raise!
    What hopes did they afford,
To earn my honoured master's praise,
    And crown his cheerful board!'

Poor Morrice, wrapt in sad surprise,
    Demands in sober mood,
'Should storms molest a man so wise,
    A man so just and good?'

Ah! Morrice, cease thy fruitless moan,
    Nor at misfortunes spurn,
Misfortune's not thy lot alone;
    Each neighbour hath his turn.

Thy prostrate peas, which low recline
    Beneath the frowns of fate,
May teach much wiser heads than thine
    Their own uncertain state.

The sprightly youth in beauty's prime,
    The lovely nymph so gay,
Oft victims fall to early time,
    And in their bloom decay.

blow] flourish or blossom, with of course an ironic pun on blow (= storm)

In vain th' indulgent father's care,
        In vain wise precepts form;
They droop, like peas, in tainted air,
        Or perish in a storm.

                                    (1749)

Joseph Warton
1722–1800

70   from *The Enthusiast*

YE green-robed dryads, often at dusky eve
By wondering shepherds seen, to forests brown,
To unfrequented meads, and pathless wilds,
Lead me from gardens decked with art's vain pomps.
Can gilt alcoves, can marble-mimic gods,
Parterres embroidered, obelisks, and urns
Of high relief; can the long, spreading lake,
Or vista lessening to the sight; can Stowe
With all her Attic fanes, such raptures raise,
As the thrush-haunted copse, where lightly leaps
The fearful fawn the rustling leaves along,
And the brisk squirrel sports from bough to bough,
While from an hollow oak the busy bees
Hum drowsy lullabies? The bards of old,
Fair nature's friends, sought such retreats, to charm
Sweet Echo with their songs; often too they met,
In summer evenings, near sequestered bowers,
Or mountain-nymph, or muse, and eager learnt
The moral strains she taught to mend mankind.
As to a secret Egeria stole
With patriotic Numa, and in silent night
Whispered him sacred laws, he listening sat
Rapt with her virtuous voice, old Tiber leant
Attentive on his urn, and hushed his waves.

Rich in her weeping country's spoils Versailles
May boast a thousand fountains, that can cast
The tortured waters to the distant heavens;

Egeria . . . Numa] water-nymph, consort and advisor of Numa, legendary king of Rome

Yet let me choose some pine-topped precipice
Abrupt and shaggy, whence a foamy stream,
Like Anio, tumbling roars; or some bleak heath,
Where straggling stand the mournful juniper,
Or yew-tree scathed; while in clear prospect round,
From the grove's bosom spires emerge, and smoke
In bluish wreaths ascends, ripe harvests wave,
Herds low, and straw-roofed cots appear, and streams
Beneath the sunbeams twinkle — The shrill lark,
That wakes the wood-man to his early task,
Or love-sick Philomel, whose luscious lays
Soothe lone night-wanderers, the moaning dove,
Pitied by listening milkmaid, far excel
The deep-mouthed viol, the soul-lulling lute,
And battle-breathing trumpet. Artful sounds!
That please not like the choristers of air,
When first they hail th' approach of laughing May.
Can Kent design like nature? Mark where Thames
Plenty and pleasure pours through Lincoln's meads;
Can the great artist, though with taste supreme
Endued, one beauty to this Eden add?
Though he, by rules unfettered, boldly scorns
Formality and method, round and square
Disdaining, plans irregularly great.
Creative Titian, can thy vivid strokes,
Or thine, O graceful Raphael, dare to vie
With the rich tints that paint the breathing mead?
The thousand-coloured tulip, violet's bell
Snow-clad and meek, the vermil-tinctured rose,
And golden crocus?

(1744)

Anonymous

71   from *The Rise and Progress of the Present Taste in
Planning Parks, Pleasure Grounds, Gardens, etc.*

O STUDY Nature! and with thought profound,
Previous to laying out with taste your ground,
O mark her beauties as they striking rise,
Bid all her adventitious charms surprise!

Philomel] legendary character metamorphosed into a nightingale   Kent] William
Kent, landscape gardener (1685–1748)

Eye all her shining, all her shadowy grace,
And to conceal them every blemish trace.
Yet there's a happiness that baffles Art,
In showing Nature great in every part,
Which chiefly flows from mingled lights and shades,
In lawns, and woods, hills, rivers, rocks and glades;
For only happy's that assemblage made,
Where force of light contends with force of shade.
But when too busy Art destroys each grace,
And shades with ornaments her lovely face,
We abdicated beauty eye with pain,
And Art presides, where Nature ought to reign . . .

But you, my lord, at Templenewsham find,
The charms of Nature gracefully combined,
Sweet waving hills, with woods and verdure crowned,
And winding vales, where murmuring streams resound;
Slopes fringed with oaks which gradual die away,
And all around romantic scenes display.
Delighted still along the park we rove,
Varied with hill and dale, with wood and grove;
O'er velvet lawns what noble prospects rise,
Fair as the scenes that Rubens' hand supplies!
But when the lake shall these sweet grounds adorn,
And bright expanding like the eye of morn,
Reflect whate'er above its surface rise,
The hills, the rocks, the woods, and varying skies,
Then will the wild and beautiful combine,
And taste and beauty grace your whole design.

But you great artist, like the source of light,
Gilds every scene with beauty and delight;
At Blenheim, Croome and Caversham we trace
Salvator's wildness, Claude's enlivening grace,
Cascades and lakes as fine as Risdale drew,
While Nature's varied in each charming view.
To paint his works would Poussin's powers require,
Milton's sublimity, and Dryden's fire;
For both the sister arts in him combined,
Enrich the great ideas of his mind;

great artist] Lancelot 'Capability' Brown, landscape gardener (1716–83)   Salvator
. . . Claude] Salvator Rosa (1615–73) and Claude Lorrain (1600–82) famous as landscape
painters   Risdale] Salomon van Ruysdael (c.1600–70) Dutch landscape painter
Poussin] either Nicolas Poussin (1593/4–1665) or, more likely, Gaspard Dughet (1615–75),
called Poussin, here invoked, like Rubens earlier, as painter of landscapes

And these still brighten all his vast designs,
For here the painter, there the poet shines!
With just contempt he spurns all former rules,
And shows true taste is not confined to schools.
He barren tracts with every charm illumes,
At his command a new creation blooms;
Born to grace Nature, and her works complete,
With all that's beautiful, sublime and great!
For him each muse enwreathes the laurel crown,
And consecrates to fame immortal Brown.

(1767)

Joseph Giles
(late eighteenth century)

72   from *The Leasowes: Or, A Poetical Description of the
        Late Mr Shenstone's Rural Retirement*

HERE circling trees, which form a shade
For contemplation fitly made,
    Surround the weeping urn:
Which tells of friendship's silken chains
Dissolved by death (in moving strains),
    And bids the reader mourn.

We now the flowery path pursue,
Which oft presents some pleasing view,
    To entertain the sight:
While fertile grounds, which all excel,
With beauteous falls, or graceful swell,
    Contribute to delight.

Here, we ascend some airy seat,
Or little temple's close retreat,
    Beneath a shady bower:
And oft some moral sentence find
To please or to instruct the mind,
    And pass each tedious hour.

Now, view the boundless prospect, fair,
And breathe a pure, sublimer air,
    While smoke involves the town:
Then those reflections soon occur
Of busy life, its noise and stir,
    Which mental pleasures drown.

Here may the thoughts expatiate free,
Embrace that friend, Philosophy,
    The jarring crowd forget:
And since those plagues my joys bereave,
With what reluctance here I leave
    This happy, blissful seat.

Hence, as we tread the flowery lawn,
We see some striking object drawn
    Among the distant trees:
Nature's chief beauties here abound!
Her liberal hand has blessed the ground,
    Her breath perfumes the breeze.

Now, through the leafy maze we stray,
There find a fragrant, winding way,
    Beneath a shady grove:
And hear the woodlark's pleasing note,
Whene'er she tries her tuneful throat
    To melting strains of love.

Here, a pure, crystal, purling stream,
Imbibes the sun's refulgent beam,
    From slope to slope falls down:
So gently flows, so soft and clear,
We see its sparkling bed appear;
    While flowers the margin crown.

Whene'er I to this grove resort,
Methinks I see the dryads sport,
    So famed of bards of yore;
And deep among the trees I scan
The temple of immortal Pan,
    Which sylvan swains adore.

Here the long vista far extends,
And like a Gothic cloister bends,
    Almost excluding day:
But hence emerged, new beauties rise,
And raise our wonder and surprise,
    As we the whole survey.

Here, woods and groves, and flowery fields
Have every blessing nature yields,
    While herds and flocks abound:
Here sloping lawns so smooth and green,
With many a beauteous, rural scene,
    Adorn the prospect round.

Though small the mansion, void of state,
The whole is beautifully neat,
    Within the centre placed:
And every grace the owner knows—
Throughout the whole true greatness flows
    With elegance and taste.

                                    (pub. 1771)

William Mason
1724–1797

from *The English Garden*

73   [*Some early gardenists*]

LONG was the night of error, nor dispelled
By him that rose at learning's earliest dawn,
Prophet of unborn Science. On thy realm,
Philosophy! his sovereign lustre spread;
Yet did he deign to light with casual glance
The wilds of taste. Yes, sagest Verulam,
'Twas thine to banish from the royal groves
Each childish vanity of crisped knot
And sculptured foliage; to the lawn restore

73 Verulam] Francis Bacon, first Lord Verulam (1561–1626), author of a celebrated essay
'Of Gardens' (1625)

Its ample space, and bid it feast the sight
With verdure pure, unbroken, unabridged:
For verdure soothes the eye, as roseate sweets
The smell, or music's melting strains the ear.

So taught the Sage, taught a degenerate reign
What in Eliza's golden day was taste.
Not but the mode of that romantic age,
The age of tourneys, triumphs, and quaint masques,
Glared with fantastic pageantry, which dimmed
The sober eye of truth, and dazzled ev'n
The Sage himself; witness his high-arched hedge,
In pillared state by carpentry upborn,
With coloured mirrors decked, and prisoned birds.
But when our step has paced his proud parterres,
And reached the heath, then Nature glads our eye
Sporting in all her lovely carelessness.
There smiles in varied tufts the velvet rose,
There flaunts the gadding woodbine, swells the ground
In gentle hillocks, and around its sides
Thro' blossomed shades the secret pathway steals.

Thus, with a poet's power, the Sage's pen
Portrayed that nicer negligence of scene,
Which Taste approves. While he, delicious swain,
Who tuned his oaten pipe by Mulla's stream,
Accordant touched the stops in Dorian mood:
What time he 'gan to paint the fairy vale,
Where stands the fane of Venus. Well I ween
That then, if ever, Colin, thy fond hand
Did steep its pencil in the well-fount clear
Of true simplicity; and 'called in Art
Only to second Nature, and supply
All that the Nymph forgot, or left forlorn'.
Yet what availed the song? or what availed
Ev'n thine, thou chief of Bards, whose mighty mind,
With inward light irradiate, mirror-like
Received, and to mankind with ray reflex
The sov'reign Planter's primal work displayed?
'That work, where not nice Art in curious knots,
But Nature's boon poured forth on hill and dale
Flowers worthy of Paradise; while all around

ween] believe   Colin] Edmund Spenser (?1552–99) who took the persona of a
shepherd, Colin Clout   chief of Bards] Milton

Umbrageous grots, and caves of cool recess,
And murmuring waters down the slope dispersed,
Or held, by fringed banks, in crystal lakes,
Compose a rural seat of various view.'
'Twas thus great Nature's herald blazoned high
That fair original impress, which she bore
In state sublime; e'er miscreated Art,
Offspring of Sin and Shame, the banner seized,
And with adulterate pageantry defiled.
Yet vainly, Milton, did thy voice proclaim
These her primeval honours. Still she lay
Defaced, deflowered, full many a ruthless year:
Alike, when Charles, the abject tool of France,
Came back to smile his subjects into slaves;
Or Belgic William, with his warrior frown,
Coldly declared them free; in fetters still
The Goddess pined, by both alike opprest.

Go to the proof! Behold what Temple called
A perfect garden. There thou shalt not find
One blade of verdure, but with aching feet
From terrace down to terrace shalt descend,
Step following step, by tedious flight of stairs:
On leaden platforms now the noon-day sun
Shall scorch thee; now the dank arcades of stone
Shall chill thy fervour; happy, if at length
Thou reach the orchard, where the sparing turf
Through equal lines, all centring in a point,
Yields thee a softer tread. And yet full oft
O'er Temple's studious hour did truth preside,
Sprinkling her lustre o'er his classic page:
There here his candour own in fashion's spite,
In spite of courtly dullness, hear it own
'There is a grace in wild variety
Surpassing rule and order.' Temple, yes,
There is a grace; and let eternal wreaths
Adorn their brows who fixed its empire here.

(1772)

Charles] Charles II   Belgic William] the Dutchman, William III   Temple] Sir
William Temple (1628–99), author of a famous essay on gardens, 'Upon the gardens of
Epicurus . . .' (1692)

74

[Alcander's flower garden]

As through a neighb'ring grove, where ancient beech
Their awful foliage flung, Alcander led
The pensive maid along. 'Tell me,' she cried,
'Why, on these forest features all-intent,
Forbears my friend some scene distinct to give
To Flora and her fragrance? Well I know
That in the general landscape's broad expanse
Their little blooms are lost; but here are glades,
Circled with shade, yet pervious to the sun,
Where, if enamelled with their rainbow-hues,
The eye would catch their splendour: Turn thy task,
Even in this grassy circle where we stand,
To form their plots; there weave a woodbine bower.
And call that bower Nerina's.' At the word
Alcander smiled; his fancy formed
The fragrant scene she wished; and Love, with Art
Uniting, soon produced the finished whole.

Down to the south the glade by Nature leaned;
Art formed the slope still softer, opening there
Its foliage, and to each Etesian gale
Admittance free dispensing; thickest shade
Guarded the rest.—His taste will best conceive
The new arrangement, whose free footsteps, used
To forest haunts, have pierced their opening dells,
Where frequent tufts of sweetbriar, box, or thorn,
Steal on the green sward, but admit fair space
For many a mossy maze to wind between.
So here did Art arrange her flowery groups
Irregular, yet not in patches quaint,
But interposed between the wandering lines
Of shaven turf which twisted to the path,
Gravel or sand, that in as wild a wave
Stole round the verdant limits of the scene;
Leading the eye to many a sculptured bust
On shapely pedestal, of sage, or bard,
Bright heirs of fame, who living loved the haunts
So fragrant, so sequestered. Many an urn
There too had place, with votive lay inscribed
To freedom, friendship, solitude, or love.

awful] awesome   Etesian gale] strong summer winds in the Aegean Sea

And now each flower that bears transplanting change,
Or blooms indigenous, adorned the scene:
Only Nerina's wish, her woodbine bower,
Remained to crown the whole. Here, far beyond
That humble wish, her lover's genius formed
A glittering fane, where rare and alien plants
Might safely flourish; where the citron sweet,
And fragrant orange, rich in fruit and flowers,
Might hang their silver stars, their golden globes,
On the same odorous stem: Yet scorning there
The glassy penthouse of ignoble form,
High on Ionic shafts he bad it tower
A proud rotunda; to its sides conjoined
Two broad piazzas in theatric curve,
Ending in equal porticos sublime.
Glass roofed the whole, and sidelong to the south
'Twixt every fluted column, lightly reared
Its wall pellucid. All within was day,
Was genial summer's day, for secret stoves
Through all the pile solstitial warmth conveyed.

(1781)

75   from *An Heroic Epistle to Sir William Chambers*

THERE was a time, 'in Esher's peaceful grove,
When Kent and Nature vied for Pelham's love',
That Pope beheld them with auspicious smile,
And owned that Beauty blest their mutual toil.
Mistaken Bard! could such a pair design
Scenes fit to live in thy immortal line?
Hadst thou been born in this enlightened day,
Felt, as we feel, taste's oriental ray,
Thy satire sure had given them both a stab,
Called Kent a driveller, and the Nymph a drab.
For what is Nature? Ring her changes round,
Her three flat notes are water, plants, and ground;
Prolong the peal, yet spite of all your clatter,
The tedious chime is still ground, plants, and water.
So, when some John his dull invention racks,
To rival Boodle's dinners, or Almack's,

75 Kent] William Kent (1685–1748), landscape gardener who landscaped Esher Place for Pelham in 1729   Pelham] Henry Pelham (?1695–1754)

Three uncouth legs of mutton shock our eyes,
Three roasted geese, three buttered apple-pies.
  Come then, prolific Art, and with thee bring
The charms that rise from thy exhaustless spring;
To Richmond come, for see, untutored Brown
Destroys those wonders which were once thy own.
Lo, from his melon-ground the peasant slave
Has rudely rushed, and levelled Merlin's Cave;
Knocked down the waxen wizzard, seized his wand,
Transformed to lawn what late was fairy land;
And marred, with impious hand, each sweet design
Of Stephen Duck, and good Queen Caroline.
Haste, bid yon livelong terrace re-ascend,
Replace each vista, straighten every bend;
Shut out the Thames; shall that ignoble thing
Approach the presence of great Ocean's king?
No! let barbaric glories feast his eyes,
August pagodas round his palace rise,
And finished Richmond open to his view,
'A work to wonder at, perhaps a' Kew . . .

  Be these the rural pastimes that attend
Great Brunswick's leisure: these shall best unbend
His royal mind, whene'er, from state withdraw'n,
He treads the velvet of his Richmond lawn;
These shall prolong his Asiatic dream,
Tho' Europe's balance trembles on its beam.
And thou, Sir William! while thy plastic hand
Creates each wonder, which thy bard has planned,
While, as thy art commands, obsequious rise
Whate'er can please, or frighten, or surprise,
O! let that bard his knight's protection claim,
And share, like faithful Sancho, Quixote's fame.

(1773)

Brown] Lancelot 'Capability' Brown, landscape gardener (1716–83)   Stephen Duck]
1705–56, the so-called 'Thresher Poet', who occasionally inhabited Merlin's Cave in
Richmond Park (see nos. 59 and 61)   Queen Caroline] wife of George II
Brunswick] the House of Brunswick

76

To a Gravel Walk

SMOOTH, simple path! whose undulating line,
  With sidelong tufts of flowery fragrance crowned,
  'Plain, in its neatness', spans my garden ground;
What, though two acres thy brief course confine,
Yet sun and shade, and hill and dale are thine,
  And use with beauty here more surely found,
  Than where, to spread the picturesque around,
Cart ruts and quarry holes their charms combine!
  Here, as thou leads't my step through lawn or grove,
Liberal though limited, restrained though free,
  Fearless of dew, or dirt, or dust, I rove,
And own those comforts all derived from thee!
  Take then, smooth path, this tribute of my love,
Thou emblem pure of legal liberty!

(1795)

Erasmus Darwin
1731–1802

from The Botanic Garden

77   [Kew]

So sits enthroned in vegetable pride
Imperial Kew by Thames's glittering side;
Obedient sails from realms unfurrowed bring
For her the unnamed progeny of spring;
Attendant nymphs her dulcet mandates hear,
And nurse in fostering arms the tender year,
Plant the young bulb, inhume the living seed,
Prop the weak stem, the erring tendril lead;
Or fan in glass-built fanes the stranger flowers
With milder gales, and steep with warmer showers.
Delighted Thames through tropic umbrage glides,
And flowers antarctic, bending o'er his tides;
Drinks the new tints, the sweets unknown inhales,
And calls the sons of science to his vales.

77 antarctic] from the southern hemisphere

In one bright point admiring Nature eyes
The fruits and foliage of discordant skies,
Twines the gay floret with the fragrant bough,
And bends the wreath round George's royal brow.
—Sometimes retiring, from the public weal
One tranquil hour the Royal Partners steal;
Through glades exotic pass with step sublime,
Or mark the growths of Britain's happier clime;
With beauty blossomed, and with virtue blazed,
Mark the fair scions, that themselves have raised;
Sweet blooms the rose, the towering oak expands,
The grace and guard of Britain's golden lands.

(1791)

William Cowper
1731–1800

78
The Shrubbery
Written in a Time of Affliction

OH, happy shades—to me unblest!
   Friendly to peace, but not to me!
How ill the scene that offers rest,
   And heart that cannot rest, agree!

This glassy stream, that spreading pine,
   Those alders quiv'ring to the breeze,
Might soothe a soul less hurt than mine,
   And please, if any thing could please.

But fixed unalterable care
   Forgoes not what she feels within,
Shows the same sadness ev'ry where,
   And slights the season and the scene.

For all that pleased in wood or lawn,
   While peace possessed these silent bow'rs,
Her animating smile withdrawn,
   Has lost its beauties and its pow'rs.

blazed] proclaimed, emblazoned

The saint or moralist should tread
   This moss-grown alley, musing, slow;
They seek, like me, the secret shade,
   But not, like me, to nourish woe!

Me fruitful scenes and prospects waste
   Alike admonish not to roam;
These tell me of enjoyments past,
   And those of sorrows yet to come.

(1782)

from *The Task*

79   ['*Who loves a garden, loves a greenhouse too*']

WHO loves a garden, loves a greenhouse too.
Unconscious of a less propitious clime,
There blooms exotic beauty, warm and snug,
While the winds whistle and the snows descend.
The spiry myrtle with unwithering leaf
Shines there and flourishes. The golden boast
Of Portugal and western India there,
The ruddier orange and the paler lime,
Peep through their polished foliage at the storm,
And seem to smile at what they need not fear.
The amomum there with intermingling flowers
And cherries hangs her twigs. Geranium boasts
Her crimson honours, and the spangled beau,
Ficoides, glitters bright the winter long.
All plants, of every leaf that can endure
The winter's frown, if screened from its shrewd bite,
Live there and prosper. Those Ausonia claims,
Levantine regions these; the Azores send
Their jessamine, her jessamine remote
Caffraria: foreigners from many lands,
They form one social shade, as if convened
By magic summons of the Orphean lyre.
Yet just arrangement, rarely brought to pass
But by a master's hand, disposing well
The gay diversities of leaf and flower,
Must lend its aid to illustrate all their charms,
And dress the regular yet various scene.
Plant behind plant aspiring, in the van
The dwarfish, in the rear retired, but still
Sublime above the rest, the statelier stand.

80 [*'Capability' Brown*]

IMPROVEMENT too, the idol of the age,
Is fed with many a victim. Lo! he comes—
The omnipotent magician, Brown, appears.
Down falls the venerable pile, the abode
Of our forefathers, a grave whiskered race,
But tasteless. Springs a palace in its stead,
But in a distant spot; where more exposed,
It may enjoy the advantage of the north,
And aguish east, till time shall have transformed
Those naked acres to a sheltering grove.
He speaks. The lake in front becomes a lawn,
Woods vanish, hills subside, and valleys rise,
And streams, as if created for his use,
Pursue the track of his directing wand,
Sinuous or straight, now rapid and now slow,
Now murmuring soft, now roaring in cascades,
Even as he bids. The enraptured owner smiles.
'Tis finished! and yet, finished as it seems,
Still wants a grace, the loveliest it could shew,
A mine to satisfy the enormous cost.
Drained to the last poor item of his wealth,
He sighs, departs, and leaves the accomplished plan
That he has touched, retouched, many a long day
Laboured, and many a night pursued in dreams,
Just when it meets his hopes, and proves the heaven
He wanted, for a wealthier to enjoy . . .
Where now the vital energy that moved,
While summer was, the pure and subtle lymph
Through the imperceptible meandering veins
Of leaf and flower? It sleeps; and the icy touch
Of unprolific winter has impressed
A cold stagnation on the intestine tide.
But let the months go round, a few short months,
And all shall be restored. These naked shoots,
Barren as lances, among which the wind
Makes wintry music, sighing as it goes,
Shall put their graceful foliage on again,
And more aspiring, and with ampler spread,
Shall boast new charms, and more than they have lost.
Then, each in its peculiar honours clad,
Shall publish, even to the distant eye,
Its family and tribe. Laburnum rich

In streaming gold; syringa ivory pure;
The scentless and the scented rose, this red
And of an humbler growth, the other tall,
And throwing up into the darkest gloom
Of neighbouring cypress, or more sable yew,
Her silver globes, light as the foamy surf
That the wind severs from the broken wave;
The lilac various in array, now white,
Now sanguine, and her beauteous head now set
With purple spikes pyramidal, as if
Studious of ornament, yet unresolved
Which hue she most approved, she chose them all;
Copious of flowers the woodbine, pale and wan,
But well compensating her sickly looks
With never-cloying odours, early and late;
Hypericum all bloom, so thick a swarm
Of flowers like flies clothing her slender rods
That scarce a leaf appears; mezereon, too,
Though leafless, well attired, and thick beset
With blushing wreaths investing every spray;
Althea with the purple eye; the broom,
Yellow and bright as bullion unalloyed
Her blossoms; and luxuriant above all
The jasmine, throwing wide her elegant sweets,
The deep dark green of whose unvarnished leaf
Makes more conspicuous, and illumines more
The bright profusion of her scattered stars.
These have been, and these shall be in their day;
And all this uniform, uncoloured scene
Shall be dismantled of its fleecy load,
And flush into variety again.

(1785)

81   *Inscription*
*For a Stone Erected at the Sowing of a Grove of Oaks at
Chillington, the Seat of T. Gifford, esq., 1790*

OTHER stones the era tell,
When some feeble mortal fell:
I stand here to date the birth
Of these hardy sons of earth.
   Which shall longest brave the sky,
Storm and frost? these oaks or I?

Pass an age or two away,
I must moulder and decay,
But the years that crumble me
Shall invigorate the tree,
Spread the branch, dilate its size,
Lift its summit to the skies.
   Cherish honour, virtue, truth!
So shalt thou prolong thy youth:
Wanting these, however fast
Man be fixed, and formed to last,
He is lifeless even now,
Stone at heart, and cannot grow.

           (1803)

82   *Inscription*
For a Moss-House in the Shrubbery at Weston

HERE, free from riot's hated noise,
Be mine, ye calmer, purer joys,
   A book or friend bestows;
Far from the storms that shake the great,
Contentment's gale shall fan my seat,
   And sweeten my repose.

           (1804)

83   *Inscription*
For an Hermitage in the Author's Garden

THIS cabin, Mary, in my sight appears,
Built as it has been in our waning years,
A rest afforded to our weary feet,
Preliminary to—the last retreat.

           (1803)

Robert Lloyd
1733–1764

84   from *The Cit's Country Box*

SOME three or four mile out of town
(An hour's ride will bring you down),
He fixes on his choice abode,
Not half a furlong from the road:
And so convenient does it lay,
The stages pass it ev'ry day:
And then so snug, so mighty pretty,
To have an house so near the city!
Take but your places at the Boar,
You're set down at the very door.

Well then, suppose them fixed at last,
White-washing, painting, scrubbing past,
Hugging themselves in ease and clover,
With all the fuss of moving over;
Lo, a new heap of whims are bred,
And wanton in my lady's head:
   'Well, to be sure, it must be owned
It is a charming spot of ground;
So sweet a distance for a ride,
And all about so *countrified!*
'Twould come to but a trifling price
To make it quite a paradise;
I cannot bear those nasty rails,
Those ugly, broken, mouldy pales:
Suppose, my dear, instead of these,
We build a railing, all Chinese.
Although one hates to be exposed,
'Tis dismal to be thus inclosed;
One hardly any object sees—
I wish you'd fell those odious trees.
Objects continual passing by
Were something to amuse the eye,
But to be pent within the walls—
One might as well be at St Paul's.

Cit] citizen, with pejorative implications of tradesman

137

Our house beholders would adore,
Was there a level lawn before,
Nothing its views to incommode,
But quite laid open to the road;
While ev'ry trav'ler in amaze
Should on our little mansion gaze,
And, pointing to the choice retreat,
Cry, "That's Sir Thrifty's country seat." '
   No doubt her arguments prevail,
For Madam's *taste* can never fail.

   Blest age! when all men may procure
The title of a connoisseur;
When noble and ignoble herd
Are governed by a single word;
Though, like the royal German dames,
It bears an hundred Christian names,
As Genius, Fancy, Judgement, Goût,
Whim, Caprice, Je-ne-sais-quoi, Virtù:
Which appellations all describe
Taste, and the modern *tasteful* tribe.

   Now bricklay'rs, carpenters and joiners,
With Chinese artists and designers,
Produce their schemes of alteration,
To work this wond'rous reformation.
The useful dome, which secret stood
Embosomed in the yew-tree's wood,
The trav'ler with amazement sees
A temple, Gothic, or Chinese,
With many a bell and tawdry rag on,
And crested with a sprawling dragon;
A wooden arch is bent astride
A ditch of water, four foot wide,
With angles, curves and zigzag lines,
From Halfpenny's exact designs.
In front, a level lawn is seen,
Without a shrub upon the green,
Where Taste would want its first great law,
But for the skulking, sly *ha-ha*,
By whose miraculous assistance,
You gain a prospect two fields' distance.

  Je-ne-sais-quoi] I don't know what, affected French phrase to use when the proper word is
not known   Halfpenny] William (d. 1755) or his son John (dates unknown) Halfpenny,
authors of pattern books from which such details could be copied

And now from Hyde-Park Corner come
The gods of Athens and of Rome.
Here squabby Cupids take their places,
With Venus and the clumsy Graces:
Apollo there, with aim so clever,
Stretches his leaden bow for ever;
And there, without the pow'r to fly,
Stands fixed a tip-toe Mercury.
    The villa thus completely graced,
All own that Thrifty has a Taste;
And Madam's female friends and cousins,
With common-council-men by dozens,
Flock ev'ry Sunday to the seat,
To stare about them, and to eat.

                  (1762)

John Langhorne
1735–1779

85   *Studley Park*

FARRAR! to thee these early lays I owe:
Thy friendship warms the heart from whence they flow.
Thee, thee I find, in all I find to please;
In this thy elegance, in that thy ease.
Come then with fancy to thy fav'rite scene,
Where Studley triumphs in her wreaths of green,
And pleased for once, while Eden smiles again,
Forget that life's inheritance is pain.
    Say, shall we muse along yon arching shades,
Whose awful gloom no brightening ray pervades;
Or down these vales where vernal flowers display
Their golden blossoms to the smiles of day;
Where the fond eye in sweet distraction strays.
Most pleased, when most it knows not where to gaze?
Here groves arranged in various order rise,
And blend their quiv'ring summits in the skies.
The regal oak high o'er the circling shade,
Exalts the hoary honours of his head.

85 Farrar] clergyman to whom the poem is dedicated

The spreading ash a diff'ring green displays,
And the smooth asp in soothing whispers plays.
The fir that blooms in Spring's eternal prime,
The spiry poplar, and the stately lime.
Here moss-clad walks, there lawns of lively green,
United form one nicely varying scene:
The varying scene still charms th'attentive sight,
Or brown with shades, or op'ning into light.
Here the gay tenants of the tuneful grove,
Harmonious breathe the raptures of their love;
Each warbler sweet that hails the genial Spring,
Tunes the glad song, and plies th' expanded wing:
The love-suggested notes in varied strains,
Fly round the vocal hills and list'ning plains:
The vocal hills and list'ning plains prolong
In varied strains the love-suggested song.
To thee, all bounteous Nature! thee they pay,
The welcome tribute of their grateful lay!
To thee, whose kindly-studious hand prepares
The fresh'ning fields and softly breathing airs;
Whose parent-bounty annual still provides
Of foodful insects such unbounded tides.
Beneath some friendly leaf supremely blest,
Each pours at large the raptures of his breast:
Nor changeful seasons mourn, nor storms unkind,
With those contented, and to these resigned.

(1759)

Anna Seward
1742–1809

86   *The Lake: Or, Modern Improvement in Landscape*

GRAND, ancient, Gothic, mark this ample dome,
Of fashion's slave, the uncongenial home!
Long have its turrets braved the varying clime,
And mocked the ravage of relentless time.

asp] aspen

The owner shrugs his shoulders, and deplores
One vile effect of his self-squandered stores,
That the triste edifice must still remain
To shock his lordship's gaze, and blot the plain;
That no gay villa may supply its place,
Rise in Italian, or in Gallic grace.

'But, yet,' he cries, 'by Fashion's aid divine,
Rescued from sylvan shrouds, my scenes may shine;
Resistless goddess, to thy votary come,
And chase the horrors of this leafy gloom!'

She comes!—the gaudy despot stands confessed,
Known by her mien assured, and motley vest;
The vest, mistaken by her servile train
For beauty's robe of sky-enwoven grain,
Decked with each varying form, each living hue,
That Nature hallowed, and her Repton drew.

Scorning their power, and reckless of expense,
The foe of beauty, and the bane of sense;
Close by my lord, and with strange projects warm,
Stalks o'er the scenes her edicts shall deform.

'Yon broad, brown wood, now darkening to the sky,
Shall prostrate soon with perished branches lie;
Yield golden treasures for our great design,
Till all the scene one glassy surface shine.'

Mid shrubs, and tangled grass, with sparkling waves,
A little vagrant brook the valley laves;
Now hid, now seen, the wanton waters speed,
Hurrying loquacious o'er their pebbly bed.

'A lake!' she cries, 'this source can never fail,
A lake shall fill our undulating dale!
No more the dingles shall sink dark and deep,
No waving hedgerows round the meadows sweep;
All must be lake this level lawn between,
And those bare hills, and rocks, that form the screen,
Peer o'er the yet-proud woods, and close the scene.'

triste] sad (affected French)   Repton] Humphry Repton (1752–1818), landscape
architect

What recks it her that, many a tedious year,
Barren and bleak its naked banks appear!
Since, though the pliant naiad swiftly pours
Her urn exhaustless to receding shores,
Sullen and tardy found, the dryad train
Are still, through circling seasons, wooed in vain,
Ere the dusk umbrage shall luxuriant flow,
And shadowy tremble o'er the lake below;
Which curtained thus, changes its leaden hue,
Rising a silver mirror to the view.

See, at the pert behest, subservient toil
Plough with the victim woods the echoing soil!
See, the forced flood th' o'erwhelmed valley laves,
O'er fields, lanes, thickets, spread the silent waves!—
No lively hue of spring they know to wear,
No gorgeous glow of the consummate year;
No tinge that gold-empurpled autumn spreads
O'er the rich woodland, sloping from the meads,
But stagnant, mute, unvarying, cold, and pale,
They meet the winter-wind, and summer-gale.

Between the base of yonder Gothic pile,
Whose towers frown sullen o'er the wat'ry spoil,
And the chill lake's uncomfortable breast,
Lo! on the lawn, with venerable crest,
A few old oaks defend the tired survey,
In part, from that dull pool's eternal grey;
While, gleaming, underneath their darksome boughs,
With better grace the torpid water shows.
Again the dame her swarthy agents calls,
Raised is the ready axe—and—ah! it falls!
They who had seen whole centuries roll away,
No more half-veil the lake, and mitigate the day.

Too late the slumbering genius of the scene
Starts from his mossy couch, with 'wildered mien;
Dismayed beholds, and all too late to save,
His graces destined to a watery grave;
His winding brook, green wood, and mead and dell,
His grassy lanes, and moss-encircled well;
And for the guardian oaks, now prostrate laid,
His winter screen, his sultry summer's shade,

Sees the weak saplings, dotted on the lawn,
With dark and clumsy fence around them drawn,
Warp in the noon-tide ray, with shrivelled rind,
And shrink, and tremble in the rising wind.

In vain he curses the fantastic power,
And the pale ravage of her idiot-hour;
But no vindictive ire the spell revokes,
Fall'n are the woods, and lawn-adorning oaks!
Fled every varied charm boon Nature gave,
No green field blossoms, and no hedgerows wave!
On the dim waters nods the useless sail,
And Eurus howls along the deluged vale.

His reign usurped, since Time can ne'er restore,
Indignant rising to return no more,
His eyes concealing with one lifted hand,
Shadowing the waters, as his wings expand,
The injured genius seeks the distant coast,
Like Abdiel, flying from the rebel host.

(1790)

Samuel Jackson Pratt
1749–1814

87   from *Cottage Pictures*

No village dames and maidens now are seen,
But madams, and the misses of the green!
Farm-house, and farm too, are in deep disgrace,
'Tis now the Lodge, the Cottage, or the Place!
Or if a farm, *ferme ornée* is the phrase!
And if a cottage, of these modern days,
Expect no more to see the straw-built shed,
But a fantastic villa in its stead!
Pride, thinly veiled in mock humility;
The name of cot, without its poverty!
By affectation, still with thatching crowned;
By affectation, still with ivy bound;

Eurus] east wind   Abdiel] an angel in Milton's *Paradise Lost* who resists Satan's
proposal to revolt

By affection, still the mantling vine
The door-way and the window-frames entwine;
The hawthorn bow'rs, and benches near the grove,
Give place to temples, and the rich alcove:
A naked Venus here, a Bacchus there,
And mimic ruins, kept in good repair;
The real rustic's sweet and simple bounds,
Quick-set and garden, changed to pleasure-grounds,
And the fresh sod, that formed the pathway green,
The strawberry bed, and currant-bush between
The honey-suckle hedge and lily tall,
Yield to the shrubbery and high-raised wall;
Then for exotics of botanic fame,
Of which the lady scarcely knows the name;
Yet, as with country friend she goes the round,
She christens them with words of learned sound.
The wall, in foreign fruits so rich and fine,
Forms the dessert, when farmer-gentry dine!
And then for water! geese and ducks no more
Have leave to puddle round a modern door;
Fair on the glassy lake they sail in state,
And seem to know a prouder change of fate;
From thence, on china served, they grace the dish,
And vie in honours with the silver fish.

(1802)

Richard Payne Knight
1750–1824

from *The Landscape*

88

[*Picturesque gardening*]

OFT when I've seen some lonely mansion stand,
Fresh from th' improver's desolating hand,
'Midst shaven lawns, that far around it creep
In one eternal undulating sweep;
And scattered clumps, that nod at one another,
Each stiffly waving to its formal brother;
Tired with th' extensive scene, so dull and bare,
To Heav'n devoutly I've addressed my prayer,—

Again the moss-grown terraces to raise,
And spread the labyrinth's perplexing maze;
Replace in even lines the ductile yew,
And plant again the ancient avenue.
Some features then, at least, we should obtain,
To mark this flat, insipid, waving plain;
Some varied tints and forms would intervene,
To break this uniform, eternal green.

E'en the trimmed hedges, that enclosed the field,
Some consolation to the eye might yield;
But even these are studiously removed,
And clumps and bareness only are approved.
Though the old system against nature stood,
At least in this, 'twas negatively good: —
Enclosed by walls, and terraces, and mounds,
Its mischiefs were confined to narrow bounds;
Just round the house, in formal angles traced,
It moved responsive to the builder's taste;
Walls answered walls, and alleys, long and thin,
Mimicked the endless passages within.

But kings of yew, and goddesses of lead,
Could never far their baneful influence spread;
Cooped in the garden's safe and narrow bounds,
They never dared invade the open grounds;
Where still the roving ox, or browsing deer,
From such prim despots kept the country clear;
While uncorrupted still, on every side,
The ancient forest rose in savage pride;
And in its native dignity displayed
Each hanging wood and ever verdant glade;
Where ev'ry shaggy shrub and spreading tree
Proclaimed the seat of native liberty;
In loose and varied groups unheeded thrown,
And never taught the planter's care to own:
Some, tow'ring upwards, spread their arms in state;
And others, bending low, appeared to wait:
While scattered thorns, browsed by the goat and deer,
Rose all around, and let no lines appear.

Such groups did Claude's light pencil often trace,
The foreground of some classic scene to grace;
Such, humble Waterloe, to nature true,
Beside the copse, or village pasture drew.

Claude] Claude Gellée, called Le Lorrain (1600–82), French painter   Waterloe]
Anthonie Waterlo, or Waterloo (1610–90) Dutch landscape painter

But ah! how different is the formal lump
Which the improver plants, and calls a clump!
Break, break, ye nymphs, the fence that guards it round!
With browsing cattle, all its forms confound!
As chance or fate will have it, let it grow;—
Here spiring high;—there cut, or trampled low.
No apter ornament can taste provide
T' embellish beauty, or defect to hide;
If trained with care and undiscovered skill,
Its just department in the scene to fill;
But with reserve and caution be it seen,
Nor e'er surrounded by the shaven green;
But in the foreground boldly let it rise,
Or joined with other features meet the eyes:
The distant mansion, seen beneath its shade,
Is often advantageously displayed:—
But here, once more, ye rural muses, weep
The ivied balustrades, and terrace steep;
Walls, mellowed into harmony by time,
O'er which fantastic creepers used to climb;
While statues, labyrinths, and alleys, pent
Within their bounds, at least were innocent!
Our modern taste, alas! no limit knows:—
O'er hill, o'er dale, through woods and fields it flows;
Spreading o'er all its unprolific spawn,
In never-ending sheets of vapid lawn.
    True composition all extremes rejects,
And just proportions still, of all, selects;
Wood, water, lawn, in just gradation joins,
And each with artful negligence combines:
But still in level, or slow-rising ground,
The wood should always form th' exterior bound;
Not as a belt, encircling the domain,
Which the tired eye attempts to trace in vain;
But as a bolder outline to the scene
Than the unbroken turf's smooth even green.
But if some distant hill o'er all arise,
And mix its azure colours with the skies;
Or some near mountain its rough summits shew,
And bound with broken crags the Alpine view;
Or rise, with even slope and gradual swell,
Like the broad cone, or wide-extended bell;—
Never attempt, presumptuous, to o'erspread
With starved plantations its bleak, barren head:

Nature herself the rash design withstands,
And guards her wilds from innovating hands;
Which, if successful, only would disgrace
Her giant limbs with fripp'ry, fringe, and lace.

(1794)

Thomas Maurice
1754–1824

from *Richmond Hill*

89   [*Chiswick*]

HAIL, beauteous Chiswick! hail, sequestered seat!
Where all that's chaste, and grand, and beauteous meet!
Fairer than e'er Palladio's fancy planned,
Or rose beneath a Jones's daring hand.
Hail thy proud portico! thy swelling dome!
Thy happy mingled scene of light and gloom,
Where, now, rich lawns, in vernal beauty bright,
Expanding to meridian suns, invite:
Now, rows of cedar cast their solemn shade,
And artificial darkness wraps the glade.
Hail thy sweet terrace! whence, with eager gaze,
To Sheen's loved bower the eye delightful strays;
Where Philomel, in hope's delightful grove,
Swells high the strain of rapture and of love
Hail thy long vistas! hail thy dark alcoves
Where genius muses, and where beauty roves;
Where Pope, delighted, led the laurelled throng,
And poured, spontaneous, the resounding song;
Where Thomson, wandering near his favourite tide,
Beheld the rolling seasons sweetly glide:
And patriot chiefs, the glory of their age,
Felt freedom's throb, and burned with Grecian rage . . .

Where'er I turn, the glorious dead arise,
In busts and statues, to my wondering eyes;
While, in the bosom of yon beauteous vale,
Where richest odours scent the verdant gale,

89 Jones] Inigo Jones (1573–1652), British architect and disciple of Palladio   Sheen]
old name for town of Richmond   Philomel] the nightingale

From thousand aromatic shrubs that rise,
The gorgeous offspring of antarctic skies!
Or the deep gloom of yon embowering wood,
With serpent folds where glides the winding flood,
The towering obelisk, and swelling dome,
And urns and statues, once the boast of Rome!
With tasteful skill, in rich profusion spread,
O'er all an air of classic grandeur shed.

(1807)

William Blake
1757–1827

90   *The Garden of Love*

I WENT to the Garden of Love,
And saw what I never had seen:
A chapel was built in the midst,
Where I used to play on the green.

And the gates of this chapel were shut,
And 'Thou shalt not' writ over the door;
So I turned to the Garden of Love
That so many sweet flowers bore;

And I saw it was filled with graves,
And tomb-stones where flowers should be;
And priests in black gowns were walking their rounds,
And binding with briars my joys and desires.

(1794)

antarctic] from the southern hemisphere

Maria Henrietta Montolieu

(dates unknown)

91   from *The Gardens* of the Abbé de Lille

THE velvet ground we now with pleasure tread,
In earlier times with burning gravel spread,
Reflecting fiery sunbeams, bare, and dry,
Distressed the aching feet, and hurt the eye.
England at length gave new improvements birth,
And bade us cover and adorn the earth.
These lawns with toil assiduous attend;
If thirsty, bid fictitious rains descend;
Let not the scythe and heavy roller rest,
But even, well selected, closely pressed,
Freed from all wild, usurping grass with care,
Let them a down as soft as ermine wear,
And in due time the spoils of age repair.
Those grounds contiguous to the sight adorn,
With this smooth turf, this luxury of lawn,
The parts remote your flocks and herds should keep,
And cultivate themselves the fruits they reap;
Around you thus shall numerous nurslings thrive,
Enrich your lands, and make the scene alive.
Then blush not, though false pride should deem it strange,
Free in your parks to let your cattle range,
The cow, the useful ox, and fleecy race,
Nor spoil their grandeur, nor my lays disgrace.
    All is not done when spacious lawns are laid;
Be they with skill designed, with taste displayed.
Insipid circles and the formal square,
Stiff uniformity avoid with care;
Now let them flourish free to sight disclosed,
In graceful sweeps, in easy slopes disposed;
By woods forsaken, now in part revealed,
Now by the clasping woods in shades concealed.
    Would you improve, and add to their effect,
Observe how Nature's fairest scenes are decked,
What prodigality of tints she yields,
What bright enamel decorates her fields.
Haste then, her sweet unstudied walks pursue,
Your gardens ask their fragrant stores of you.

Nature more beauteous seems adorned with flowers;
To paint their colours Art exerts her powers;
Affection's simple token still they prove,
Offered by Friendship, hazarded by Love;
The laurel lets them in her glory share;
Their pride it is to ornament the fair ...

(1798)

Robert Burns
1759–1796

92   *The Gardener wi' his Paidle—Or, The Gardener's March*

WHEN rosy May comes in wi' flowers
To deck her gay, green, spreading bowers;
Then busy, busy are his hours,
     The gardener wi' his paidle.—

The crystal waters gently fa';
The merry birds are lovers a';
The scented breezes round him blaw,
     The gardener wi' his paidle.—

When purple morning starts the hare
To steal upon her early fare;
Then thro' the dews he maun repair,
     The gardener wi' his paidle.—

When Day, expiring in the west,
The curtain draws of Nature's rest;
He flies to her arms he lo'es the best,
     The gardener wi' his paidle.—

(1790)

92 paidle] garden hoe, with implication of fumbling about   maun] must

93   *Extempore—On Being Shown a Beautiful Country Seat*
       Belonging to Maxwell of Cardoness

WE grant they're thine, those beauties all,
    So lovely in our eye:
Keep them, thou eunuch, C[ardone]ss,
    For others to enjoy!

(1793)

George Colman, The Younger
1762–1836

from *London Rurality*

94   [*'Vulgar Tusculum'* or *'Suburban Picturesque'*]

PEACE to each swain, who rural rapture owns,
As soon as past a toll, and off the stones!
Whose joy, if buildings solid bliss bestow,
Cannot, for miles, an interruption know:
Save when a gap, of some half-dozen feet,
Just breaks the continuity of street;
Where the prig architect with style in view,
Has doled his houses forth, in two by two;
And reared a row upon the plan, no doubt,
Of old men's jaws, with every third tooth out.
Or where, still greater lengths in taste, to go,
He warps his tenements into a bow;
Nails a scant canvas, propped on slight deal sticks,
Nicknamed veranda, to the first-floor bricks;
Before the whole, in one snug segment drawn,
Claps half a rood of turf he calls a lawn;
Then, chuckling at his lath and plaster bubble,
Dubs it the Crescent—and the rents are double . . .

And, here and there, thrown back, a few yards deep
Some staring coxcombry pretends to peep;
Low paled in front, and shrubbed, with laurels, in,
That, sometimes, flourish higher than your chin.

94 prig] fashionable, foppish

Here modest ostentation sticks a plate,
Or daubs Egyptian letters on the gate,
Informing passengers 'tis 'Cowslip Cot'
Or 'Woodbine Lodge', or 'Pummock's Grot'.
Oh! why not, Vanity! since dolts bestow
Such names on dog-holes, squeezed out from a row,
The title of 'Horn Hermitage' entail
Upon the habitation of a snail?
Why not inscribe ('twould answer quite as well)
'Marine Pavilion' on an oyster-shell?

See, in these roads, scarce conscious of a field,
What uniform varieties they yield!—
Row smirks at row, each band-box has a brother,
And half the causeway just reflects the other.
To beautify each close-wedged neighbour's door,
A strip of garden aims at length, before;
Gritty, in sunshine;—yet, in showers, 'twill do,
Between a coach and house, to wet you through:
But, soon, the public path, in envious sort,
Crosses,—and cuts it, at right angles, short:
Then, up the jemmy rail, with tenters topped,
Like virtue from necessity, is popped:—
Behind it pine, to decorate the grounds,
And mark with greater elegance their bounds,
Three thin, aquatic poplars, parched with drought,
Vying with lines of lamp-posts, fixed without.
Still may the scene some rustic thoughts supply,
When sounds and objects strike the ear and eye:
For, here, the gardener bawls his greens and leeks,
And (jostling funerals) the waggon creaks;
Oxen, though pastureless, each hour appear,
And bellow, though the drover's in the rear;
While flocks of sheep enrich the turnpike trust,
And bleat their way to Smithfield, through the dust.

(1816)

jemmy] neatly made   tenters] stretched cloth (to hide public path?)

Richard Alfred Milliken
1767–1815

The Groves of Blarney

THE groves of Blarney
They look so charming,
Down by the purling
   Of sweet, silent brooks,
Being banked with posies
That spontaneous grow there,
Planted in order
   By the sweet 'Rock Close'.
'Tis there the daisy
And the sweet carnation,
The blooming pink
   And the rose so fair,
The daffydowndilly,
Likewise the lily,
All flowers that scent
   The sweet, fragrant air.

'Tis Lady Jeffers
That owns this station;
Like Alexander
   Or Queen Helen fair
There's no commander
In all the nation,
For emulation,
   Can with her compare.
Such walls surround her,
That no nine-pounder
Could dare to plunder
   Her place of strength;
But Oliver Cromwell
Her he did pommell,
And made a breach
   In her battlement.

There's gravel walks there
For speculation
And conversation
   In sweet solitude.

'Tis there the lover
May hear the dove, or
The gentle plover
   In the afternoon;
And if a lady
Would be so engaging
As to walk alone in
   Those shady bowers,
'Tis there the courtier
He may transport her
Into some fort, or
   All underground.

For 'tis there's a cave where
No daylight enters,
But cats and badgers
   Are for ever bred;
Being mossed by nature,
That makes it sweeter
Than a coach-and-six or
   A feather bed.
'Tis there the lake is,
Well stored with perches,
And comely eels in
   The verdant mud;
Besides the leeches,
And groves of beeches,
Standing in order
   For to guard the flood.

There's statues gracing
This noble place in—
All heathen gods
   And nymphs so fair;
Bold Neptune, Plutarch,
And Nicodemus,
All standing naked
   In the open air!
So now to finish
This brave narration,
Which my poor genii
   Could not entwine;

But were I Homer,
Or Nebuchadnezzar,
'Tis in every feature
I would make it shine.

(1821)

William Wordsworth
1770–1850

96   *Inscription for the Moss-Hut at Dove Cottage*

No whimsy of the purse is here,
No pleasure-house forlorn;
Use, comfort, do this roof endear;
A tributary shed to cheer
The little cottage that is near,
To help it and adorn.

(wr. 1804)

97   from *The Excursion*

HER cottage, then a cheerful object, wore
Its customary look,—only, it seemed,
The honeysuckle, crowding round the porch,
Hung down in heavier tufts; and that bright weed,
The yellow stone-crop, suffered to take root
Along the window's edge, profusely grew
Blinding the lower panes. I turned aside,
And strolled into her garden. It appeared
To lag behind the season, and had lost
Its pride of neatness. Daisy-flowers and thrift
Had broken their trim border-lines, and straggled
O'er paths they used to deck: carnations, once
Prized for surpassing beauty, and no less
For the peculiar pains they had required,
Declined their languid heads, wanting support.
The cumbrous bind-weed, with its wreaths and bells,
Had twined about her two small rows of peas,
And dragged them to the earth.

        Ere this an hour
Was wasted.—Back I turned my restless steps;
A stranger passed; and, guessing whom I sought,
He said that she was used to ramble far.—
The sun was sinking in the west; and now
I sat with sad impatience. From within
Her solitary infant cried aloud;
Then, like a blast that dies away self-stilled,
The voice was silent. From the bench I rose;
But neither could divert nor soothe my thoughts.
The spot, though fair, was very desolate—
The longer I remained, more desolate:
And, looking round me, now I first observed
The corner stones, on either side the porch,
With dull red stains discoloured, and stuck o'er
With tufts and hairs of wool, as if the sheep,
That fed upon the common, thither came
Familiarly, and found a couching-place
Even at her threshold. Deeper shadows fell
From these tall elms; the cottage-clock struck eight;—
I turned, and saw her distant a few steps.
Her face was pale and thin—her figure, too,
Was changed. As she unlocked the door, she said,
'It grieves me you have waited here so long,
But, in good truth, I've wandered much of late;
And, sometimes—to my shame I speak—have need
Of my best prayers to bring me back again.'

            (1814)

98 *In a Garden in the Grounds of Coleorton, Leicestershire*

OFT is the medal faithful to its trust
When temples, columns, towers, are laid in dust;
And 'tis a common ordinance of fate
That things obscure and small outlive the great:
Hence, when yon mansion and the flowery trim
Of this fair garden, and its alleys dim,
And all its stately trees, are passed away,
This little niche, unconscious of decay,
Perchance may still survive. And be it known
That it was scooped within the living stone,—
Not by the sluggish and ungrateful pains
Of labourer plodding for his daily gains,

But by an industry that wrought in love;
With help from female hands, that proudly strove
To aid the work, what time these walks and bowers
Were shaped to cheer dark winter's lonely hours.

(1815)

99   *A Farewell*

FAREWELL, thou little nook of mountain-ground,
Thou rocky corner in the lowest stair
Of that magnificent temple which doth bound
One side of our whole vale with grandeur rare;
Sweet garden-orchard, eminently fair,
The loveliest spot that man hath ever found,
Farewell!—we leave thee to Heaven's peaceful care,
Thee, and the cottage which thou dost surround.

Our boat is safely anchored by the shore,
And there will safely ride when we are gone;
The flowering shrubs that deck our humble door
Will prosper, though untended and alone:
Fields, goods, and far-off chattels we have none:
These narrow bounds contain our private store
Of things earth makes, and sun doth shine upon:
Here are they in our sight—we have no more.

Sunshine and shower be with you, bud and bell!
For two months now in vain we shall be sought;
We leave you here in solitude to dwell
With these our latest gifts of tender thought;
Thou, like the morning, in thy saffron coat,
Bright gowan, and marsh-marigold, farewell!
Whom from the borders of the lake we brought,
And placed together near our rocky well.

We go for One to whom ye will be dear;
And she will prize this bower, this Indian shed,
Our own contrivance, building without peer!
—A gentle maid, whose heart is lowly bred,
Whose pleasures are in wild fields gatherèd,
With joyousness, and with a thoughtful cheer,
Will come to you; to you herself will wed;
And love the blessed life that we lead here.

Dear spot! which we have watched with tender heed,
Bringing thee chosen plants and blossoms blown
Among the distant mountains, flower and weed,
Which thou hast taken to thee as thy own,
Making all kindness registered and known;
Thou for our sakes, though Nature's child indeed,
Fair in thyself and beautiful alone,
Hast taken gifts which thou dost little need.

And O most constant, yet most fickle place,
That hast thy wayward moods, as thou dost show
To them who look not daily on thy face;
Who, being loved, in love no bounds dost know,
And say'st, when we forsake thee, 'Let them go!'
Thou easy-hearted thing, with thy wild race
Of weeds and flowers, till we return be slow,
And travel with the year at a soft pace.

Help us to tell her tales of years gone by,
And this sweet spring, the best beloved and best;
Joy will be flown in its mortality;
Something must stay to tell us of the rest.
Here, thronged with primroses, the steep rock's breast
Glittered at evening like a starry sky;
And in this bush our sparrow built her nest,
Of which I sang one song that will not die.

O happy garden! whose seclusion deep
Hath been so friendly to industrious hours;
And to soft slumbers, that did gently steep
Our spirits, carrying with them dreams of flowers,
And wild notes warbled among leafy bowers;
Two burning months let summer overleap,
And, coming back with Her who will be ours,
Into thy bosom we again shall creep.

(1815)

Samuel Taylor Coleridge
1772–1834

This Lime-Tree Bower my Prison

WELL, they are gone, and here must I remain,
This lime-tree bower my prison! I have lost
Beauties and feelings, such as would have been
Most sweet to my remembrance even when age
Had dimmed mine eyes to blindness! They, meanwhile,
Friends, whom I never more may meet again,
On springy heath, along the hilltop edge,
Wander in gladness, and wind down, perchance,
To that still roaring dell, of which I told;
The roaring dell, o'crwooded, narrow, deep,
And only speckled by the midday sun;
Where its slim trunk the ash from rock to rock
Flings arching like a bridge;—that branchless ash,
Unsunned and damp, whose few poor yellow leaves
Ne'er tremble in the gale, yet tremble still,
Fanned by the water-fall! and there my friends
Behold the dark green file of long lank weeds,
That all at once (a most fantastic sight!)
Still nod and drip beneath the dripping edge
Of the blue clay-stone.

            Now, my friends emerge
Beneath the wide wide Heaven—and view again
The many-steepled tract magnificent
Of hilly fields and meadows, and the sea,
With some fair bark, perhaps, whose sails light up
The slip of smooth clear blue betwixt two isles
Of purple shadow! Yes! they wander on
In gladness all; but thou, methinks, most glad,
My gentle-hearted Charles! for thou hast pined
And hungered after Nature, many a year,
In the great City pent, winning thy way
With sad yet patient soul, through evil and pain
And strange calamity! Ah! slowly sink
Behind the western ridge, thou glorious sun!
Shine in the slant beams of the sinking orb,
Ye purple heath-flowers! richlier burn, ye clouds!

Charles] Charles Lamb (1775–1834), the essayist

Live in the yellow light, ye distant groves!
And kindle, thou blue ocean! So my Friend
Struck with deep joy may stand, as I have stood,
Silent with swimming sense; yea, gazing round
On the wide landscape, gaze till all doth seem
Less gross than bodily; and of such hues
As veil the Almighty Spirit, when yet he makes
Spirits perceive his presence.

                A delight
Comes sudden on my heart, and I am glad
As I myself were there! Nor in this bower,
This little lime-tree bower, have I not marked
Much that has soothed me. Pale beneath the blaze
Hung the transparent foliage; and I watched
Some broad and sunny leaf, and loved to see
The shadow of the leaf and stem above
Dappling its sunshine! And that walnut-tree
Was richly tinged, and a deep radiance lay
Full on the ancient ivy, which usurps
Those fronting elms, and now, with blackest mass
Makes their dark branches gleam a lighter hue
Through the late twilight: and though now the bat
Wheels silent by, and not a swallow twitters,
Yet still the solitary humble bee
Sings in the bean-flower! Henceforth I shall know
That Nature ne'er deserts the wise and pure;
No plot so narrow, be but Nature there,
No waste so vacant, but may well employ
Each faculty of sense, and keep the heart
Awake to Love and Beauty! and sometimes
'Tis well to be bereft of promised good,
That we may lift the Soul, and contemplate
With lively joy the joys we cannot share.
My gentle-hearted Charles! when the last rook
Beat its straight path along the dusky air
Homewards, I blest it! deeming, its black wing
(Now a dim speck, now vanishing in light)
Had crossed the mighty orb's dilated glory,
While thou stood'st gazing; or when all was still,
Flew creaking o'er thy head, and had a charm
For thee, my gentle-hearted Charles, to whom
No sound is dissonant which tells of Life.

                        (1800)

101 ### from *Kubla Khan*

IN Xanadu did Kubla Khan
A stately pleasure-dome decree:
Where Alph, the sacred river, ran
Through caverns measureless to man
Down to a sunless sea.
So twice five miles of fertile ground
With walls and towers were girdled round:
And here were gardens bright with sinuous rills,
Where blossomed many an incense-bearing tree;
And here were forests ancient as the hills,
Enfolding sunny spots of greenery.

(1816)

Leigh Hunt
1784–1859

102 ### from *The Story of Rimini*

A NOBLE range it was, of many a rood,
Walled and tree-girt, and ending in a wood.
A small sweet house o'erlooked it from a nest
Of pines:—all wood and garden was the rest,
Lawn, and green lane, and covert:—and it had
A winding stream about it, clear and glad,
With here and there a swan, the creature born
To be the only graceful shape of scorn.
The flower-beds all were liberal of delight;
Roses in heaps were there, both red and white,
Lilies angelical, and gorgeous glooms
Of wall-flowers, and blue hyacinths, and blooms
Hanging thick clusters from light boughs; in short,
All the sweet cups to which the bees resort,
With plots of grass, and leafier walks between
Of red geraniums, and of jessamine,
And orange, whose warm leaves so finely suit,
And look as if they shade a golden fruit;
And midst the flow'rs, turfed round beneath a shade
Of darksome pines, a babbling fountain played,

And 'twixt their shafts you saw the water bright,
Which through the tops glimmered with show'ring light.
So now you stood to think what odours best
Made the air happy in that lovely nest;
And now you went beside the flowers, with eyes
Earnest as bees, restless as butterflies;
And then turned off into a shadier walk
Close and continuous, fit for lover's talk;
And then pursued the stream, and as you trod
Onward and onward o'er the velvet sod,
Felt on your face an air, watery and sweet,
And a new sense in your soft-lighting feet.
At last you entered shades indeed, the wood,
Broken with glens and pits, and glades far-viewed,
Through which the distant palace now and then
Looked lordly forth with many-windowed ken;
A land of trees,—which reaching round about
In shady blessing stretched their old arms out;
With spots of sunny openings, and with nooks
To lie and read in, sloping into brooks,
Where at her drink you startled the slim deer,
Retreating lightly with a lovely fear.
And all about, the birds kept leafy house,
And sung and darted in and out the boughs;
And all about, a lovely sky of blue
Clearly was felt, or down the leaves laughed through;
And here and there, in every part, were seats,
Some in the open walks, some in retreats,—
With bowering leaves o'erhead, to which the eye
Looked up half sweetly and half awfully,—
Places of nestling green, for poets made,
Where, when the sunshine struck a yellow shade,
The rugged trunks, to inward peeping sight,
Thronged in dark pillars up the gold green light.

But 'twixt the wood and flowery walks, half-way,
And formed of both, the loveliest portion lay,—
A spot, that struck you like enchanted ground:—
It was a shallow dell, set in a mound
Of sloping orchards,—fig, and almond trees,
Cherry and pine, with some few cypresses;
Down by whose roots, descending darkly still,
(You saw it not, but heard) there gushed a rill,

Whose low sweet talking seemed as if it said
Something eternal to that happy shade.
The ground within was lawn, with fruits and flowers
Heaped towards the centre, half of citron bowers;
And in the middle of those golden trees,
Half seen amidst the globy oranges,
Lurk'd a rare summer-house, a lovely sight,—
Small, marble, well-proportioned creamy white,
Its top with vine-leaves sprinkled,—but no more,—
And a young bay-tree either side the door.
The door was to the wood, forward and square,
The rest was domed at top, and circular;
And through the dome the only light came in,
Tinged as it entered by the vine-leaves thin.

It was a beauteous piece of ancient skill,
Spared from the rage of war, and perfect still;
By some supposed the work of fairy hands,—
Famed for luxurious taste, and choice of lands,
Alcina or Morgana,—who from fights
And errant fame inveigled amorous knights,
And lived with them in a long round of blisses,
Feasts, concerts, baths, and bower-enshaded kisses.
But 'twas a temple, as its sculpture told.
Built to the nymphs that haunted there of old;
For o'er the door was carved a sacrifice
By girls and shepherds brought, with reverend eyes,
Of sylvan drinks and foods, simple and sweet,
And goats with struggling horns and planted feet:
And round about, ran, on a line with this,
In like relief, a world of pagan bliss,
That showed, in various scenes, the nymphs themselves;
Some by the water-side, on bowery shelves
Leaning at will,—some in the stream at play,—
Some pelting the young fauns with buds of May,—
Or half-asleep pretending not to see
The latter in the brakes come creepingly,
While from their careless urns, lying aside
In the long grass, the straggling waters glide.
Never, be sure, before or since was seen
A summer-house so fine in such a nest of green.

(1816)

Alcina ... Morgana] enchantresses in Ariosto's *Orlando Furioso*

103   from *The Sensitive Plant*

A SENSITIVE Plant in a garden grew,
And the young winds fed it with silver dew,
And it opened its fan-like leaves to the light,
And closed them beneath the kisses of night.

And the Spring arose on the garden fair,
Like the Spirit of Love felt every where;
And each flower and herb on Earth's dark breast
Rose from the dreams of its wintry rest.

But none ever trembled and panted with bliss
In the garden, the field, or the wilderness,
Like a doe in the noon tide with love's sweet want,
As the companionless Sensitive Plant.

The snow-drop, and then the violet,
Arose from the ground with warm rain wet,
And their breath was mixed with fresh odour, sent
From the turf, like the voice and the instrument.

Then the pied wind-flowers and the tulip tall,
And narcissi, the fairest among them all,
Who gaze on their eyes in the stream's recess,
Till they die of their own dear loveliness;

And the naiad-like lily of the vale,
Whom youth makes so fair and passion so pale,
That the light of its tremulous bells is seen
Through their pavilions of tender green;

And the hyacinth purple, and white, and blue,
Which flung from its bells a sweet peal anew
Of music so delicate, soft, and intense,
It was felt like an odour within the sense;

And the rose like a nymph to the bath addrest,
Which unveiled the depth of her glowing breast,
Till, fold after fold, to the fainting air
The soul of her beauty and love lay bare:

And the wand-like lily, which lifted up,
As a maenad, its moonlight-coloured cup,
Till the fiery star, which is its eye,
Gazed through clear dew on the tender sky;

And the jessamine faint, and the sweet tuberose,
The sweetest flower for scent that blows;
And all rare blossoms from every clime
Grew in that garden in perfect prime.

(1820)

John Clare
1793–1864

104   from *The Wish*

AND now a garden pland with nicest care
Should be my next attention to prepare;
For this I'd search the soil of different grounds
Nor small nor great should mark its homley bounds:
Between these two extreems the plan should be
Compleat throughout and large enough for me;
A strong brick wall should bound the outward fence
Where by the suns allcheering influence
Walltrees should flourish in a spreading row
And Peach and Pear in ruddy lustre glow.
A five foot bed should follow from the wall
To look compleat or save the trees withall
On which small seeds for sallading I'd sow
While curl-leaf Parsley should for edges grow.
My Garden in four quarters I'd divide
To show good taste and not a gaudy pride;
In this the middle walk should be the best
Being more to sight exposed than the rest,

104 Walltrees] walnut trees

At whose southend a harbour should be made
So well belov'd in summer for its shade:
For this the rose would do or jessamine
With virginbower or the sweet woodbine,
Each one of these would form exactly well
A compleat harbour both for shade or smell.
Here would I sit when leisure did agree
To view the pride of summer scenery
See the productions promis'd from my spade
While blest with liberty and cooling shade.
But now a spot should be reserv'd for flowers
That would amuse me in those vacant hours
When books and study cease their charms to bring
And Fancy sits to prune her shatterd wing,
Then is the time I'd view the flowrets eye
And all loose stragglers with scotch-mattin tye;
The borders too I'd clean with nicest care
And not one smothering weed should harbour there:
In trifling thus I should such pleasure know
As nothing but such trifles could bestow.
This charming spot should boast a charming place
Southwardly plan'd my cottage front to grace.
There a nice gras plat should attract the eye
Mow'd every week more level then the dye.
Ah! think how this would decorate the scene
So fine a level and a finer green.
My borders they should lie a little flue
And rear the finest flowers that sip the dew
The roses blush the lilies vying snow
Should uniform their namles beauties show,
With fine ranuncullus and jonquil fair
That sweet perfumer of the evening air
The scabious too so jocolatley dusk
Should there be seen with tufts of smelling musk
The woodbine tree should all her sweets unfurl
Close to my door in many a wanton curl.
Aside my wall the vine should find a place
While damask roses did my window grace:
And now a walk as was the plan before
Exactly coresponding with the door
Should lead my footsteps to another bower
Whenever leisure gave the pleasent hour.

harbour] arbour   scotch-mattin] matting, i.e. raffia for tying up   plat] flat plot
dye] dice   flue] shallow   jocolatley] chocolatey

But once again the greens delightful spot
Should wear a ornament I quite forgot;
A little pond within a circle laid
It would look nice and might be useful made:
The side with freestone should be walled round
And steps the same to bevel with the ground.
There sweet Nymphea lover of the tide
Should deck my mimic pool with spangling pride.
Oft would I seek the steps in midday hour
When sol mounts high in full meredian power
To see its leaves that on the surface lie
Prove Boats of Pleasure to the dragon flye.
Ah scenes so happy void of all controul
Your seeming prospects heightens up my soul;
E'en now so bright the fairy vision flies,
I mark its flight as with possesing eyes
But thats in vain—to hope the wish was gave
It clogs the mind and binds the heart a slave.
Tis nothing but a wish one vents at will
Still vainly wishing and be wanting still
For when a wishing mind enjoys the view
He dont expect it ever will come true,
Yet when he cherishes the pleasing thought
He still keeps wishing till he wants for nought,
And so will I—

(wr. 1808–9)

John Greenleaf Whittier
1807–1892

105   *Garden*

O PAINTER of the fruits and flowers,
    We own Thy wise design,
Whereby these human hands of ours
    May share the work of Thine!

Apart from Thee we plant in vain
    The root and sow the seed;
Thy early and Thy later rain,
    Thy sun and dew we need.

Our toil is sweet with thankfulness,
   Our burden is our boon;
The curse of Earth's gray morning is
   The blessing of its noon.

Why search the wide world everywhere
   For Eden's unknown ground?
That garden of the primal pair
   May nevermore be found.

But, blest by Thee, our patient toil
   May right the ancient wrong,
And give to every clime and soil
   The beauty lost so long.

Our homestead flowers and fruited trees
   May Eden's orchard shame;
We taste the tempting sweets of these
   Like Eve, without her blame.

And, north and south and east and west,
   The pride of every zone,
The fairest, rarest, and the best
   May all be made our own.

Its earliest shrines the young world sought
   In hill-groves and in bowers,
The fittest offerings thither brought
   Were Thy own fruits and flowers.

And still with reverent hands we cull
   Thy gifts each year renewed;
The good is always beautiful,
   The beautiful is good.

(1882)

Alfred, Lord Tennyson
1809–1892

Recollections of The Arabian Nights

WHEN the breeze of a joyful dawn blew free
In the silken sail of infancy,
The tide of time flowed back with me,
　The forward-flowing tide of time;
And many a sheeny summer-morn,
Adown the Tigris I was borne,
By Bagdat's shrines of fretted gold,
High-wallèd gardens green and old;
True Mussulman was I and sworn,
　For it was in the golden prime
　　Of good Haroun Alraschid.

Anight my shallop, rustling through
The low and bloomèd foliage, drove
The fragrant, glistening deeps, and clove
The citron-shadows in the blue:
By garden porches on the brim,
The costly doors flung open wide,
Gold glittering through lamplight dim,
And broidered sofas on each side:
　In sooth it was a goodly time,
　For it was in the golden prime
　　Of good Haroun Alraschid.

Often where clear-stemmed platans guard
The outlet, did I turn away
The boat-head down a broad canal
From the main river sluiced, where all
The sloping of the moon-lit sward
Was damask-work, and deep inlay
Of braided blooms unmown, which crept
Adown to where the water slept.
　A goodly place, a goodly time,
　For it was in the golden prime
　　Of good Haroun Alraschid.

shallop] little boat or sloop

A motion from the river won
Ridged the smooth level, bearing on
My shallop through the star-strown calm,
Until another night in night
I entered, from the clearer light,
Imbowered vaults of pillared palm,
Imprisoning sweets, which, as they clomb
Heavenward, were stayed beneath the dome
   Of hollow boughs.—A goodly time,
    For it was in the golden prime
      Of good Haroun Alraschid.

Still onward; and the clear canal
Is rounded to as clear a lake.
From the green rivage many a fall
Of diamond rillets musical,
Through little crystal arches low
Down from the central fountain's flow
Fallen silver-chiming, seemed to shake
The sparkling flints beneath the prow.
   A goodly place, a goodly time,
    For it was in the golden prime
      Of good Haroun Alraschid.

Above through many a bowery turn
A walk with vary-coloured shells
Wandered engrained. On either side
All round about the fragrant marge
From fluted vase, and brazen urn
In order, eastern flowers large,
Some dropping low their crimson bells
Half-closed, and others studded wide
   With disks and tiars, fed the time
    With odour in the golden prime
      Of good Haroun Alraschid.

Far off, and where the lemon grove
In closest coverture upsprung,
The living airs of middle night
Died round the bulbul as he sung;
Not he: but something which possessed
The darkness of the world, delight,
Life, anguish, death, immortal love,
Ceasing not, mingled, unrepressed,

Apart from place, withholding time,
But flattering the golden prime
Of good Haroun Alraschid.

Black the garden-bowers and grots
Slumbered: the solemn palms were ranged
Above, unwooed of summer wind:
A sudden splendour from behind
Flushed all the leaves with rich gold-green,
And, flowing rapidly between
Their interspaces, counterchanged
The level lake with diamond-plots
Of dark and bright. A lovely time,
For it was in the golden prime
Of good Haroun Alraschid.

Dark-blue the deep sphere overhead,
Distinct with vivid stars inlaid,
Grew darker from that under-flame:
So, leaping lightly from the boat,
With silver anchor left afloat,
In marvel whence that glory came
Upon me, as in sleep I sank
In cool soft turf upon the bank,
Entrancèd with that place and time,
So worthy of the golden prime
Of good Haroun Alraschid.

Thence through the garden I was drawn—
A realm of pleasance, many a mound,
And many a shadow-chequered lawn
Full of the city's stilly sound,
And deep myrrh-thickets blowing round
The stately cedar, tamarisks,
Thick rosaries of scented thorn,
Tall orient shrubs, and obelisks
Graven with emblems of the time,
In honour of the golden prime
Of good Haroun Alraschid.

With dazèd vision unawares
From the long alley's latticed shade
Emerged, I came upon the great
Pavilion of the Caliphat.

Right to the carven cedarn doors,
Flung inward over spangled floors,
Broad-basèd flights of marble stairs
Ran up with golden balustrade,
   After the fashion of the time,
   And humour of the golden prime
     Of good Haroun Alraschid.

The fourscore windows all alight
As with the quintessence of flame,
A million tapers flaring bright
From twisted silvers looked to shame
The hollow-vaulted dark, and streamed
Upon the moonèd domes aloof
In inmost Bagdat, till there seemed
Hundreds of crescents on the roof
   Of night new-risen, that marvellous time
   To celebrate the golden prime
     Of good Haroun Alraschid.

Then stole I up, and trancedly
Gazed on the Persian girl alone,
Serene with argent-lidded eyes
Amorous, and lashes like to rays
Of darkness, and a brow of pearl
Tressèd with redolent ebony,
In many a dark delicious curl,
Flowing beneath her rose-hued zone;
   The sweetest lady of the time,
   Well worthy of the golden prime
     Of good Haroun Alraschid.

Six columns, three on either side,
Pure silver, underpropt a rich
Throne of the massive ore, from which
Down-drooped, in many a floating fold,
Engarlanded and diapered
With inwrought flowers, a cloth of gold.
Thereon, his deep eye laughter-stirred
With merriment of kingly pride,
   Sole star of all that place and time,
   I saw him—in his golden prime,
     THE GOOD HAROUN ALRASCHID.

                     (1842)

107 *Song*

A SPIRIT haunts the year's last hours
Dwelling amid these yellowing bowers:
   To himself he talks;
For at eventide, listening earnestly,
At his work you may hear him sob and sigh
   In the walks;
   Earthward he boweth the heavy stalks
Of the mouldering flowers:
  Heavily hangs the broad sunflower
   Over its grave i' the earth so chilly;
  Heavily hangs the hollyhock,
   Heavily hangs the tiger-lily.

The air is damp, and hushed, and close,
As a sick man's room when he taketh repose
   An hour before death;
My very heart faints and my whole soul grieves
At the moist rich smell of the rotting leaves,
   And the breath
   Of the fading edges of box beneath,
And the year's last rose.
  Heavily hangs the broad sunflower
   Over its grave i' the earth so chilly;
  Heavily hangs the hollyhock,
   Heavily hangs the tiger-lily.

                (1830)

108   from *The Gardener's Daughter*

LIGHTLY he laughed, as one that read my thought,
And on we went; but ere an hour had passed,
We reached a meadow slanting to the north;
Down which a well-worn pathway courted us
To one green wicket in a privet hedge;
This, yielding, gave into a grassy walk
Through crowded lilac-ambush trimly pruned;
And one warm gust, full-fed with perfume, blew
Beyond us, as we entered in the cool.
The garden stretches southward. In the midst
A cedar spread his dark-green layers of shade.
The garden-glasses glanced, and momently
The twinkling laurel scattered silver lights.

'Eustace,' I said, 'this wonder keeps the house.'
He nodded, but a moment afterwards
He cried, 'Look! look!' Before he ceased I turned,
And, ere a star can wink, beheld her there.

For up the porch there grew an Eastern rose,
That, flowering high, the last night's gale had caught,
And blown across the walk. One arm aloft—
Gowned in pure white, that fitted to the shape—
Holding the bush, to fix it back, she stood,
A single stream of all her soft brown hair
Poured on one side: the shadow of the flowers
Stole all the golden gloss, and, wavering
Lovingly lower, trembled on her waist—
Ah, happy shade—and still went wavering down,
But, ere it touched a foot, that might have danced
The greensward into greener circles, dipt,
And mixed with shadows of the common ground!
But the full day dwelt on her brows, and sunned
Her violet eyes, and all her Hebe bloom,
And doubled his own warmth against her lips,
And on the bounteous wave of such a breast
As never pencil drew. Half light, half shade,
She stood, a sight to make an old man young.

(1842)

109   from *The Princess*

So sang the gallant glorious chronicle;
And, I all rapt in this, 'Come out,' he said,
'To the Abbey: there is Aunt Elizabeth
And sister Lilia with the rest.' We went
(I kept the book and had my finger in it)
Down through the park: strange was the sight to me;
For all the sloping pasture murmured, sown
With happy faces and with holiday.
There moved the multitude, a thousand heads:
The patient leaders of their Institute
Taught them with facts. One reared a font of stone
And drew, from butts of water on the slope,
The fountain of the moment, playing, now
A twisted snake, and now a rain of pearls,
Or steep-up spout whereon the gilded ball

174

Danced like a wisp: and somewhat lower down
A man with knobs and wires and vials fired
A cannon: Echo answered in her sleep
From hollow fields: and here were telescopes
For azure views; and there a group of girls
In circle waited, whom the electric shock
Dislinked with shrieks and laughter: round the lake
A little clock-work steamer paddling plied
And shook the lilies: perched about the knolls
A dozen angry models jetted steam:
A petty railway ran: a fire-balloon
Rose gem-like up before the dusky groves
And dropt a fairy parachute and past:
And there through twenty posts of telegraph
They flashed a saucy message to and fro
Between the mimic stations; so that sport
Went hand in hand with Science; otherwhere
Pure sport: a herd of boys with clamour bowled
And stumped the wicket; babies rolled about
Like tumbled fruit in grass; and men and maids
Arranged a country dance, and flew through light
And shadow, while the twangling violin
Struck up with Soldier-laddie, and overhead
The broad ambrosial aisles of lofty lime
Made noise with bees and breeze from end to end.

    Strange was the sight and smacking of the time;
And long we gazed, but satiated at length
Came to the ruins. High-arched and ivy-claspt,
Of finest Gothic lighter than a fire,
Through one wide chasm of time and frost they gave
The park, the crowd, the house; but all within
The sward was trim as any garden lawn.

(1847)

110   from *In Memoriam*

LXXXIX

Witch-elms that counterchange the floor
    Of this flat lawn with dusk and bright;
    And thou, with all thy breadth and height
Of foliage, towering sycamore;

How often, hither wandering down,
  My Arthur found your shadows fair,
  And shook to all the liberal air
The dust and din and steam of town:

He brought an eye for all he saw;
  He mixt in all our simple sports;
  They pleased him, fresh from brawling courts
And dusty purlieus of the law.

O joy to him in this retreat,
  Immantled in ambrosial dark,
  To drink the cooler air, and mark
The landscape winking through the heat:

O sound to rout the brood of cares,
  The sweep of scythe in morning dew,
  The gust that round the garden flew,
And tumbled half the mellowing pears!

O bliss, when all in circle drawn
  About him, heart and ear were fed
  To hear him, as he lay and read
The Tuscan poets on the lawn:

Or in the all-golden afternoon
  A guest, or happy sister, sung,
  Or here she brought the harp and flung
A ballad to the brightening moon:

Nor less it pleased in livelier moods,
  Beyond the bounding hill to stray,
  And break the livelong summer day
With banquet in the distant woods;

Whereat we glanced from theme to theme,
  Discussed the books to love or hate,
  Or touched the changes of the state,
Or threaded some Socratic dream;

But if I praised the busy town,
  He loved to rail against it still,
  For 'ground in yonder social mill
We rub each other's angles down,

'And merge' he said 'in form and gloss
    The picturesque of man and man.'
    We talked: the stream beneath us ran,
The wine-flask lying couched in moss,

Or cooled within the glooming wave;
    And last, returning from afar,
    Before the crimson-circled star
Had fallen into her father's grave,

And brushing ankle-deep in flowers,
    We heard behind the woodbine veil
    The milk that bubbled in the pail,
And buzzings of the honied hours.

CI

Unwatched, the garden bough shall sway,
    The tender blossom flutter down,
    Unloved, that beech will gather brown,
This maple burn itself away;

Unloved, the sun-flower, shining fair,
    Ray round with flames her disk of seed,
    And many a rose-carnation feed
With summer spice the humming air;

Unloved, by many a sandy bar,
    The brook shall babble down the plain,
    At noon or when the lesser wain
Is twisting round the polar star;

Uncared for, gird the windy grove,
    And flood the haunts of hern and crake;
    Or into silver arrows break
The sailing moon in creek and cove;

Till from the garden and the wild
    A fresh association blow,
    And year by year the landscape grow
Familiar to the stranger's child;

As year by year the labourer tills
   His wonted glebe, or lops the glades;
   And year by year our memory fades
From all the circle of the hills.

           (1850)

III   from *Maud*

COME into the garden, Maud,
   For the black bat, night, has flown,
Come into the garden, Maud,
   I am here at the gate alone;
And the woodbine spices are wafted abroad,
   And the musk of the rose is blown.

For a breeze of morning moves,
   And the planet of Love is on high,
Beginning to faint in the light that she loves
   On a bed of daffodil sky,
To faint in the light of the sun she loves,
   To faint in his light, and to die.

All night have the roses heard
   The flute, violin, bassoon;
All night has the casement jessamine stirred
   To the dancers dancing in tune;
Till a silence fell with the waking bird,
   And a hush with the setting moon.

I said to the lily, 'There is but one
   With whom she has heart to be gay.
When will the dancers leave her alone?
   She is weary of dance and play.'
Now half to the setting moon are gone,
   And half to the rising day;
Low on the sand and loud on the stone
   The last wheel echoes away.

I said to the rose, 'The brief night goes
   In babble and revel and wine.
O young lord-lover, what sighs are those,
   For one that will never be thine?
But mine, but mine,' so I sware to the rose,
   'For ever and ever, mine.'

And the soul of the rose went into my blood,
   As the music clashed in the hall;
And long by the garden lake I stood,
   For I heard your rivulet fall
From the lake to the meadow and on to the wood,
   Our wood, that is dearer than all;

From the meadow your walks have left so sweet
   That whenever a March-wind sighs
He sets the jewel-print of your feet
   In violets blue as your eyes,
To the woody hollows in which we meet
   And the valleys of Paradise.

The slender acacia would not shake
   One long milk-bloom on the tree;
The white lake-blossom fell into the lake
   As the pimpernel dozed on the lea;
But the rose was awake all night for your sake,
   Knowing your promise to me;
The lilies and roses were all awake,
   They sighed for the dawn and thee.

Queen rose of the rosebud garden of girls,
   Come hither, the dances are done,
In gloss of satin and glimmer of pearls,
   Queen lily and rose in one;
Shine out, little head, sunning over with curls,
   To the flowers, and be their sun.

There has fallen a splendid tear
   From the passion-flower at the gate.
She is coming, my dove, my dear;
   She is coming, my life, my fate;
The red rose cries, 'She is near, she is near;'
   And the white rose weeps, 'She is late;'
The larkspur listens, 'I hear, I hear;'
   And the lily whispers, 'I wait.'

She is coming, my own, my sweet;
   Were it ever so airy a tread,
My heart would hear her and beat,
   Were it earth in an earthy bed;

My dust would hear her and beat,
   Had I lain for a century dead;
Would start and tremble under her feet,
   And blossom in purple and red.

(1855)

Robert Browning
1812–1889

from *Sordello*, Book IV

112   ['*Passing Through the Rare Garden*']

Our dropping Autumn morning clears apace,
And poor Ferrara puts a softened face
On her misfortunes. Let us scale this tall
Huge foursquare line of red brick garden-wall
Bastioned within by trees of every sort
On three sides, slender, spreading, long and short;
Each grew as it contrived, the poplar ramped,
The fig-tree reared itself,—but stark and cramped,
Made fools of, like tamed lions: whence, on the edge,
Running 'twixt trunk and trunk to smooth one ledge
Of shade, were shrubs inserted, warp and woof,
Which smothered up that variance. Scale the roof
Of solid tops, and o'er the slope you slide
Down to a grassy space level and wide,
Here and there dotted with a tree, but trees
Of rarer leaf, each foreigner at ease,
Set by itself: and in the centre spreads,
Borne upon three uneasy leopards' heads,
A laver, broad and shallow, one bright spirt
Of water bubbles in. The walls begirt
With trees leave off on either hand; pursue
Your path along a wondrous avenue
Those walls abut on, heaped of gleamy stone,
With aloes leering everywhere, grey-grown
From many a Moorish summer: how they wind
Out of the fissures! likelier to bind
The building than those rusted cramps which drop
Already in the eating sunshine. Stop,

You fleeting shapes above there! Ah, the pride
Or else despair of the whole country-side!
A range of statues, swarming o'er with wasps,
God, goddess, woman, man, the Greek rough-rasps
In crumbling Naples marble—meant to look
Like those Messina marbles Constance took
Delight in, or Taurello's self conveyed
To Mantua for his mistress, Adelaide,
A certain font with caryatides
Since cloistered at Goito; only, these
Are up and doing, not abashed, a troop
Able to right themselves—who see you, stoop
O' the instant after you their arms! Unplucked
By this or that, you pass; for they conduct
To terrace raised on terrace, and, between,
Creatures of brighter mould and braver mien
Than any yet, the choicest of the Isle
No doubt. Here, left a sullen breathing-while,
Up-gathered on himself the Fighter stood
For his last fight, and, wiping treacherous blood
Out of the eyelids just held ope beneath
Those shading fingers in their iron sheath,
Steadied his strengths amid the buzz and stir
Of the dusk hideous amphitheatre
At the announcement of his over-match
To wind the day's diversions up, dispatch
The pertinacious Gaul: while, limbs one heap,
The Slave, no breath in her round mouth, watched leap
Dart after dart forth, as her hero's car
Clove dizzily the solid of the war
—Let coil about his knees for pride in him.
We reach the farthest terrace, and the grim
San Pietro Palace stops us.

(1840)

Garden Fancies

I. The Flower's Name

HERE'S the garden she walked across,
 Arm in my arm, such a short while since:
Hark, now I push its wicket, the moss
 Hinders the hinges and makes them wince!

113

She must have reached this shrub ere she turned,
 As back with that murmur the wicket swung;
For she laid the poor snail, my chance foot spurned,
 To feed and forget it the leaves among.

Down this side of the gravel-walk
 She went while her robe's edge brushed the box:
And here she paused in her gracious talk
 To point me a moth on the milk-white phlox.
Roses, ranged in valiant row,
 I will never think that she passed you by!
She loves you noble roses, I know;
 But yonder, see, where the rock-plants lie!

This flower she stopped at, finger on lip,
 Stooped over, in doubt, as settling its claim;
Till she gave me, with pride to make no slip,
 Its soft meandering Spanish name:
What a name! Was it love or praise?
 Speech half-asleep or song half-awake?
I must learn Spanish, one of these days,
 Only for that slow sweet name's sake.

Roses, if I live and do well,
 I may bring her, one of these days,
To fix you fast with as fine a spell,
 Fit you each with his Spanish phrase;
But do not detain me now; for she lingers
 There, like sunshine over the ground,
And ever I see her soft white fingers
 Searching after the bud she found.

Flower, you Spaniard, look that you grow not,
 Stay as you are and be loved for ever!
Bud, if I kiss you 'tis that you blow not:
 Mind, the shut pink mouth opens never!
For while it pouts, her fingers wrestle,
 Twinkling the audacious leaves between,
Till round they turn and down they nestle—
 Is not the dear mark still to be seen?

Where I find her not, beauties vanish;
 Whither I follow her, beauties flee;
Is there no method to tell her in Spanish
 June's twice June since she breathed it with me?

Come, bud, show me the least of her traces,
    Treasure my lady's lightest footfall!
—Ah, you may flout and turn up your faces—
    Roses, you are not so fair after all!

II. *Sibrandus Schafnaburgensis*

Plague take all your pedants, say I!
    He who wrote what I hold in my hand,
Centuries back was so good as to die,
    Leaving this rubbish to cumber the land;
This, that was a book in its time,
    Printed on paper and bound in leather,
Last month in the white of a matin-prime
    Just when the birds sang all together.

Into the garden I brought it to read,
    And under the arbute and laurustine
Read it, so help me grace in my need,
    From title-page to closing line.
Chapter on chapter did I count,
    As a curious traveller counts Stonehenge;
Added up the mortal amount;
    And then proceeded to my revenge.

Yonder's a plum-tree with a crevice
    An owl would build in, were he but sage;
For a lap of moss, like a fine pont-levis
    In a castle of the Middle Age,
Joins to a lip of gum, pure amber;
    When he'd be private, there might he spend
Hours alone in his lady's chamber:
    Into this crevice I dropped our friend.

Splash, went he, as under he ducked,
    —At the bottom, I knew, rain-drippings stagnate:
Next, a handful of blossoms I plucked
    To bury him with, my bookshelf's magnate;
Then I went in-doors, brought out a loaf,
    Half a cheese, and a bottle of Chablis;
Lay on the grass and forgot the oaf
    Over a jolly chapter of Rabelais.

Sibrandus Schafnaburgensis] Sibrandus of Aschafenburg, here the epitome of pedants
pont-levis] drawbridge

Now, this morning, betwixt the moss
    And gum that locked our friend in limbo,
A spider had spun his web across,
    And sat in the midst with arms akimbo:
So, I took pity, for learning's sake,
    And, *de profundis, accentibus laetis,*
Cantate! quoth I, as I got a rake;
    And up I fished his delectable treatise.

Here you have it, dry in the sun,
    With all the binding all of a blister,
And great blue spots where the ink has run,
    And reddish streaks that wink and glister
O'er the page so beautifully yellow:
    Oh, well have the droppings played their tricks!
Did he guess how toadstools grow, this fellow?
    Here's one stuck in his chapter six!

How did he like it when the live creatures
    Tickled and toused and browsed him all over,
And worm, slug, eft, with serious features,
    Came in, each one, for his right of trover?
—When the water-beetle with great blind deaf face
    Made of her eggs the stately deposit,
And the newt borrowed just so much of the preface
    As tiled in the top of his black wife's closet?

All that life and fun and romping,
    All that frisking and twisting and coupling,
While slowly our poor friend's leaves were swamping
    And clasps were cracking and covers suppling!
As if you had carried sour John Knox
    To the play-house at Paris, Vienna or Munich,
Fastened him into a front-row box,
    And danced off the ballet with trousers and tunic.

Come, old martyr! What, torment enough is it?
    Back to my room shall you take your sweet self.
Good-bye, mother-beetle; husband-eft, *sufficit!*
    See the snug niche I have made on my shelf!

de profundis . . . Cantate] from the depths, with glad accents, sing   toused] pulled and tugged about   eft] newt or lizard   trover] taking into possession   *sufficit*] that's enough

A.'s book s...   ...ll cover you,
    H...   ... D. to be gay,
And...   ...F. right over you,
    ...   ...e Judgment-day!

(1844)

Walt Whitman
1819–1892

114   *This Compost*

I

Something startles me where I thought I was safest,
I withdraw from the still woods I loved,
I will not go now on the pastures to walk,
I will not strip the clothes from my body to meet
                              my lover the sea,
I will not touch my flesh to the earth as to other flesh
                              to renew me.

O how can it be that the ground itself does not sicken?
How can you be alive you growths of spring?
How can you furnish health you blood of herbs,
                              roots, orchards, grain?
Are they not continually putting distemper'd
                              corpses within you?
Is not every continent work'd over and over
                              with sour dead?

Where have you disposed of their carcasses?
Those drunkards and gluttons of so many generations?
Where have you drawn off all the foul liquid and meat?
I do not see any of it upon you to-day, or perhaps
                              I am deceiv'd,
I will run a furrow with my plough, I will press my
         spade through the sod and turn it up underneath,
I am sure I shall expose some of the foul meat.

II

Behold this compost! behold it well!
Perhaps every mite has once form'd part of a sick
                                  person—yet behold!
The grass of spring covers the prairies,
The bean bursts noiselessly through the mould
                                  in the garden,
The delicate spear of the onion pierces upward,
The apple-buds cluster together on the apple-branches,
The resurrection of the wheat appears with pale visage
                                  out of its graves,
The tinge awakes over the willow-tree and the
                                  mulberry-tree,
The he-birds carol mornings and evenings while the
                                  she-birds sit on their nests,
The young of poultry break through the hatch'd eggs,
The new-born of animals appear, the calf is dropt from
                                  the cow, the colt from the mare,
Out of its little hill faithfully rise the potato's dark
                                  green leaves,
Out of its hill rises the yellow maize-stalk, the lilacs
                                  bloom in the dooryards,
The summer growth is innocent and disdainful above
                                  all those strata of sour dead.

What chemistry!
That the winds are really not infectious,
That this is no cheat, this transparent green-wash of
                                  the sea which is so amorous after me,
That it is safe to allow it to lick my naked body all over
                                  with its tongues,
That it will not endanger me with the fevers that have
                                  deposited themselves in it,
That all is clean forever and forever,
That the cool drink from the well tastes so good,
That blackberries are so flavorous and juicy,
That the fruits of the apple-orchard and the
        orange-orchard, that melons, grapes, peaches, plums,
                                  will none of them poison me,
That when I recline on the grass I do not catch
                                  any disease,
Though probably every spear of grass rises out of what
                                  was once a catching disease.

Now I am terrified at the Earth, it is that calm
                                  and patient,
It grows such sweet things out of such corruptions,
It turns harmless and stainless on its axis, with such
                    endless successions of diseas'd corpses,
It distills such exquisite winds out of such infused fetor,
It renews with such unwitting looks its prodigal,
                              annual, sumptuous crops,
It gives such divine materials to men, and accepts such
                      leavings from them at last.

(1867)

Matthew Arnold
1822–1888

115   *Lines Written in Kensington Gardens*

In this lone, open glade I lie,
Screened by deep boughs on either hand;
And at its end, to stay the eye,
Those black-crowned, red-boled pine-trees stand!

Birds here make song, each bird has his,
Across the girdling city's hum.
How green under the boughs it is!
How thick the tremulous sheep-cries come!

Sometimes a child will cross the glade
To take his nurse his broken toy;
Sometimes a thrush flit overhead
Deep in her unknown day's employ.

Here at my feet what wonders pass,
What endless, active life is here!
What blowing daisies, fragrant grass!
An air-stirred forest, fresh and clear.

Scarce fresher is the mountain-sod
Where the tired angler lies, stretched out,
And, eased of basket and of rod,
Counts his day's spoil, the spotted trout.

In the huge world, which roars hard by,
Be others happy if they can!
But in my helpless cradle I
Was breathed on by the rural Pan.

I, on men's impious uproar hurled,
Think often, as I hear them rave,
That peace has left the upper world
And now keeps only in the grave.

Yet here is peace for ever new!
When I who watch them am away,
Still all things in this glade go through
The changes of their quiet day.

Then to their happy rest they pass!
The flowers upclose, the birds are fed,
The night comes down upon the grass,
The child sleeps warmly in his bed.

Calm soul of all things! make it mine
To feel, amid the city's jar,
That there abides a peace of thine,
Man did not make, and cannot mar.

The will to neither strive nor cry,
The power to feel with others give!
Calm, calm me more! nor let me die
Before I have begun to live.

(1853)

Francis Turner Palgrave
1824–1897

116 *Eutopia*

THERE is a garden where lilies
And roses are side by side;
And all day between them in silence
The silken butterflies glide.

I may not enter the garden,
  Though I know the road thereto;
And morn by morn to the gateway
  I see the children go.

They bring back light on their faces;
  But they cannot bring back to me
What the lilies say to the roses,
  Or the songs of the butterflies be.

(1871)

Christina Rossetti
1830–1894

117   *An October Garden*

IN my Autumn garden I was fain
  To mourn among my scattered roses;
  Alas for that last rosebud that uncloses
To Autumn's languid sun and rain
When all the world is on the wane!
  Which has not felt the sweet constraint of June,
  Nor heard the nightingale in tune.

Broad-faced asters by my garden walk,
  You are but coarse compared with roses:
  More choice, more dear that rosebud which uncloses,
Faint-scented, pinched, upon its stalk,
That least and last which cold winds balk;
  A rose it is though least and last of all,
  A rose to me though at the fall.

(1878)

T. E. Brown
1830–1897

118   *My Garden*

A GARDEN is a lovesome thing, God wot!
Rose plot,
Fringed pool,
Ferned grot—
The veriest school
Of peace; and yet the fool
Contends that God is not—
Not God! in gardens! when the eve is cool?
Nay, but I have a sign;
'Tis very sure God walks in mine.

(1893)

Algernon Charles Swinburne
1837–1900

119   from *The Two Dreams* (after Boccaccio)

ALL things felt sweet were felt sweet overmuch;
The rose-thorn's prickle dangerous to touch,
And flecks of fire in the thin leaf-shadows;
Too keen the breathèd honey of the rose,
Its red too harsh a weight on feasted eyes;
They were so far gone in love's histories,
Beyond all shape and colour and mere breath,
Where pleasure has for kinsfolk sleep and death,
And strength of soul and body waxen blind
For weariness, and flesh entoiled with mind,
When the keen edge of sense foretasteth sin.
    Even this green place the summer caught them in
Seemed half deflowered and sick with beaten leaves
In their strayed eyes; these gold flower-fumèd eves
Burnt out to make the sun's love-offering,
The midnoon's prayer, the rose's thanksgiving,

The trees' weight burdening the strengthless air,
The shape of her stilled eyes, her coloured hair,
Her body's balance from the moving feet—
All this, found fair, lacked yet one grain of sweet
It had some warm weeks back: so perisheth
On May's new lip the tender April breath;
So those same walks the wind sowed lilies in
All April through, and all their latter kin
Of languid leaves whereon the Autumn blows—
The dead red raiment of the last year's rose—
The last year's laurel, and the last year's love,
Fade, and grow things that death grows weary of.

(1866)

120   *A Forsaken Garden*

IN a coign of the cliff between lowland and highland,
    At the sea-down's edge between windward and lee,
Walled round with rocks as an inland island,
    The ghost of a garden fronts the sea.
A girdle of brushwood and thorn encloses
    The steep square slope of the blossomless bed
Where the weeds that grew green from the graves of its roses
      Now lie dead.

The fields fall southward, abrupt and broken,
    To the low last edge of the long lone land.
If a step should sound or a word be spoken,
    Would a ghost not rise at the strange guest's hand?
So long have the grey bare walks lain guestless,
    Through branches and briars if a man make way,
He shall find no life but the sea-wind's, restless
      Night and day.

The dense hard passage is blind and stifled
    That crawls by a track none turn to climb
To the strait waste place that the years have rifled
    Of all but the thorns that are touched not of time.
The thorns he spares when the rose is taken;
    The rocks are left when he wastes the plain.
The wind that wanders, the weeds wind-shaken,
      These remain.

Not a flower to be pressed of the foot that falls not;
  As the heart of a dead man the seed-plots are dry;
From the thicket of thorns whence the nightingale calls not,
  Could she call, there were never a rose to reply.
Over the meadows that blossom and wither
  Rings but the note of a sea-bird's song;
Only the sun and the rain come hither
    All year long.

The sun burns sere and the rain dishevels
  One gaunt bleak blossom of scentless breath.
Only the wind here hovers and revels
  In a round where life seems barren as death.
Here there was laughing of old, there was weeping,
  Haply, of lovers none ever will know,
Whose eyes went seaward a hundred sleeping
    Years ago.

Heart handfast in heart as they stood, 'Look thither,'
  Did he whisper? 'look forth from the flowers to the sea;
For the foam-flowers endure when the rose-blossoms wither,
  And men that love lightly may die—but we?'
And the same wind sang and the same waves whitened,
  And or ever the garden's last petals were shed,
In the lips that had whispered, the eyes that had lightened,
    Love was dead.

Or they loved their life through, and then went whither?
  And were one to the end—but what end who knows?
Love deep as the sea as a rose must wither,
  As the rose-red seaweed that mocks the rose.
Shall the dead take thought for the dead to love them?
  What love was ever as deep as a grave?
They are loveless now as the grass above them
    Or the wave.

All are at one now, roses and lovers,
  Not known of the cliffs and the fields and the sea.
Not a breath of the time that has been hovers
  In the air now soft with a summer to be.
Not a breath shall there sweeten the seasons hereafter
  Of the flowers or the lovers that laugh now or weep,
When as they that are free now of weeping and laughter
    We shall sleep.

Here death may deal not again for ever;
  Here change may come not till all change end.
From the graves they have made they shall rise up never,
  Who have left nought living to ravage and rend.
Earth, stones, and thorns of the wild ground growing,
  While the sun and the rain live, these shall be;
Till a last wind's breath upon all these blowing
      Roll the sea.

Till the slow sea rise and the sheer cliff crumble,
  Till terrace and meadow the deep gulfs drink,
Till the strength of the waves of the high tides humble
  The fields that lessen, the rocks that shrink,
Here now in his triumph where all things falter,
  Stretched out on the spoils that his own hand spread,
As a god self-slain on his own strange altar,
      Death lies dead.

(1878)

121   *The Mill Garden*

STATELY stand the sunflowers, glowing down the garden-side,
Ranged in royal rank arow along the warm grey wall,
Whence their deep disks burn at rich midnoon afire with pride,
Even as though their beams indeed were sunbeams, and the tall
Sceptral stems bore stars whose reign endures, not flowers that fall.
Lowlier laughs and basks the kindlier flower of homelier fame,
Held by love the sweeter that it blooms in Shakespeare's name,
Fragrant yet as though his hand had touched and made it thrill,
Like the whole world's heart, with warm new life and gladdening flame.
Fair befall the fair green close that lies below the mill!

Softlier here the flower-soft feet of refluent seasons glide,
Lightlier breathes the long low note of change's gentler call.
Wind and storm and landslip feed the lone sea's gulf outside,
Half a seamew's first flight hence; but scarce may these appal
Peace, whose perfect seal is set for signet here on all.
Steep and deep and sterile, under fields no plough can tame,
Dip the cliffs full-fledged with poppies red as love or shame,
Wide wan daisies bleak and bold, or herbage harsh and chill;
Here the full clove pinks and wallflowers crown the love they claim.
Fair befall the fair green close that lies below the mill!

All the place breathes low, but not for fear lest ill betide,
Soft as roses answering roses, or a dove's recall.
Little heeds it how the seaward banks may stoop and slide,
How the winds and years may hold all outer things in thrall,
How their wrath may work on hoar church tower and boundary wall.
Far and wide the waste and ravin of their rule proclaim
Change alone the changeless lord of things, alone the same:
Here a flower is stronger than the winds that work their will,
Or the years that wing their way through darkness toward their aim.
Fair befall the fair green close that lies below the mill!

Friend, the home that smiled us welcome hither when we came,
When we pass again with summer, surely should reclaim
Somewhat given of heart's thanksgiving more than words fulfil—
More than song, were song more sweet than all but love, might frame.
Fair befall the fair green close that lies below the mill!

(1884)

Thomas Hardy
1840–1928

122   *Domicilium*

IT faces west, and round the back and sides
High beeches, bending, hang a veil of boughs,
And sweep against the roof. Wild honeysucks
Climb on the walls, and seem to sprout a wish
(If we may fancy wish of trees and plants)
To overtop the apple-trees hard by.

Red roses, lilacs, variegated box
Are there in plenty, and such hardy flowers
As flourish best untrained. Adjoining these
Are herbs and esculents; and farther still
A field; then cottages with trees, and last
The distant hills and sky.

122 title] Latin for domicile, place where one usually lives

Behind, the scene is wilder. Heath and furze
Are everything that seems to grow and thrive
Upon the uneven ground. A stunted thorn
Stands here and there, indeed; and from a pit
An oak uprises, springing from a seed
Dropped by some bird a hundred years ago.

                                    In days bygone—
Long gone—my father's mother, who is now
Blest with the blest, would take me out to walk.
At such a time I once inquired of her
How looked the spot when first she settled here.
The answer I remember. 'Fifty years
Have passed since then, my child, and change has marked
The face of all things. Yonder garden-plots
And orchards were uncultivated slopes
O'ergrown with bramble bushes, furze and thorn:
That road a narrow path shut in by ferns,
Which, almost trees, obscured the passer-by.
Our house stood quite alone, and those tall firs
And beeches were not planted. Snakes and efts
Swarmed in the summer days, and nightly bats
Would fly about our bedrooms. Heathcroppers
Lived on the hills, and were our only friends;
So wild it was when first we settled here.'

                                              (1916)

123   *The Frozen Greenhouse*

            'THERE was a frost
            Last night!' she said,
            'And the stove was forgot
            When we went to bed,
            And the greenhouse plants
            Are frozen dead!'

            By the breakfast blaze
            Blank-faced spoke she,
            Her scared young look
            Seeming to be
            The very symbol
            Of tragedy.

    efts] lizards   Heathcroppers] wild ponies

The frost is fiercer
Than then to-day,
As I pass the place
Of her once dismay,
But the greenhouse stands
Warm, tight, and gay,

While she who grieved
At the sad lot
Of her pretty plants—
Cold, iced, forgot—
Herself is colder,
And knows it not.

(1925)

124   *The Lodging-House Fuchsias*

Mrs Masters's fuchsias hung
Higher and broader, and brightly swung,
    Bell-like, more and more
Over the narrow garden-path,
Giving the passer a sprinkle-bath
    In the morning.

She put up with their pushful ways,
And made us tenderly lift their sprays,
    Going to her door:
But when her funeral had to pass
They cut back all the flowery mass
    In the morning.

(1928)

Henry Austin Dobson
1840–1921

125   *A Garden Song*

HERE, in this sequestered close,
Bloom the hyacinth and rose;
Here beside the modest stock
Flaunts the flaring hollyhock;
Here, without a pang, one sees
Ranks, conditions, and degrees.

All the seasons run their race
In this quiet resting place;
Peach, and apricot, and fig
Here will ripen, and grow big
Here is store and overplus,—
More had not Alcinous!

Here, in alleys cool and green,
Far ahead the thrush is seen;
Here along the southern wall
Keeps the bee his festival;
All is quiet else-afar
Sounds of toil and turmoil are.

Here be shadows large and long;
Here be spaces meet for song;
Grant, O garden-god, that I,
Now that mood and moment please,—
Find the fair Pierides!

(1885)

126   *The Sundial*

'TIS an old dial, dark with many a stain;
    In summer crowned with drifting orchard bloom,
Tricked in the autumn with the yellow rain,
    And white in winter like a marble tomb;

125 Alcinous] King of the Phaeacians in Homer's *Odyssey*: see no. 49 for his fabled gardens
Pierides] the Muses, born in Pieria

And round about its gray, time-eaten brow
   Lean letters speak—a worn and shattered row:
I am a Shade: a Shadowe too arte thou:
   I marke the Time: saye, Gossip, dost thou soe?

Here would the ringdoves linger, head to head;
   And here the snail a silver course would run,
Beating old Time; and here the peacock spread
   His gold-green glory, shutting out the sun.

Robert Bridges
1844–1930

127   *The Garden in September*

Now thin mists temper the slow-ripening beams
Of the September sun: his golden gleams
On gaudy flowers shine, that prank the rows
Of high-grown hollyhocks, and all tall shows
That Autumn flaunteth in his bushy bowers;
Where tomtits, hanging from the drooping heads
Of giant sunflowers, peck the nutty seeds;
And in the feathery aster bees on wing
Seize and set free the honied flowers,
Till thousand stars leap with their visiting:
While ever across the path mazily flit,
Unpiloted in the sun,
The dreamy butterflies
With dazzling colours powdered and soft glooms,
White, black and crimson stripes, and peacock eyes,
Or on chance flowers sit,
With idle effort plundering one by one
The nectaries of deepest-throated blooms.

With gentle flaws the western breeze
Into the garden saileth,
Scarce here and there stirring the single trees,
For his sharpness he vaileth:
So long a comrade of the bearded corn,
Now from the stubbles whence the shocks are borne,

O'er dewy lawns he turns to stray,
As mindful of the kisses and soft play
Wherewith he enamoured the light-hearted May,
Ere he deserted her;
Lover of fragrance, and too late repents;
Nor more of heavy hyacinth now may drink,
Nor spicy pink,
Nor summer's rose, nor garnered lavender,
But the few lingering scents
Of streakèd pea, and gillyflower, and stocks
Of courtly purple, and aromatic phlox.

And at all times to hear are drowsy tones
Of dizzy flies, and humming drones,
With sudden flap of pigeon wings in the sky,
Or the wild cry
Of thirsty rooks, that scour ascare
The distant blue, to watering as they fare
With creaking pinions, or—on business bent,
If aught their ancient polity displease,—
Come gathering to their colony, and there
Settling in ragged parliament,
Some stormy council hold in the high trees.

(1893)

Edgar Bateman

(dates unknown)

128 *The Cockney's Garden* (to music by Geo Le Brunn)

IF you saw my little backyard, 'Wot a pretty spot!' you'd cry—
    It's a picture on a sunny summer day;
Wiv the turnip-tops and cabbages wot people doesn't buy
    I makes it on a Sunday look so gay.
The neighbours fink I grows 'em, and you'd fancy you're in Kent,
    Or at Epsom, if you gaze into the mews;
It's a wonder as the landlord doesn't want to raise the rent,
    Because we've got such nobbly distant views.

Chorus

Oh! it really is a werry pretty garden,
And Chingford to the eastward could be seen;
Wiv a ladder and some glasses,
You could see to 'Ackney Marshes,
If it wasn't for the 'ouses in between.

We're as countrified as can be wiv a clothes-prop for a tree,
The tub-stool makes a rustic little stile;
Every time the blooming clock strikes there's a cuckoo sings to me,
And I've painted up 'To Leather Lane, a mile.'
Wiv tom-ar-toes and wiv radishes wot 'adn't any sale,
The backyard looks a puffick mass o' bloom;
And I've made a little beehive wiv some beetles in a pail,
And a pitchfork wiv the 'andle o' the broom.

Chorus

Oh! it really is a werry pretty garden,
An' the Rye 'Ouse from the cockloft could be seen,
Where the chickweed man undresses,
To bathe among the watercresses,
If it wasn't for the 'ouses in between.

There's the bunny shares 'is egg-box wiv the cross-eyed cock and hen,
Though they 'as got the pip, and 'im the morf;
In a dog's-'ouse on the line-post there was pigeons nine or ten,
Till some one took'd a brick and knocked it off.
The dust-cart, though it seldom comes, is just like 'arvest 'ome
And we mean to rig a dairy up some'ow;
Put the donkey in the wash'ouse wiv some imitation 'orns,
For we're teaching 'im to moo just like a kah.

Chorus

Oh! it really is a werry pretty garden,
And 'Endon to the westward could be seen;
And by clinging to the chimbley,
You could see across to Wembley,
If it wasn't for the 'ouses in between.

---

puffick] perfect   morf] morfound, a chill affecting livestock   kah] cow

Though the gas works isn't wiolets, they improve the rural scene—
  For mountains they would werry nicely pass;
There's the mushrooms in the dust-hole, with the cowcumbers so
                                        green—
  It only wants a bit o' 'ot-'ouse glass.
I wears this milkman's nightshirt, and I sits outside all day,
  Like the plough-boy cove what mizzled o'er the Lea;
And when I goes indoors at night they dunno what I say,
  'Cause my language gets as yokel as can be.

Chorus

Oh! it really is a werry pretty garden,
And the soap works from the 'ouse-tops could be seen;
  If I got a rope and pulley,
  I'd enjoy the breeze more fully,
If it wasn't for the 'ouses in between.

                                        (First performed 1894)

George R. Sims
1847–1922

129   *A Garden Song*

I SCORN the doubts and cares that hurt
    The world and all its mockeries,
My only care is now to squirt
    The ferns among my rockeries.

In early youth and later life
    I've seen an up and seen a down,
And now I have a loving wife
    To help me peg verbena down.

Of joys that come to womankind
    The loom of fate doth weave her few,
But here are summer joys entwined
    And bound with golden feverfew,

mizzled] lounged or absconded (usually to take oneself off)

201

GEORGE R. SIMS

I've learnt the lessons one and all
  With which the world its sermon stocks,
Now, heedless of a rise or fall,
  I've Brompton and I've German stocks.

In peace and quiet pass our days,
  With nought to vex our craniums,
Our middle beds are all ablaze
  With red and white geraniums.

And like a boy I laugh when she,
  In Varden hat and Varden hose,
Comes slyly up the lawn at me
  To squirt me with the garden hose.

Let him who'd have the peace he needs
  Give all his worldly mumming up,
Then dig a garden, plant the seeds,
  And watch the product coming up.

(1879)

Philip Yorke II
1849–1922

130   ['*Our Gardener*' *at Erddig*]

OUR Gardener here, James Phillips see,
A Bachelor of Husbandry,
Who did from garden-boy become
The finished grower of the Plum,
Scarce ever absent from our ground
Then only some few miles around.
This Garden formed his chief delight,
And was as Eden in his sight.

Old-fashioned, in his notions, he
With foreign names did not agree
'Quatre-Saisons' 'Quarter-Sessions' meant,
The 'Bijou' as the 'By Joe' went,

Varden] character in Dickens's *Barnaby Rudge*

'Glory to die John' was the Rose,
Which each as 'Gloire de Dijon' knows.
No Green-house here 'twas his advice
The Antique Frames would well suffice.

Invited by a friend was he
To Leasowe Castle by the Sea
And a day's holiday he took
That he on that Estate might look.
Little regard to it he paid,
This one remark was all he made,
That they, whose Gardens he was shown,
Did 'a fine sheet of water' own.

He in his boyhood once did try
A verse of Psalm to glorify
'Blow up the trumpet in new moon
The time appointed for its tune'.
And thus to Marchwiel Church he brought
That instrument in Wrexham bought,
And on the solemn Feast-day played
To give effect to what was said.

For three and forty years his name
Was known to all who hither came:
Our gardens under his employ
Did great fertility enjoy:
And visitors did oft declare
They ne'er did taste so good a pear
As 'Winter-nellie', by him grown,
And at our local Contests shown.

This faithful steward, just and true
Died here, in eighteen eighty two,
At the full age of fifty eight,
Like 'shock of corn', mayhap of wheat;
When 'as bare grain' his body sank
Were nigh four thousand pounds in Bank.
A search for next of kin was made,
And to a niece the same was paid.

(After 1882)

Robert Louis Stevenson
1850–1894

131

The Gardener

THE gardener does not love to talk,
He makes me keep the gravel walk;
And when he puts his tools away,
He locks the door and takes the key.

Away behind the currant row
Where no one else but cook may go,
Far in the plots, I see him dig
Old and serious, brown and big.

He digs the flowers, green, red and blue,
Nor wishes to be spoken to.
He digs the flowers and cuts the hay,
And never seems to want to play.

Silly gardener! summer goes,
And winter comes with pinching toes,
When in the garden bare and brown
You must lay your barrow down.

Well now, and while the summer stays
To profit by these garden days
O how much wiser you would be
To play at Indian wars with me!

(1885)

132

To a Gardener

FRIEND, in my mountain-side demesne
My plain-beholding, rosy, green
And linnet-haunted garden-ground,
Let still the esculents abound.
Let first the onion flourish there,
Rose among roots, the maiden-fair,
Wine-scented and poetic soul
Of the capacious salad bowl.

Let thyme the mountaineer—to dress
The tinier birds—and wading cress,
The lover of the shallow brook,
From all my plots and borders look.
Nor crisp and ruddy radish, nor
Pease-cods for the child's pinafore
Be lacking; nor of salad clan
The last and least that ever ran
About great nature's garden-beds.
Nor thence be missed the speary heads
Of artichoke; nor thence the bean
That gathered innocent and green
Outsavours the belauded pea.

These tend, I prithee; and for me,
Thy most long-suffering master, bring
In April, when the linnets sing
And the days lengthen more and more
At sundown to the garden door.
And I, being provided thus,
Shall, with superb asparagus,
A book, a taper, and a cup
Of country wine, divinely sup.

(1887)

from *Translations from Martial*

[*De Hortis Julii Martialis, IV. 64*]

133

My Martial owns a garden, famed to please,
Beyond the glades of the Hesperides;
Along Janiculum lies the chosen block
Where the cool grottos trench the hanging rock.
The moderate summit, something plain and bare,
Tastes overhead of a serener air;
And while the clouds besiege the vales below,
Keeps the clear heaven and doth with sunshine glow.
To the June stars that circle in the skies
The dainty roofs of that tall villa rise.
Hence do the seven imperial hills appear;
And you may view the whole of Rome from here:

133 Janiculum] one of the hills of ancient Rome famed for its gardens

Beyond, the Alban and the Tuscan hills;
And the cool groves and the cool falling rills.
Rubre Fidenae, and with virgin blood
Anointed once Perenna's orchard wood.
Thence the Flaminian, the Salarian way,
Stretch far abroad below the dome of day;
And lo! the traveller toiling toward his home;
And all unheard, the chariot speeds to Rome!
For here no whisper of the wheels; and tho'
The Mulvian Bridge, above the Tiber's flow,
Hangs all in sight, and down the sacred stream
The sliding barges vanish like a dream,
The seaman's shrilling pipe not enters here,
Nor the rude cries of porters on the pier.
And if so rare the house, how rarer far
The welcome and the weal that therein are!
So free the access, the doors so widely thrown
You half imagine all to be your own.

(1895)

E. Nesbit
1858–1924

134

At Parting

AND you could leave me now—
After the first remembered whispered vow
Which sings for ever and ever in my ears—
The vow which God among His Angels hears—
After the long-drawn years,
The slow, hard tears,
Could break new ground, and wake
A new strange garden to blossom for your sake,
And leave me here alone,
In the old garden that was once our own?

How should I learn to bear
Our garden's pleasant ways and pleasant air,
Her flowers, her fruits, her lily, her rose and thorn,
When only in the picture these appear—

Rubre Fidenae] examples given by Martial of 'cool retreats' near Rome

These, once alive, and always over-dear?
Ah—think again: the rose you used to wear
Must still be more than other roses be
The flower of flowers. Ah, pity, pity me!

For in my acres is no plot of ground
Whereon could any garden site be found:
I have but little skill
To water, weed, and till,
And make the desert blossom like the rose;
Yet our old garden knows
If I have loved its ways and walks and kept
The garden watered, and the pleasance swept.

Yet—if you must—go now:
Go, with my blessing filling both your hands,
And, mid the desert sands
Which life drifts deep round every garden wall
Make your new festival
Of bud and blossom—red rose and green leaf.
No blight born of my grief
Shall touch your garden, love; but my heart's prayer
Shall draw down blessings on you from the air,
And all we learned of leaf and plant and tree
Shall serve you when you walk no more with me
In garden ways; and when with her you tread
The pleasant ways with blossoms overhead,
And when she asks, 'How did you come to know
The secrets of the way these green things grow?'
Then you will answer—and I, please God, hear,
'I had another garden once, my dear.'

(1905)

Arthur Symons
1865–1945

135   *L'Allée* (after Paul Verlaine)

As in the age of shepherd king and queen,
Painted and frail amid her nodding bows,
Under the sombre branches and between
The green and mossy garden-ways she goes,

With little mincing airs one keeps to pet
A darling and provoking perroquet.
Her long-trained robe is blue, the fan she holds
With fluent fingers girt with heavy rings,
So vaguely hints of vague erotic things
That her eye smiles, musing among its folds.
—Blonde too, a tiny nose, a rosy mouth,
Artful as that sly patch that makes more sly,
In her divine unconscious pride of youth,
The slightly simpering sparkle of the eye.

(1896)

William Butler Yeats
1865–1939

136 . ### *Ancestral Houses*

SURELY among a rich man's flowering lawns,
Amid the rustle of his planted hills,
Life overflows without ambitious pains;
And rains down life until the basin spills,
And mounts more dizzy high the more it rains
As though to choose whatever shape it wills
And never stoop to a mechanical
Or servile shape, at others' beck and call.

Mere dreams, mere dreams! Yet Homer had not sung
Had he not found it certain beyond dreams
That out of life's own self-delight had sprung
The abounding glittering jet; though now it seems
As if some marvellous empty sea-shell flung
Out of the obscure dark of the rich streams,
And not a fountain, were the symbol which
Shadows the inherited glory of the rich.

Some violent bitter man, some powerful man
Called architect and artist in, that they,
Bitter and violent men, might rear in stone
The sweetness that all longed for night and day,
The gentleness none there had ever known;
But when the master's buried mice can play,

And maybe the great-grandson of that house,
For all its bronze and marble, 's but a mouse.

O what if gardens where the peacock strays
With delicate feet upon old terraces,
Or else all Juno from an urn displays
Before the indifferent garden deities;
O what if levelled lawns and gravelled ways
Where slippered Contemplation finds his ease
And Childhood a delight for every sense,
But take our greatness with our violence?

What if the glory of escutcheoned doors,
And buildings that a haughtier age designed,
The pacing to and fro on polished floors
Amid great chambers and long galleries, lined
With famous portraits of our ancestors;
What if those things the greatest of mankind
Consider most to magnify, or to bless,
But take our greatness with our bitterness?

(1928)

137   *Coole Park and Ballylee, 1931*

UNDER my window-ledge the waters race,
Otters below and moor-hens on the top,
Run for a mile undimmed in Heaven's face
Then darkening through 'dark' Raftery's 'cellar' drop,
Run underground, rise in a rocky place
In Coole demesne, and there to finish up
Spread to a lake and drop into a hole.
What's water but the generated soul?

Upon the border of that lake's a wood
Now all dry sticks under a wintry sun,
And in a copse of beeches there I stood,
For Nature's pulled her tragic buskin on
And all the rant's a mirror of my mood:
At sudden thunder of the mounting swan
I turned about and looked where branches break
The glittering reaches of the flooded lake.

Another emblem there! That stormy white
But seems a concentration of the sky;
And, like the soul, it sails into the sight
And in the morning's gone, no man knows why;
And is so lovely that it sets to right
What knowledge or its lack had set awry,
So arrogantly pure, a child might think
It can be murdered with a spot of ink.

Sound of a stick upon the floor, a sound
From somebody that toils from chair to chair;
Beloved books that famous hands have bound,
Old marble heads, old pictures everywhere;
Great rooms where travelled men and children found
Content or joy; a last inheritor
Where none has reigned that lacked a name and fame
Or out of folly into folly came.

A spot whereon the founders lived and died
Seemed once more dear than life; ancestral trees,
Or gardens rich in memory glorified
Marriages, alliances and families,
And every bride's ambition satisfied.
Where fashion or mere fantasy decrees
We shift about—all that great glory spent—
Like some poor Arab tribesman and his tent.

We were the last romantics—chose for theme.
Traditional sanctity and loveliness;
Whatever's written in what poets name
The book of the people; whatever most can bless
The mind of man or elevate a rhyme;
But all is changed, that high horse riderless,
Though mounted in that saddle Homer rode
Where the swan drifts upon a darkening flood.

(1933)

Rudyard Kipling
1865–1936

The Glory of the Garden

OUR England is a garden that is full of stately views,
Of borders, beds and shrubberies and lawns and avenues,
With statues on the terraces and peacocks strutting by;
But the Glory of the Garden lies in more than meets the eye.

For where the old thick laurels grow, along the thin red wall,
You find the tool- and potting-sheds which are the heart of all;
The cold-frames and the hot-houses, the dungpits and the tanks,
The rollers, carts and drain-pipes, with the barrows and the planks.

And there you'll see the gardeners, the men and 'prentice boys
Told off to do as they are bid and do it without noise;
For, except when seeds are planted and we shout to scare the birds,
The Glory of the Garden it abideth not in words.

And some can pot begonias and some can bud a rose,
And some are hardly fit to trust with anything that grows;
But they can roll and trim the lawns and sift the sand and loam,
For the Glory of the Garden occupieth all who come.

Our England is a garden, and such gardens are not made
By singing:—'Oh, how beautiful!' and sitting in the shade,
While better men than we go out and start their working lives
At grubbing weeds from gravel-paths with broken dinner-knives.

There's not a pair of legs so thin, there's not a head so thick,
There's not a hand so weak and white, nor yet a heart so sick,
But it can find some needful job that's crying to be done,
For the Glory of the Garden glorifieth every one.

Then seek your job with thankfulness and work till further orders,
If it's only netting strawberries or killing slugs on borders;
And when your back stops aching and your hands begin to harden,
You will find yourself a partner in the Glory of the Garden.

Oh, Adam was a gardener, and God who made him sees
That half a proper gardener's work is done upon his knees,
So when your work is finished, you can wash your hands and pray
For the Glory of the Garden, that it may not pass away!
And the Glory of the Garden it shall never pass away!

(1911)

Richard Le Gallienne
1866–1947

139   *A Library in a Garden*

'A Library in a garden! The phrase seems to contain the whole
felicity of man.'—Mr Edmund Gosse in *Gossip in a Library*.

A WORLD of books amid a world of green,
Sweet song without, sweet song again within
Flowers in the garden, in the folios too:
O happy Bookman, let me live with you!

(1892)

W. H. Davies
1871–1940

140   *The Hill-Side Park*

SOME banks cropped close, and lawns smooth mown and green,
Where, when a daisy's guiltless face was seen,
Its pretty head came sacrifice to pride
Of human taste—I saw upon the side
Of a steep hill. Without a branch of wood
Plants, giant-leaved, like boneless bodies stood.
The flowers had colonies, not one was seen
To go astray from its allotted green,
But to the light like mermaids' faces came
From waves of green, and scarce two greens the same.
And everywhere man's ingenuity
On fence and bordering: for I could see

The tiny scaffolding to hold the heads
And faces overgrown of flowers in beds
On which their weak-developed frames must fall,
Had they not such support upright and tall.
There was a fountain, and its waters' leap
Was under a full-quivered Cupid's keep.
And from his mother's lips the spray was blown
Upon adjusted rock, selected stone;
And so was placed that all the waters fell
Into a small ravine in a small dell,
And made a stream, where that wee river raved,
Though gold his rocks and margent amber paved.
This park, it was a miracle of care,
But sweeter far to me the prospects there:
The far beyond, where lived Romance near seas
And pools in haze, and in far realms of trees.
I saw where Severn had run wide and free,
Out where the Holms lie flat upon a sea
Whose wrinkles wizard Distance smoothed away,
And still sails flecked its face of silver-grey.

(1905)

141   *No Man's Wood*

SHALL I have jealous thoughts to nurse,
When I behold a rich man's house?
Not though his windows, thick as stars,
    Number the days in every year;
I, with one window for each month,
    Am rich in four or five to spare.

But when I count his shrubberies,
His fountains there, and clumps of trees,
Over the palings of his park
    I leap with my primeval blood;
Down wild ravines to Ocean's rocks,
    Clean through the heart of No-man's Wood.

(1925)

the Holms] islands in the Bristol Channel off Weston-super-Mare, probably the same two
'isles' observed by Coleridge (see no. 100)

Walter De La Mare
1875–1956

142   *The Three Cherry Trees*

THERE were three cherry trees once,
  Grew in a garden all shady;
And there for delight of so gladsome a sight,
  Walked a most beautiful lady,
  Dreamed a most beautiful lady.

Birds in those branches did sing,
  Blackbird and throstle and linnet,
But she walking there was by far the most fair—
  Lovelier than all else within it,
  Blackbird and throstle and linnet.

But blossoms to berries do come,
  All hanging on stalks light and slender,
And one long summer's day charmed that lady away,
  With vows sweet and merry and tender;
  A lover with voice low and tender.

Moss and lichen the green branches deck;
  Weeds nod in its paths green and shady:
Yet a light footstep seems there to wander in dreams,
  The ghost of that beautiful lady,
  That happy and beautiful lady.

(1912)

143   *Two Gardens*

Two gardens see!—this, of enchanted flowers,
Strange to the eye, and more than earthly-sweet;
Small rivulets running, song-reëchoing bowers;
And green-walled pathways which, ere parting, meet;
And there a lion-like sun in heaven's delight
Breathes plenitude from dayspring to the night.

The other:—walls obscure, and chaces of trees,
Ilex and yew, and dream-enticing dark,
Hid pools, moths, creeping odours, silentness,
Luna its deity, and its watchword, *Hark!*
A still and starry mystery, wherein move
Phantoms of ageless wonder and of love.

Two gardens for two children—in one mind:
But ah, how seldom open now their gates I find!

(1945)

Mary Ursula Bethell
1874–1945

144

Time

'ESTABLISHED' is a good word, much used in garden books,
'The plant, when established' . . .
Oh, become established, quickly, quickly, garden!
For I am fugitive, I am very fugitive—

Those that come after me will gather these roses,
And watch, as I do now, the white wistaria
Burst, in the sunshine, from its pale green sheath.

Planned. Planted. Established. Then neglected,
Till at last the loiterer by the gate will wonder
At the old, old cottage, the old wooden cottage,
And say, 'One might build here, the view is glorious;
This must have been a pretty garden once.'

(1929)

chaces] (as if) engraved in relief

Alfred Noyes
1880–1958

145

The Butterfly Garden

'Then there is that more capricious close of happy surprises—the
butterfly garden. By keeping a sheltered corner for the colours and
scents that they like best, you may have not only the anchored sort of
flowers, but what our forefathers would have called a pretty pleasance
of winged flowers, flowers that have cut their stalky cables, and sail as
they please upon the sunlit air.'—*Orchard's Bay.*

HERE, by this crumbling wall
    We'll spread the feast, then watch what guests it brings.
Earth-rooted flowers to flowers of heaven shall call,
    And all the gorgeous air shall wink with wings.

We'll choose what they love most
    As all men must whose guests are of the sky;
Not lavender, of lost gardens the sweet ghost;
    But heliotrope, young Psyche's cherry-pie.

Be sure she does not pine
    For any phantom feast, that heavenly Maid!
'Tis we that make a wraith of things divine,
    And think the very soul into a shade.

The Chilian orange-ball
    First of the shrubs that Tortoise-shells prefer,
Must hang its honeyed clusters over all
    And tempt the freckled blues to flutter near;

With globes of fragrant gold
    Luring the Green-veined White from near and far,
While faultless Painted Ladies here unfold
    Their pearly fans, inlaid with moon and star;

Till later buddleias trail
    Their long racemes of violet and rose,
Round which the glorious Admirals dip and sail,
    And swarthy Peacocks flit and sip and doze.

Hedging them closely round
  Veronica must spread her spikes of blue,
That sun and flowers may in one sleep be drowned
  Yet keep her own Fritillaries fluttering, too.

Blue is their heart's delight.
  Therefore, though crimson petals also please,
And soft white wings will sail to bridal white
  Like yachts with orange tips on blossoming seas,

We'll make them doubly blest
  With this, the deepening blue of children's eyes;
For wingèd creatures love that colour best,
  Which smiled upon them, once, in Paradise.

(1930)

Wallace Stevens
1883–1963

146   *A Room on a Garden*

          O STAGNANT east-wind, palsied mare,
          Giddap! The ruby roses' hair
          Must blow.

          Behold how order is the end
          Of everything. The roses bend
          As one.

          Order, the law of hoes and rakes,
          May be perceived in windy quakes
          And squalls.

          The gardener searches earth and sky
          The truth in nature to espy
          In vain.

          He well might find that eager balm
          In lilies' stately-statued calm;
          But then

          He well might find it in this fret
          Of lilies rusted, rotting, wet
          With rain.

                                    (1957)

William Carlos Williams
1883–1963

147   *The Tulip Bed*

THE May sun—whom
all things imitate—
that glues small leaves to
the wooden trees
shone from the sky
through bluegauze clouds
upon the ground.
Under the leafy trees
where the suburban streets
lay crossed,
with houses on each corner,
tangled shadows had begun
to join
the roadway and the lawns.
With excellent precision
the tulip bed
inside the iron fence
upreared its gaudy
yellow, white and red,
rimmed round with grass,
reposedly.

(1921)

148   *The Italian Garden*
[*Gratwick Farm, nr. Pavilion, NY*]

WHEN she married years ago
her romantic ideas dominated
the builders

nightingale and hermit thrush
then the garden
fell into disuse.

Now her son has taken up her
old ideas formally
shut out

by high walls from the sheep run.
It is a scene from Comus
transported

to upper New York State. I remember
it already ruined
in

early May the trees crowded
with orioles chickadees
robins

brown-thrashers cardinals
in their scarlet
coats

vocal at dawn among pools
reft of their
lilies

and rarer plants flowers
given instead to
mallows

pampas-grass and cattails by
drought and winter
winds

where now hummingbirds touch
without touching.
Moss-covered

benches fallen apart among
sunken gardens
where

The Faerie Queene was read to
strains from
Campion

and the scent of wild strawberries
mingled with that
of eglantine

Comus] the masque by John Milton first acted in 1634 at Ludlow Castle   Campion]
Thomas Campion (1567–1620), poet, composer, physician

and verbena. Courtesy has revived
with visitors who
have

begun to stroll the paths
as in the quattrocento
covertly.

Maybe it will drive them to
be more civil
love

more jocosely (a good word) as
we presume they did
in that famous

garden where Boccaccio and
his friends hid
themselves

from the plague and rude manners
in the woods
of that garden

as we would similarly today
to escape the plague
of

our cars which cannot
penetrate
hers.

(1962)

Siegfried Sassoon
1886–1967

149   *In Heytesbury Wood*

Not less nor more than five and forty years ago
The old lord went along the ornamental ride;
For the last time he walked there, tired and very slow;
Saw the laburnum's golden chains, the glooming green
Of bowery box-trees; stood and looked farewell, and sighed
For roots that held his heart and summers that he'd seen.

And then, maybe, he came again there, year by year,
To watch, as dead men do, and see—who knows how clear?—
That vista'd paradise which in his time had thriven;
Those trees to which in cogitating strolls he'd given
Perennial forethought,—branches that he'd lopped and cherished:
Came, and saw sad neglect; dense nettles; favourites felled
Or fallen in gales and left to rot; came and beheld
How with succeeding seasons his laburnums perished.

'Return', I think, 'next summer, and you'll find such change,—
Walking, some low-lit evening, in the whispering wood,—
As will refresh your eyes and do them ghostly good;
See redolence befriend, neglect no more estrange;
See plumed acacia and the nobly tranquil bay;
Laburnums too, now small as in the prosperous prime
Of your well-ordered distant mid-Victorian time . . .'
Thus I evoke him; thus he looks and goes his way
Along that path we call the ornamental ride—
The old slow lord, the ghost whose trees were once his pride.

(1940)

Edith Sitwell
1887–1964

150   *Gardener Janus Catches a Naiad*

BASKETS of ripe fruit in air
The bird-songs seem, suspended where

Between the hairy leaves trills dew,
All tasting of fresh green anew.

Ma'am, I've heard your laughter flare
Through your waspish-gilded hair:

    Feathered masks,
    Pots of peas,
    Janus asks
    Naught of these.

Creaking water
Brightly stripèd,
Now, I've caught her—
Shrieking biped.
Flute sounds jump
And turn together,
Changing clumps
Of glassy feather.
In among the
Pots of peas
Naiad changes—
Quick as these.

(1925)

Dorothy Wellesley, Duchess of Wellington
1889–1956

151   *Walled Garden*

ABOVE the walls the west light hangs, until
The White Tea Roses, staring where deep shade is,
Ghosts of old lovely ladies,
Whisper and stir till all the flowers fill
The living darkness with a sense of sound;
The flowers wake and speak, in that walled ground.

The Lily of the Incas spoke: 'I clung
Among red rocks, where like crustaceans grew
Giant mosses on the mountains of Peru;
There, half on earth, and half from heaven hung,
A-swing in mist and cold,
I saw below the High Priest set the bourn,
And the rayed Emperor turn
The year's first furrow with a plough of gold.'

Then cried great curly lilies slashed with brown:
'We stood where cloudy torrents thunder down
Slender, for ever wet,
From falls that carry cannonading trees
Through riven clefts, and the collapsing screes
Besiege farm doors on scar sides of Tibet.'

Scented Magnolias in the darkness said:
'Sensuous and pale like a dark woman's skin,
Sealed, secret, with a core of gold within,
And anthers tipped with red,
What is our business in this English air?'

The Water-lilies there,
Great cups of lighted sulphur, streaked with green,
Tugged at their drags, darted like floats about,
Complainingly cried out:
'We decked Nilotic barges for a Queen.'

Blue lilies, sprung between three oceans, said:
'Grinding, and half atilt
The light swung boulders rock upon the veldt:
We bloom by lions dead
Of old age in the wild.'

                    Windflowers then
Cried suddenly, as when
Kites' tails of crackling leaves before a gust
Sweep over porous cork-woods on the hills:
'We star the sites of lost volcanic vills
And tufa tombs: we are Etruria's dust
Which grew the rustling maize,
And painted slim-loined panthers on a frieze.'

Then cried a voice: 'The scholars know me well,
Shining in verse, or springing from a plinth
By the dark stairway of a labyrinth:
This yellow of the Cretan asphodel.'

White Prickly Poppies sighed: 'We used to know
Warm vales of Mexico.'
The tall Camassias chattered in their sleep:
'How great the stars above the granite shone
On the Blue Mountains in dim Oregon.'
The Amethyst Sea Holly cried: 'I keep
The sea-coast colour: brine has painted me,
Blustered like tattered shags,
For aeons on the legendary crags,
My stems are stained to the Dalmatian Sea.'

The Persian Pink. 'On painted miniature
I posed with pretty boy, and gold gazelle,
Petals of peach that fell,
Fat men in love, all framed in foliature;
And with a fine disdain,
Heard water falling on the white laced courts,
And noted, likely through the sweets and sports
Sweet Sheherazade telling lies again.'

Heathers from highlands of Madeira sighed:
'Gold gods looked sea-ward from the marble docks;
In the flint cottages with weathercocks
The children dreamed night-terrors of the tide;
For there the streams and tarns
Fell glancing through Atlantean villages
Where housewives slapped the linen.
                              Memories
Live on, when runes are blotted from the sarns.'

Silence was heard; and all the flowers within
The walls were hushed. The wider world awoke,
And in the garden spoke
Their foreign kin;
The wild wine-netted Irises that spring
From the hot silver of the Caspian sand
Kindled, a clamouring band;
With bud and bloom that grow
In tracts no man can know:
Those bred in heat, with apes and birds, that cling
Twisted in tendrilled darkness till they die,
Without a glimpse of sky;
Where pyramids and towns
Under the oozy orchids sleep obscure,
In vegetation hostile, sexed, impure,
And faces jabber in the dark like clowns,
And snakes sail down the forest ways like ships,
High prowed, and out to ram
The lesser craft, and trees go down and jam,
Leaving the forest lighted up in strips.

Growing, a tumbled rout
Of sound the flowers sang out;

sarns] sarsen-stone

The fiery tongues of Heaven
Seeking their souls were given,
The blooms black convicts bind about the yoke
Of island elephants, dragging crimson trunks
To rafts upon the river-race, for Junks
To ship them at the mouth.
                    All blossom spoke:
The flower of cotton, and the bloom of tea,
Apples of Sodom from shores of the Dead Sea,
   Singing from hills and waves,
From desert mounds, where like white window slats
Dead camel ribs let light through; rockier flats,
Where wasted saints, with lions, possessed the caves,
And mixed with fossil shells in secret grow
   Roses of Jericho.
From ships on sunken reefs with mouldered hulls,
That cake with orange lichen till they glow,
And where among the heaps of rags below
The brilliant mosses map the piteous skulls.
From bells of Pieris ranged below the ice;
From pats of rose on a moist precipice;
From those clean plants lighting the slushy dips,
   Starring the wet moraine,
That swept by avalanches spring again
Among the limestone chips.
From flowers on Asian plains; where, chewing corn,
Preparing for the march, long, long ago,
Dim gathering hordes lashed the humped buffalo,
Sinister in the hush of Tartar dawn.

'Renewal and renewal', and once more:
'Renew our hearts', they cried: 'Who lives receives.'
Outside the walls the wind whipped up the leaves
And like a thresher drove the dark before.
Shouting from East to West he came; the waves
Beating beyond Formosa felt the lash,
And feathered to their tips; the hollow wash
Of water in closed caves
Boomed on a deeper tone; the sleepy ships
Shuddered in spasm; all the blind, obscured
Lives of the nether sea, one second stirred,
Throbbing to guess his whips
Lashing the world awake.

Snow-spirals swirled
On Everest Peaks; and here the Cottage Rose,
Rude shaken from repose,
Scattered her petals on the rolling world.

(1925)

W. J. Turner
1889–1946

152   *Magic*

I LOVE a still conservatory
   That's full of giant, breathless palms,
Azaleas, clematis and vines
   Whose quietness great Trees becalms
Filling the air with foliage,
   A curved and dreamy statuary . . .

I love the mossy quietness
   That grows upon the great stone flags,
The dark tree-ferns, the staghorn ferns,
   The prehistoric, antlered stags
That carven stand and stare among
   The silent, ferny wilderness . . .

I like to hear a cold, pure rill
   Of water trickling low, afar
With sudden littler jerks and purls
   Into a tank or stoneware jar,
The song of a tiny sleeping bird
   Held like a shadow in its trill.

I watch a white Nyanza float
   Upon a green, untroubled pool,
A fairyland Ophelia, she
   Has cast herself in water cool,
And lies while fairy cymbals ring
   Drowned in her fairy castle moat.

Still as a great jewel is the air
  With boughs and leaves smooth-carved in it,
And rocks and trees and giant ferns,
  And blooms with inner radiance lit,
And naked water like a nymph
  That dances tireless, slim and bare.

Silent the Cattleyas blaze
  And thin red orchid shapes of Death
Peer savagely with twisted lips
  Sucking an eerie, phantom breath
With that bright, spotted, fever'd lust
  That watches lonely travellers craze.

Gigantic, mauve and hairy leaves
  Hang like obliterated faces
Full of dim unattained expression
  Such as haunts virgin forest places
When Silence leaps among the trees
  And the echoing heart deceives.

                                 (1916)

Arthur Waley
1889–1966

153   *Planting Flowers on the Eastern Embankment*
                (after Po Chu-I)
        written when Governor of Chung-Chou

I TOOK money and bought flowering trees
And planted them out on the bank to the east of the Keep.
I simply bought whatever had most blooms,
Not caring whether peach, apricot, or plum.
A hundred fruits, all mixed together;
A thousand branches, flowering in due rotation.
Each has its season coming early or late;
But to all alike the fertile soil is kind.
The red flowers hang like a sunset mist;
The white flowers gleam like a fall of snow.
The wandering bees cannot bear to leave them;
The sweet birds also come there to roost.
In front there flows an ever-running stream;
Beneath there is built a little flat terrace.

Sometimes I sweep the flagstones of the terrace;
Sometimes, in the wind, I raise my cup and drink.
The flower-branches screen my head from the sun;
The flower-buds fall down into my lap.
Alone drinking, alone singing my songs
I do not notice that the moon is level with the steps.
The people of Pa do not care for flowers;
All the spring no one has come to look.
But their Governor General, alone with his cup of wine
Sits till evening and will not move from the place!

(1918)

Cole Porter
1891–1964

154   *An Old-Fashioned Garden*

ONE summer day,
I chanced to stray
To a garden of flowers blooming wild.
It took me once more
To the dear days of yore
And a spot that I loved as a child.

There were the phlox,
Tall hollyhocks,
Violets perfuming the air,
Frail eglantines,
Shy columbines,
And marigolds everywhere ...

> It was an old-fashioned garden,
> Just an old-fashioned garden,
> But it carried me back
> > To that dear little shack
> > > In the land of long ago ...

> I saw an old-fashioned missus
> Getting old-fashioned kisses,
> In that old-fashioned garden,
> > From an old-fashioned beau.

(1919)

Vita Sackville-West
1892–1962

from *The Land*

WHEN skies are gentle, breezes bland,
When loam that's warm within the hand
Falls friable between the tines,
Sow hollyhocks and columbines,
The tufted pansy, and the tall
Snapdragon in the broken wall,
Not for this summer, but for next,
Since foresight is the gardener's text,
And though his eyes may never know
How lavishly his flowers blow,
Others will stand and musing say
'These were the flowers he sowed that May.'

But for this summer's quick delight
Sow marigold, and sow the bright
Frail poppy that with noonday dies
But wakens to a fresh surprise;
Along the pathway stones be set
Sweet Alysson and mignonette,
That when the full midsummer's come
On scented clumps the bees may hum,
Golden Italians, and the wild
Black humble-bee alike beguiled:
And lovers who have never kissed
May sow the cloudy Love-in-Mist.

Nor be the little space forgot
For herbs to spice the kitchen pot:
Mint, pennyroyal, bergamot,
Tarragon and melilot,
Dill for witchcraft, prisoners' rue,
Coriander, costmary,
Tansy, thyme, Sweet Cicely,
Saffron, balm, and rosemary
That since the Virgin threw her cloak
Across it,—so say cottage folk—
Has changed its flowers from white to blue.

But have a care that seeds be strewn
One night beneath a waxing moon,
And pick when the moon is on the wane,
Else shall your toil be all in vain . . .

And gardener, let your spud be sharp to ridge
The loam from spiny hedge to hedge;
Labour within your garden square
Till back be broke and light grow rare,
But never heed the sinews' pain
If you may snatch before the rain
Crisp days when clods will turn up rough;
Gentleman robin brown as snuff
With spindle legs and bright round eye
Shall be your autumn company.
Trench deep; dig in the rotting weeds;
Slash down the thistle's greybeard seeds;
Then make the frost your servant; make
His million fingers pry and break
The clods by glittering midnight stealth
Into the necessary tilth.
Then may you shoulder spade and hoe,
And heavy-booted homeward go,
For no new flowers shall be born
Save hellebore on Christmas morn,
And bare gold jasmine on the wall,
And violets, and soon the small
Blue netted iris, like a cry
Startling the sloth of February.

(1927)

156   from *The Garden*

HERE, in his lamp-lit parable, he'll scan
Catalogues bright with colour and with hope,
Dearest delusions of creative mind,
His lamp-lit walls, his lamp-lit table painting
Fabulous flowers flung as he desires.
Fantastic, tossed, and all from shilling packet
—An acre sprung from one expended coin,—
Visions of what might be.

spud] spade

We dream our dreams.
What should we be, without our fabulous flowers?
The gardener dreams his special own alloy
Of possible and the impossible.

He dreams an orchard neatly pruned and spurred,
Where Cox' Orange jewels with the red
Of Worcester Permain, and the grass beneath
Blows with narcissus and the motley crocus,
Rich as Crivelli, fresh as Angelo,
Poliziano, or our English Chaucer
Or Joachim du Bellay, turn by turn.
He dreams again, extravagant, excessive,
Of planted acres most unorthodox
Where Scarlet Oaks would flush our English fields
With passionate colour as the Autumn came,
Quercus coccinea, that torch of flame
Blown sideways as by some Atlantic squall
Between its native north America
And this our moderate island. Or again
He dreams of forests made of flow'ring trees
Acre on acre, thousands in their pride,
Cherry and almond, crab and peach and plum,
Not like their working cousins grown for use
But in an arrant spendthrift swagger cloak
Squandered across th' astonished countryside . . .

And this, in these invented woods, may take
The place of underwood, replace the tall
Thirteen-year chestnut, fit for poles and spiles;
Here is romance, in this imagined forest,
These different rides of laylock and Forsythia;
Azalea in a peaty soil; magnolia
Cupping its goblets down the narrow aisles;
Vines and solanum wreathing Silver Birches,
Wild waving overhead, to lift the eyes
Surfeited with the wealth on lower level.

Think, and imagine: this might be your truth;
Follow my steps, oh gardener, down these woods.
Luxuriate in this my startling jungle.

Crivelli . . . Angelo] Carlo Crivelli (active 1457–93) and Michelangelo (?1475–1564) Italian
Renaissance artists   Poliziano] Angelo Poliziano (1454–94) Italian Renaissance poet
Joachim du Bellay] French Renaissance poet (1522–60)

I dream, this winter eve. A millionaire
Could plant these forests of a poet's dream.
A poet's dream costs nothing; yet is real.

The gardener sits in lamplight, soberer
Than I who mix such lyrical and wild
Impossibilities with what a sober man
Considers sense. Yet I, poor poet, I
Am likewise a poor practised gardener
Knowing the Yes and better still the No.
Sense must prevail, nor waste extravagant
Such drunken verse on such December dreams.
Yet I do find it difficult indeed
To break away from visions in this drear
Winter of northern island. I must love
The warmer sun and with nostalgia pine
For those my birthright climates on the coast
Mediterranean of southern Spain.
Homesick we are, and always, for another
And different world.
                          And so the traveller
Down the long avenue of memory
Sees in perfection that was never theirs
Gardens he knew, and takes his steps of thought
Down paths that, half-imagined and half-real,
Are wholly lovely with a loveliness
Suffering neither fault, neglect, nor flaw;
By visible hands not tended, but by angels
Or by St Phocas, gentlest patron saint
Of gardeners . . . Such wisdom of perfection
Never was ours in fact though ours in faith,
And since we live in fabric of delusion
Faith may well serve a turn in place of fact.

(1946)

Osbert Sitwell
1892–1969

157   *In the Potting Shed*

OH, for words with which
To paint him there from life,
As he stands in the potting-shed
    With the bass like golden hair,
    And with his insignia,
      Scissors, basket and pruning-knife,
Amid a universe
Of unripe pears and golden bulbs,
    As the stove burns warmly,
The stove crackles brightly,
And there is a smell of warm wood,
A warm wooden smell as of trees growing
    (Do not ask why the trees are growing,
    Do not ask why the trees are growing).

Here is harboured
The strength of the garden,
Enough growing-power
To make the whole country-side flicker
Next year
With the red and pink candles of the early spring,
And to illumine again
That little hill
On which for ever in our memories
Stands Mrs Hague.

                        (1928)

158   *In the Winter*

UMBERTO
    Always worked hard —
But unfortunately, the harder he worked,
    The fewer flowers grew.
For though his warm and vivid gift of life
Communicated itself to his own kind
It never prospered
    Green things growing.

So today, as yesterday, and every day
  This impressive Zeus
Fumbled and jumbled for hours among the flower-beds
Tying to stakes, and thereby breaking the necks of,
The few heavy-headed blooms,
  Monsters in a delicate winter,
  Leafy anomalies half-way to everlasting flowers,
  With their dry crinkling rattle,
Or fashioned seemingly of creased velvet
And coloured out of the same palette as
  A turkey's hanging chins—
But in the damp umbrageous confines of the garden,
Where the ferns grew and the violets,
In a mossy stone vase
  On the top of a tall stone fountain,
  Safely out of Umberto's reach,
Arum lilies flowered with magnificent impunity.

          (1958)

Herbert Read
1893–1968

159   *Garden Party*

I HAVE assumed a conscious sociability,
Pressed unresponding hands,
Sipped tea,
And chattered aimlessly
All afternoon,
Achieving spontaneity
Only
When my eyes lit at the sight
Of a scarlet spider
Running over the bright
Green mould of an apple tree.

        (1946)

Robert Graves
1895–1985

160

Gardener

LOVELIEST flowers, though crooked in their border,
And glorious fruit, dangling from ill-pruned boughs—
Be sure the gardener had not eye enough
To wheel a barrow between the broadest gates
Without a clumsy scraping.

Yet none could think it simple awkwardness;
And when he stammered of a garden-guardian,
Said the smooth lawns came by angelic favour,
The pinks and pears in spite of his own blunders,
They nudged at this conceit.

Well, he had something, though he called it nothing—
An ass's wit, a hairy-belly shrewdness
That would appraise the intentions of the angel
By the very yard-stick of his own confusion,
And bring the most to pass.

                                                  (1931)

Edmund Blunden
1896–1974

161

One Among the Roses

WHILE by the rosebed gay you stood, and revelled in the multitude
Of blooms with unfamiliar names, and tints and folds new-found,
     new-sweet,
We wondered much at the rich power which breeds so many and many
     a flower
Not like the myriads known before, and each one lovely and complete.

And while you touched the leaves and bowed your bright head there
    among the crowd,
Murmuring of roses you would have in the small garden of your dream,
I wondered much at the great grace which fashioned your clear rosy
    face,
After the myriads gone before, a beauty new and now supreme.

(1944)

Ruth Pitter
1897–1992

162   *The Diehards*

WE go, in winter's biting wind,
On many a short-lived winter day,
With aching back but willing mind
To dig and double-dig the clay.

All in November's soaking mist
We stand and prune the naked tree,
While all our love and interest
Seem quenched in blue-nosed misery.

We go in withering July
To ply the hard incessant hoe;
Panting beneath the brazen sky
We sweat and grumble, but we go.

We go to plead with grudging men,
And think it is a bit of luck
When we can wangle now and then
A load or two of farmyard muck.

What do we look for as reward?
Some little sounds, and scents, and scenes:
A small hand darting strawberry-ward,
A woman's apron full of greens.

A busy neighbour, forced to stay
By sight and smell of wallflower-bed;
The plum-trees on an autumn day,
Yellow, and violet, and red.

Tired people sitting on the grass,
Lulled by the bee, drugged by the rose,
While all the little winds that pass
Tell them the honeysuckle blows.

The sense that we have brought to birth
Out of the cold and heavy soil,
These blessed fruits and flowers of earth
Is large reward for all our toil.

(1941)

163   *Other People's Glasshouses*

WHILE gazing round this dear ramshackle one
(Not even my own, but which I help to run),
I think of what such pleasances can be,
And dream of them in tender reverie.
Those which begin with excavated sites,
Well reared with brick foundations, pressed-steel lights,
The latest heating, cunning ventilation,
Water laid on, and kind anticipation
Of all a tender plant can well demand;
With all the stores laid ready to the hand
Of richest turfy loam, manure, and peat,
Sand, sphagnum, oakleaf-mould so dark and sweet,
With stacks of clean red pots and labels white,
And every ware to forward the delight.
I muse, and faintly hope that one glad day
Some genial Duke or great rich man will say
'We have some Glass which you may like to see;
It will not bore you? Good! Then follow me.'
(Note that the Duke but grows to please himself,
Perhaps for shows, but not for sordid pelf;
So no Tomato-vistas I expect,
Nor endless Cucumbers, nor those erect
Chrysanths disbudded to but one a plant,
Which markets, but not Christians, seem to want.)

The Duke, so portly in his ancient tweeds,
Crosses a yard designed for glasshouse needs:
My eye, already ravished, straight begins
To dote on potting-sheds and compost-bins,

237

Remarks a fruit-store, and yet always keeps
Reverting to the stables' juicy heaps;
Nor can I well contain the envious sigh
Where scores of tons of leaf-mould tower high.

But of these background joys I say no more;
The Duke is beckoning from an open door,
Through which appear Azaleas' dawny hues,
The starry Cinerarias' endless blues,
Rare Primulas, far-gathered from the snows
From which they rear their coronets of rose,
By stout adventurers, who boldly face
Strange Lamas, and the savage holy place,
To win the trophy of enchanting grace:
Ranks of Carnations, to all ladies dear,
Of whose sweet taste I write approval here,
For these pre-eminent myself I think,
As long as you don't overdo the pink.

Another door—a damp delicious heat,
Odours half sinister, or languid-sweet,
And glistening pseudo-bulbs and strangest flowers
Stand massed in pans, or else depend in showers.
The Orchid-House! where all my being owns
A deep delight; where these my northern bones
Thaw, and the frugal cautious northern eye,
Abandoned to a tropic revelry,
Gazes its hungry fill; the northern nose
Its usual criterion, the rose,
Forgets awhile, and sniffs exotic scent
With large expansion and profound content;
While the incorrigible northern mind
Ponders the wonder of the orchid kind,
And though enchanted has a corner free
To marvel at their strange biology.

Forward, to where in borders, pots and tubs
Stand sturdy and delicious Trees and Shrubs!
Well-dressed Camellias flourish with the Bay,
Which is as stately, not so bright as they.
Glorious Camellias, whose hardy green
Defies our winter, and whose flowers are seen
Crowding in February, rich and fair,
When all our native shrubs are poor and bare;

And here, where they are sheltered, flower at will,
Though snow be drifted up on every sill.
Ye simple gardeners, why do you not grow
This vigorous Beauty which delights us so?

But look where Orange-trees in fruit and bud
Bless our cold eyes, and stir nostalgic blood
To pine, as ever, for their odorous groves,
Their fireflies, and their Mediterranean loves!
The poets' Myrtle, now so seldom seen,
With small spiced bloom and neat and sober green;
The glorious Fuchsia (call it Farthingale),
So fair in every kind from dark to pale,
So neat, so perfect; could a gardener want
A lovelier object, or a kindlier plant?
And ranging round, the genial showman comes
To his own favourites, the Geraniums,
(And, I confess it, favourites of mine,
So do not call the Duke a Philistine).
Not in small pots, but in the border, these
Ascend a trellis, and are tall as trees:
Bright, clear, and simple, easy to content,
At home in palace or in tenement,
Sumptuous, scented, flowering so long,
Dear to the heart, if not renowned in song.

And in this Shrub-house there are sure to be
Some curious things from far beyond the sea,
Such rarities as roving uncles seek:
Many uncommon, one or two unique;
Some gifts of princes, some of gardening aunts;
But all are notable and wondrous plants.

And now the Duke has left the Shrubs, and flits
Stately but eager past the forcing-pits,
To show the lean-to where his Fig-tree spreads
A solemn, large-leaved shade above our heads.
Grave, reverend plant! its leaden limbs are smooth,
The thoughtful eye and loving hand to soothe,
And the rich sober fruit can take the mind
Back to old Vergil and his worthy kind.
Long could I sit beneath this solemn tree,
Well entertained with thoughts of piety;
Likening good men to this fruit, with skin
Of modest hue, but bright and sweet within.

Now my enthusiastic Mentor reaches
The fair abode of Nectarines and Peaches,
Whose gracile twigs, with willowy leaves, are tied
Neat to the well-spaced wire on either side,
While their rich burdens, red or golden-pale,
Delicious breathings on the air exhale,
So that we seem absolved from sin and woe,
And Adam's curse is lifted, as we go
Wandering slowly in delicious ease
Along this blessed colonnade of trees,
Forgetting fortune and our different birth,
And only thankful that we walk the earth:
Lose Adam's curse in Adam's primal right,
Strangely absolved by mutual delight!

But let me not too selfishly impose
On my kind host, who may have gouty toes.
The Melons and the Mushrooms I will pass
And all the other glories of the glass.
I will forgo even the lordly Pines,
If I may thoroughly inspect—the Vines!
Ah sacred sight, the grand symbolic Plant,
Assuaging many a deep-felt human want,
Filling the eye with beauty, and the mind
With old associations deep and kind,
Ay, solemn too; which for the body's use
Distils that peerless and poetic juice,
So evident a blessing from above,
Whoso rejects it, him I cannot love.

Here let me wander, seeking till I find
Of the whole race the one, the peerless kind.
Not the Black Hamburg, though full well I know
This is the best for such as I to grow,
For in ramshackle houses with no heat
The willing creature ripens black and sweet:
Not the *Gross* Colmar, though this be so much
Grown for the market by the clever Dutch;
Not Canon Hall, for though 'tis large and fair
The flavour is too often wanting there.
For but a lingering moment I survey
The sweet, delicious, but too small Tokay,
But from the whole Sweetwater tribe escape—
Their flavour is unworthy of the grape;

And all the other kinds I wander by,
All good, yet only one can satisfy.
Ah! here at last we find its shy retreat;
A special Span or Dome, with extra heat.

Take the whole garden, friend, but leave me this,
The Alexandrian Muscat, plant of bliss,
With long and taper bunches hanging down,
(The best and ripest darkening into brown),
Which cracked society's capricious flukes
Deny to poets, and concede to dukes!
Whose savour reconciles the glee of youth
With the grave mellowness of heavenly truth;
Which when I taste, perception seems to be
Translated into purest poetry,
My griefs transfigured to supernal gold,
At once by nature and by art consoled.

The Duke will read my longing in my eyes,
With ready secateur will sympathise;
And while we munch, I know we shall agree
On Progress and Perfectibility;
For none can disbelieve the promised bliss,
Or immortality, while tasting this.
The Alexandrian in fruit or flower
Forbids impiety, or lust for power;
And where he shoots, to man there are restored
Some ells of Eden: here the flaming sword
Is sheathed; those Sentinels so dread and bright
Sit down with us, and share in our delight . . .

Vain vision! when the changing world each day
Sees some such lordly pleasance pass away;
When the mere stripling knows my symbols all
Worn tokens, heaven hypothetical,[1]
Nature indifferent, and the dreams of men
Figments of longing which we must condemn.
Yet keep these plants, O Man! a kindlier time
May yet be moved by them to better rhyme,
Or moved, like me, to place his pleasure low,
On the firm Earth, whence Men and Blossoms grow.

[1] To say the least.

(1941)

Horace Gregory
1898–1991

The Chinese Garden

Near the city of Washington, DC, there is a Chinese Garden. Few
visit it; the place seems singularly deserted and remote.

O YES, the Chinese Garden! Do you remember
Sun beating behind clouds? One felt the air
Shaken by streams of yellow light through aether,
And yet late summer stillness in each turn
Of paths that ran between the fading grasses,
The well-deep, glassy pool, and the damp smell,
And clouded light around us everywhere—
The half-lit madness we can never cure.

You see them now! I mean the water lilies,
White petals open as a China cup
Rising above the surface of a tray:
They are here—just out of reach—and there, the water,
The half-light in far corners of the park,
Trees fallen around it through the pale arbutus.
Do you feel the grey light at the farthest clearing
Thrusting as snow against plate glass, then gone?

Beneath the cloud-white lilies, hairy roots,
Invisible lips that breathe the cool well water
Wavering in darkness down to dreamless sleep:
The streams to walk below the net of grasses
That close above the ripples of the soul.

There were no signs to warn us: 'Walks ill-tended,
The bridges gone beneath the deeper grasses—'
Reach toward the lilies? Not that afternoon.
If one were tempted to lean out that far? . . .
No, no, not now! No one would dare to hear us.
'The water has turned black.' We turned away:
It was like leaving a forbidden city,
Earth falling away behind us into darkness:
We heard a woman cry, 'But O the flowers,
Where are the flowers? The beautiful white flowers!'

(1961)

Hart Crane
1899–1932

165   *Garden Abstract*

THE apple on its bough is her desire, —
Shining suspension, mimic of the sun.
The bough has caught her breath up, and her voice,
Dumbly articulate in the slant and rise
Of branch on branch above her, blurs her eyes.
She is prisoner of the tree and its green fingers.

And so she comes to dream herself the tree,
The wind possessing her, weaving her young veins,
Holding her to the sky and its quick blue,
Drowning the fever of her hands in sunlight.
She has no memory, nor fear, nor hope
Beyond the grass and shadows at her feet.

(1920)

Lawrence Durrell
1902–1990

166   *In the Garden: Villa Cleobolus*

THE mixtures of this garden
Conduct at night the pine and oleander,
Perhaps married to dust's thin edge
Or lime where the cork-tree rubs
The quiet house, bruising the wall:

And dense the block of thrush's notes
Press like a bulb and keeping time
In this exposure to the leaves,
And as we wait the servant comes,

A candle shielded in the warm
Coarse coral of her hand, she weaves
A pathway for her in the golden leaves,
Gathers the books and ashtrays in her arm
Walking towards the lighted house,

Brings with her from the uninhabited
Frontiers of the darkness to the known
Table and tree and chair
Some half-remembered passage from a fugue
Played from some neighbour's garden
On an old horn-gramophone,

And you think: if given once
Authority over the word,
Then how to capture, praise or measure
The full round of this simple garden,
All its nonchalance at being,
How to adopt and raise its pleasure?

Press as on a palate this observed
And simple shape, like wine?
And from the many undeserved
Tastes of the mouth select the crude
Flavour of fruit in pottery
Coloured among this lovely neighbourhood?

Beyond, I mean, this treasure hunt
Of selves, the pains we sort to be
Confined within the loving chamber of a form,
Within a poem locked and launched
Along the hairline of the normal mind?

Perhaps not this: but somehow, yes,
To outflank the personal neurasthenia
That lies beyond in each expiring kiss:
Bring joy, as lustrous on this dish
The painted dancers motionless in play
Spin for eternity, describing for us all
The natural history of the human wish.

(1948)

Edwin Denby
1903–1983

Villa D'Este

BENEATH me this dark garden plunges, buoyant
Drops through the trees to basins furtive below
Under me wobbles the tip of a mast-thick fountain
I laugh and run down; the fat trunks heavily grow;
Then cypress, ilex rise reflected immense
Melancholy, and the great fount thrusts forceful
Tiny, their seclusion perches over the plains
For plains billow far below toward Rome remorseful;
But rilling streams draw me back in, up above
To the spurt, dribble, gush, sheath of secret water
Plash, and droves of Italians childish as love
Laughing, taking pictures of laughter, of water
Discovering new fountlets; so dense, so dark
Single on a desert mountain drips the locked park.

(1956)

Patrick Kavanagh
1904–1967

The Long Garden

IT was the garden of the golden apples,
A long garden between a railway and a road,
In the sow's rooting where the hen scratches
We dipped our fingers in the pockets of God.

In the thistly hedge old boots were flying sandals
By which we travelled through the childhood skies,
Old buckets rusty-holed with half-hung handles
Were drums to play when old men married wives.

The pole that lifted the clothes-line in the middle
Was the flag-pole on a prince's palace when
We looked at it through fingers crossed to riddle
In evening sunlight miracles for men.

It was the garden of the golden apples,
And when the Carrick train went by we knew
That we could never die till something happened
Like wishing for a fruit that never grew,

Or wanting to be up on Candle-Fort
Above the village with its shops and mill.
The racing cyclists' gasp-gapped reports
Hinted of pubs where life can drink his fill.

And when the sun went down into Drumcatton
And the New Moon by its little finger swung
From the telegraph wires, we knew how God had happened
And what the blackbird in the whitethorn sang.

It was the garden of the golden apples,
The half-way house where we had stopped a day
Before we took the west road to Drumcatton
Where the sun was always setting on the play.

(1947)

Cecil Day Lewis
1904–1972

169   *Snowfall on a College Garden*

WHILE we slept, these formal gardens
Worked into their disguise. The Warden's
Judas and tulip trees awake
In ermine. Here and there a flake
Of white falls from the painted scene,
Or a dark scowl of evergreen
Glares through the shroud, or a leaf dumps
Its load and the soft burden slumps
Earthward like a fainting girl.
No movement else. The blizzard's whirl
Froze to this cataleptic trance
Where nature sleeps and sleep commands
A transformation. See this bush
Furred and fluffed out like a thrush

Against the cold: snow which could snap
A robust veteran branch, piled up
On the razor edge of a weak spray,
Plumping it out in mimicry
Of white buddleia. Like the Elect
Ghosts of summer resurrect
In snowy robes. Only the twangling
Noise of unseen sparrows wrangling
Tells me that my window-view
Holds the garden I once knew.

(1977)

Leonard Clark
1905–1981

170   *Ground Elder*

FOR nearly a week that open-aired autumn
we worked, slowly digging the pestilence out,
spades slicing the heavy soil, sun and rain,
fingers sore, and, clawing at the matted root-stocks,
cursing the small veins creeping all ways like paralysis.
Ground Elder. I hate the coarse and greedy plant.
Nothing to look at, it has neither mercy nor modesty,
insignificant flowers, seeds in league with the wind,
'growing of itselfe without seting or sowing,
fruitful in its increase', as Gerard wrote in anger,
watching the vile herb stealing his Holborn garden,
garroting and smothering all other vegetation.

Yet the weed has virtues,
or thought the old monks who planted it
innocently in their cider orchards to cure the gout
or fed apple-glutted pigs to keep them from sudden death.
They called it Bishopweed, out of reverence;
Culpepper would have you eat its young leaves for paleness.

170 Gerard] John Gerard (1545–1612), author of *Herball* (1597).

Truth or, herbal nonsense? Enemy or friend?
I, who fought it for five broken-nailed days,
found no answer, but condemned its persistence,
preferring all my joints to ache, even the fiery gout,
to those endless furrows of cruel Ground Elder.

A cunning deceiver, its white impudence will come again
with next summer's cuckoos.

(1974)

Geoffrey Grigson
1905–1985

171   *The Landscape Gardeners*

BRUTAL shuddering machines, yellow, bite into given earth.
Only rich Whigs, commanding labour,
Once had earth shifted, making lakes, and said
—And it was true—'We are improving Nature.'

(1974)

172   *In the Spring Garden*

GRASS purpled by fallen Judas flowers,
Lilacs, between yews, in flower,
A yellow watering-can;
And I have taken a child

To the train; and leaves shiver
When hit by the heavy drops of the rain.
The senses—no, the senses
Or some senses do not harden.

But what expectancy
Have I now, in the rain, now
In the white of the May
In this late spring garden?

(1980)

William Empson
1906–1984

173   *Rolling the Lawn*

YOU can't beat English lawns. Our final hope
Is flat despair. Each morning therefore ere
I greet the office, through the weekday air,
Holding the Holy Roller at the slope
(The English fetish, not the Texas Pope)
Hither and thither on my toes with care
I roll ours flatter and flatter. Long, in prayer,
I grub for daisies at whose roots I grope.

Roll not the abdominal wall; the walls of Troy
Lead, since a plumb-line ordered, could destroy.
Roll rather, where no mole dare sap, the lawn,
And ne'er his tumuli shall tomb your brawn.
World, roll yourself; and bear your roller, soul,
As martyrs gridirons, when God calls the roll.

(1935)

W. H. Auden
1907–1973

174   *Their Lonely Betters*

As I listened from a beach-chair in the shade
To all the noises that my garden made,
It seemed to me only proper that words
Should be withheld from vegetables and birds.

A robin with no Christian name ran through
The Robin-Anthem which was all it knew,
And rustling flowers for some third party waited
To say which pairs, if any, should get mated.

Not one of them was capable of lying,
There was not one which knew that it was dying
Or could have with a rhythm or a rhyme
Assumed responsibility for time.

Let them leave language to their lonely betters
Who count some days and long for certain letters;
We, too, make noises when we laugh or weep,
Words are for those with promises to keep.

(1965)

Theodore Roethke
1908–1963

175   *Transplanting*

WATCHING hands transplanting,
Turning and tamping,
Lifting the young plants with two fingers,
Sifting in a palm-full of fresh loam,—
One swift movement,—
Then plumping in the bunched roots,
A single twist of the thumbs, a tamping and turning,
All in one,
Quick on the wooden bench,
A shaking down, while the stem stays straight,
Once, twice, and a faint third thump,—
Into the flat-box it goes,
Ready for the long days under the sloped glass:

The sun warming the fine loam,
The young horns winding and unwinding,
Creaking their thin spines,
The underleaves, the smallest buds
Breaking into nakedness,
The blossoms extending
Out into the sweet air,
The whole flower extending outward,
Stretching and reaching.

(1949)

176 *Cuttings*

STICKS-IN-A-DROWSE droop over sugary loam,
Their intricate stem-fur dries;
But still the delicate slips keep coaxing up water;
The small cells bulge;

One nub of growth
Nudges a sand-crumb loose,
Pokes through a musty sheath
Its pale tendrilous horn.

177 *Cuttings*
(later)

THIS urge, wrestle, resurrection of dry sticks,
Cut stems struggling to put down feet,
What saint strained so much,
Rose on such lopped limbs to a new life?

I can hear, underground, that sucking and sobbing,
In my veins, in my bones I feel it,—
The small waters seeping upward,
The tight grains parting at last.
When sprouts break out,
Slippery as fish,
I quail, lean to beginnings, sheath-wet.

(1949)

Phoebe Hesketh
1909–

178 *Death of a Gardener*

HE rested through the winter, watched the rain
On his cold garden, slept, awoke to snow
Padding the window, thatching the roof again
With silence. He was grateful for the slow

Nights and undemanding days; the dark
Protected him; the pause grew big with cold.
Mice in the shed scuffled like leaves; a spark
Hissed from his pipe as he dreamed beside the fire.

All at once light sharpened; earth drew breath,
Stirred; and he woke to strangeness that was spring,
Stood on the grass, felt movement underneath
Like a child in the womb; hope troubled him to bring
Barrow and spade once more to the waiting soil.
Slower his lift and thrust; a blackbird filled
Long intervals with song; a worm could coil
To safety underneath the hesitant blade.
Hands tremulous as cherry branches kept
Faith with struggling seedlings till the earth
Kept faith with him, claimed him as he slept
Cold in the sun beside his upright spade.

(1966)

A. H. Snow
1910–

179 ### Gardener

he loved to pull out his clasp-knife
cut a five pound cabbage
bring it back proudly
as if he were nursing his grandson

or pick pale beans
straight as willow wands
inches too long for his trug

potatoes were different

lifting the first root
was ritual pillage of a tumulus

every year they amazed him
exposed so suddenly
to sprawl in the ruins of their crumbled cache
tender-skinned and naked

spiking one was a torture
that drove the flat-tined fork
through his own flesh

when it came to cooking
he'd have no truck with parsley or mint

any smothering of that earthy tang
was blasphemy to him

imagine, he'd say
using fancy flavours
to spice the holy bread

(1982)

Elizabeth Bishop
1911–1979

180   *Sleeping on the Ceiling*

IT is so peaceful on the ceiling!
It is the Place de la Concorde.
The little crystal chandelier
is off, the fountain is in the dark.
Not a soul is in the park.

Below, where the wallpaper is peeling,
the Jardin des Plantes has locked its gates.
Those photographs are animals.
The mighty flowers and foliage rustle;
under the leaves the insects tunnel.

We must go under the wallpaper
to meet the insect-gladiator,
to battle with a net and trident,
and leave the fountain and the square.
But oh, that we could sleep up there . . .

(1946)

George Barker

1913–1991

181   *The Gardens of Ravished Psyche*

Do not speak to us of dreams, speak to us of autumn in
the garden of ravished Psyche where the golden haired
                                        laburnum
has long since burnt itself to ashes and the old apple tree
stands blackened and rotten and the ground around it lies
covered with dead fruit and the salt of the dead sea.

Now those arbours are forsaken and the trellis vines
                                        decaying;
the rats huddle and nibble in the skulls of the demigods;
the lake has taken wing and the lovers have forgotten
why they were born, and the golden apples from the
                                        branches
have long since fallen, my love, long since fallen.

                                        (1976)

Dylan Thomas

1914–1953

182   *Walking in Gardens*

WALKING in gardens by the sides
Of marble bathers toeing the garden ponds,
Skirting the ordered beds of paint-box flowers,
We spoke of drink and girls, for hours
Touched on the outskirts of the mind,
Then stirred a little chaos in the sun.
A new divinity, a god of wheels
Destroying souls and laying waste,
Trampling to dust the bits and pieces
Of faulty men and their diseases,
Rose in our outworn brains. We spoke our lines,
Made, for the bathers to admire,
Dramatic gestures in the air.

Ruin and revolution
Whirled in our words, then faded.
We might have tried light matches in the wind.
Over and round the ordered garden hummed,
There was no need of a new divinity,
No tidy flower moved, no bather gracefully
Lifted her marble foot, or lowered her hand
To brush upon the waters of the pond.

(1971)

Randall Jarrell
1914–1965

183   *In a Hospital Garden*

(*Henrikas Radauskas*)

THROUGH a hospital window
The chloroform from a broken bottle
Flows into the twilit garden,
And the feet of the poplar fall asleep
And its arms get lost in a dream.

The petals of the wild roses
Gasp for air like fish.
A bush shudders, starts to fall,
Tries to hang on with its branches
To a low cloud, collapses.

And the nightingale
Cannot any longer count to three:
The tune, in its third trill, goes to pieces,
Falls into the yellow pond
—And all at once the garden is lighted.

Beside my suspended casket
I burn like a wake candle,
And I run down into the bottomless
Box, and the weathervane
Thrashes about in its turret, creaking feverish

Prayers to scare away the chloroform
From the poplar, the rose, the nightingale;
And then, having forgotten my name,
It spins round and round, hysterical,
Squeaks at the top of its voice, and strangles.

(1965)

Octavio Paz
1914–

184 *Stanzas for an Imaginary Garden*

THE first eight lines describe a somewhat rural, provincial garden. A small
enclosure with two entrances. Apart from the palm tree already there, you
should plant bougainvillaeas, heliotropes, an ash and a pine. You should
also install a well. This first text could be placed on one of the entrances to
the little garden either as one stanza on the lintel or on the pediment, or
divided into two quartets on each of the door posts:

> Four adobe walls. Bougainvillaeas.
> In its quiet flames eyes
> can bathe themselves. The wind passes through
> leaves
> singing praises and herbs on their knees.
>
> The heliotrope crosses over with purple steps,
> wrapped in its own aroma. There is a prophet:
> the ash tree—and a meditative: the pine.
> The garden is small, the sky infinite.

These four lines could be placed on the other entrance, on the lintel or
pediment:

> Happy rectangle: some palm trees,
> jade fountains; time flows,
> water sings, the stone is silent, the soul,
> suspended in a moment of time, is a fountain.

This text could be placed in the inside of the garden. For example, on the
fountain. I imagine a wall over which a curtain of transparent water falls as
you read the four lines:

> Rain, dancing feet and loosened hair,
> ankle bitten by lightning,
> falls down accompanied by drums:
> the tree opens its eyes, revives.

Colophon

Written after visiting the place:

> Populous wasteland, a few palms,
> plucked feather dusters, hammering
> of motors, a prison wall,
> dust and rubbish, nobody's home.

Written remembering the imaginary garden:

> Green survives in my ruins:
> in my eyes you look and touch yourself,
> you know yourself in me and in me think yourself,
> in me you survive, in me you vanish.

(1989)

Robert Lowell
1917–1977

185   *The Public Garden*

> BURNISHED, burned-out, still burning as the year
> you lead me to our stamping ground.
> The city and its cruising cars surround
> the Public Garden. All's alive —
> the children crowding home from school at five,
> punting a football in the bricky air,
> the sailors and their pick-ups under trees
> with Latin labels. And the jaded flock
> of swanboats paddles to its dock.
> The park is drying.
> Dead leaves thicken to a ball
> inside the basin of a fountain, where
> the heads of four stone lions stare
> and suck on empty fawcets. Night
> deepens. From the arched bridge, we see
> the shedding park-bound mallards, how they keep
> circling and diving in the lanternlight,
> searching for something hidden in the muck.
> And now the moon, earth's friend, that cared so much
> for us, and cared so little, comes again —
> always a stranger! As we walk,
> it lies like chalk
> over the waters. Everything's aground.

Remember summer? Bubbles filled
the fountain, and we splashed. We drowned
in Eden, while Jehovah's grass-green lyre
was rustling all about us in the leaves
that gurgled by us, turning upside down . . .
The fountain's failing waters flash around
the garden. Nothing catches fire.

(1965)

Margaret Stanley-Wrench
1917–1974

186   *Hinterland*

I LIKE the backs of houses. Fronts are smug,
Stiff and formal, masks which smile at neighbours.
These roofs, shrugging, relaxed, these sun-warmed bricks,
Smooth, rounded bays, they are like lovers in bed
At ease, knowing and known. Cats stalk here.
The wagging lines of washing wave, the knobs
Of hollyhocks knock and stroke the walls. A sunflower
Rises, bearded god with a black face.
And the swarthy, smiling, grape-bloomed neighbours stand
Amazed between the vines, the flowers, the walls,
Themselves placid yet savage deities
Of these long gardens, of these hinterlands
Green, warm and secret territory, here
Like love behind the street's correct façade,
Love, fierce and unexpected, sharp, uneven,
Sun and flower, the darkness and the sap
Surging through leaf and body, the quick flashed
Recognition of opened windows, white
Glances meeting, and doors, doors opened wide.

(wr. 1970s)

Muriel Spark
1918–

187   *Kensington Gardens*

OLD ladies and tulips, model boats,
Compact babies, mobile mothers,
Distant buses like parakeets,
Lonely men with mackintoshes
Over their arms—where do they go?
Where come from? now that summer's
Paraphernalia and splash is
Out, as if planted a year ago.

(1967)

Michael Bullock
1918–

188   *Garden*

IN the garden
I seek the essence of the garden
the lucid flowers
shine with an inner light

Shadows are small and few
the air and water bright
no bosky darkness
threatens or allures

Catalpa blossoms
muslin white
strike the keynote
of the garden's chord.

(1988)

Howard Nemerov

1920–1991

The Salt Garden

for S. M. S.

I

A GOOD house, and ground whereon
With an amateur's toil
Both lawn and garden have been won
From a difficult, shallow soil
That, now inland, was once the shore
And once, maybe, the ocean floor.
Much patience, and some sweat,
Have made the garden green,
An even green the lawn.
Turnip and bean and violet
In a decent order set,
Grow, flourish and are gone;
Even the ruins of stalk and shell,
The vine when it goes brown,
Look civil and die well.
Sometimes in the late afternoon
I sit out with my wife,
Watching the work that we have done
Bend in the salt wind,
And think that here our life
Might be a long and happy one;
Though restless over the sand
The ocean's wrinkled green
Maneuvers in its sleep,
And I despise what I had planned,
Every work of the hand,
For what can man keep?

II

Restless, rising at dawn,
I saw the great gull come from the mist
To stand upon the lawn.
And there he shook his savage wing
To quiet, and stood like a high priest
Bird-masked, mantled in grey.

Before his fierce austerity
My thought bowed down, imagining
The wild sea lanes he wandered by
And the wild waters where he slept
Still as a candle in the crypt.
Noble, and not courteous,
He stared upon my green concerns,
Then, like a merchant prince
Come to some poor province,
Who, looking all about, discerns
No spice, no treasure house,
Nothing that can be made
Delightful to his haughty trade,
And so spreads out his sail,
Leaving to savage men
Their miserable regimen;
So did he rise, making a gale
About him by his wings,
And fought his huge freight into air
And vanished seaward with a cry—
A strange tongue but the tone clear.
He faded from my troubled eye
There where the ghostly sun
Came from the mist.
                When he was gone
I turned back to the house
And thought of wife, of child,
And of my garden and my lawn
Serene in the wet dawn;
And thought that image of the wild
Wave where it beats the air
Had come, brutal, mysterious,
To teach the tenant gardener,
Green fellow of this paradise,
Where his salt dream lies.

(1955)

D. J. Enright
1920–

A Kyoto Garden

HERE you could pass your holidays,
    trace and retrace the turning ways,
a hundred yards of stepping stones, you feel
    yourself a traveller; alone

you skirt a range of moss, you cross
    and cross again what seem new Rubicons,
a *tan* of land will make ten prefectures,
    a tideless pond a great pacific sea;

each vista, you remark, seems the intended prize—
    like Fuji through a spider's web or else
between a cooper's straining thighs—
    the eyes need never be averted, nor the nose;

across a two-foot fingered canyon, an Amazon of dew,
    a few dwarf maples
lose you in a forest, then you gain a mole-hill's
    panoramic view,

and company enough, a large anthology—
    the golden crow, the myriad leaves,
the seven autumn flowers, the seven herbs of spring,
    the moon sends down a rice-cake and a cassia-tree—

till under a sliding foot a pebble shrieks:
    you hesitate—
what feeds this corpulent moss, whose emptied blood,
    what demon mouths await?—

but then you notice that the pines wear crutches—
    typhoons show no respect for art or craft;
you sigh with happiness, the garden comes alive:
    like us, these princelings feel the draught.

(1956)

tan] approximately a quarter of an acre

191 *Flowers*

THE town was proud of the town's gardens,
People came from all over to view them.
I was taken there on Thursday afternoons
Or Sundays, when admission was free.

You couldn't play games in the Jephson Gardens,
Except for miniature golf at sixpence a round.

The aesthetic sense lay stillborn in me,
Those masses of flowers did nothing to me.

Later, having reached the Pathetic Fallacy,
I looked at them more closely: they were emblematic
Of something, I couldn't make out what.

On Sundays those masses of flowers pressed round me,
Muttering, muttering too softly for me to hear.
Their language, in my inept translation,
Was thick with portentous clichés.

I never learnt their true names.
If I looked at them now,
I would only see the sound of Sunday church bells.

(1973)

Edwin Morgan
1920–

192 *My Greenhouse*

I AM pleased with a frame of four lights,
doubtful whether the few pines it contains
    will ever be worth a farthing;
amuse myself with a greenhouse
which Lord Bute's gardener could take upon his back
    and walk away with;

192 Lord Bute] 3rd Earl of Bute (1713–92), who established a fine botanical garden at
Luton Hoo, Bedfordshire

and when I have paid it the accustomed visit
and watered it and given it air
I say to myself, This is not mine,
it is a plaything lent me for the present;
    I must leave it soon.

                   (1990)

Richard Wilbur
1921–

193   *Caserta Garden*

THEIR garden has a silent tall stone-wall
So overburst with drowsing trees and vines,
None but a stranger would remark at all
The barrier within the fractured lines.

I doubt they know it's there, or what it's for—
To keep the sun-impasted road apart,
The beggar, soldier, renegade and whore,
The dust, the sweating ox, the screeching cart.

They'd say, 'But this is how a garden's made':
To fall through days in silence dark and cool,
And hear the fountain falling in the shade
Tell changeless time upon the garden pool.

See from the tiptoe boy—the dolphin throats—
The fine spray bending; jets collapse in rings
Into the round pool, and each circle floats
Wide to the verge, and fails in shimmerings.

A childhood by this fountain wondering
Would leave impress of circle-mysteries:
One would have faith that the unjustest thing
Had geometric grace past what one sees.

How beauties will grow richer walled about!
This tortile trunk, old paradigm of pain,
These cherished flowers—they dream and look not out,
And seem to have no need of earth or rain.

In heavy peace, walled out necessity,
How devious the lavish grapevine crawls,
And trails its shade, irrelevant and free,
In delicate cedillas on the walls.

And still without, the dusty shouting way,
Hills lazar-skinned, with hungry-rooted trees.
And towns of men, below a staring day,
Go scattered to the turning mountain frieze.

The garden of the world, which no one sees,
Never had walls, is fugitive with lives;
Its shapes escape our simpler symmetries;
There is no resting where it rots and thrives.

(1947)

194   *A Baroque Wall-Fountain in the Villa Sciarra*

UNDER the bronze crown
Too big for the head of the stone cherub whose feet
    A serpent has begun to eat,
Sweet water brims a cockle and braids down

    Past spattered mosses, breaks
On the tipped edge of a second shell, and fills
    The massive third below. It spills
In threads then from the scalloped rim, and makes

    A scrim or summery tent
For a faun-ménage and their familiar goose.
    Happy in all that ragged, loose
Collapse of water, its effortless descent

    And flatteries of spray,
The stocky god upholds the shell with ease,
    Watching, about his shaggy knees,
The goatish innocence of his babes at play;

    His fauness all the while
Leans forward, slightly, into a clambering mesh
    Of water-lights, her sparkling flesh
In a saecular ecstasy, her blinded smile

Bent on the sand floor
Of the trefoil pool, where ripple-shadows come
   And go in swift reticulum,
More addling to the eye than wine, and more

   Interminable to thought
Than pleasure's calculus. Yet since this all
   Is pleasure, flash, and waterfall,
Must it not be too simple? Are we not

   More intricately expressed
In the plain fountains that Maderna set
   Before St Peter's—the main jet
Struggling aloft until it seems at rest

   In the act of rising, until
The very wish of water is reversed,
   That heaviness borne up to burst
In a clear, high, cavorting head, to fill

   With blaze, and then in gauze
Delays, in a gnatlike shimmering, in a fine
   Illumined version of itself, decline,
And patter on the stones its own applause?

   If that is what men are
Or should be, if those water-saints display
   The pattern of our areté,
What of these showered fauns in their bizarre,

   Spangled, and plunging house?
They are at rest in fulness of desire
   For what is given, they do not tire
Of the smart of the sun, the pleasant water-douse

   And riddled pool below,
Reproving our disgust and our ennui
   With humble insatiety.
Francis, perhaps, who lay in sister snow

   Before the wealthy gate
Freezing and praising, might have seen in this
   No trifle, but a shade of bliss—
That land of tolerable flowers, that state

As near and far as grass
Where eyes become the sunlight, and the hand
Is worthy of water: the dreamt land
Toward which all hungers leap, all pleasures pass.

(1956)

Donald Davie
1922–

Gardens No Emblems

MAN with a scythe: the torrent of his swing
Finds its own level; and is not hauled back
But gathers fluently, like water rising
Behind the watergates that close a lock.

The gardener eased his foot into a boot;
Which action like the mower's had its mould,
Being itself a sort of taking root,
Feeling for lodgement in the leather's fold.

But forms of thought move in another plane
Whose matrices no natural forms afford
Unless subjected to prodigious strain:
Say, light proceeding edgewise, like a sword.

(1957)

Anthony Hecht
1923–

196

The Gardens of the Villa D'Este

THIS is Italian. Here
Is cause for the undiminished bounce
Of sex, cause for the lark, the animal spirit
To rise, aerated, but not beyond our reach, to spread
Friction upon the air, cause to sing loud for the bed
Of jonquils, the linen bed, and established merit
Of love, and grandly to pronounce
Pleasure without peer.

Goddess, be with me now;
Commend my music to the woods.
There is no garden to the practised gaze
Half so erotic: here the sixteenth century thew
Rose to its last perfection, this being chiefly due
To the provocative role the water plays.
Tumble and jump, the fountains' moods
Teach the world how.

But, ah, who ever saw
Finer proportion kept. The sum
Of intersecting limbs was something planned.
Ligorio, the laurel! Every turn and quirk
Weaves in this waving green and liquid world to work
Its formula, binding upon the gland,
Even as molecules succumb
To Avogadro's law.

The intricate mesh of trees,
Sagging beneath a lavender snow
Of wisteria, wired by creepers, perfectly knit
A plot to capture alive the migrant, tourist soul
In its corporeal home with all the deft control
And artifice of an Hephaestus' net.
Sunlight and branch rejoice to show
Sudden interstices.

The whole garden inclines
The flesh as water falls, to seek
For depth. Consider the top balustrade,
Where twinned stone harpies, with domed and virgin breasts,
Spurt from their nipples that no pulse or hand has pressed
Clear liquid arcs of benefice and aid
To the chief purpose. They are Greek
Versions of valentines

Ligorio] Pirro Ligorio (1500–83), Italian antiquarian and architect who devised the iconographical programme for the gardens of the Villa D'Este   Avogadro's law] Italian physicist (1776–1856) who discovered law concerning the molecular content of gases Hephaestus] Greek god of fire, who used a net to trap his faithless wife Aphrodite with the god Ares

And spend themselves to fill
The celebrated flumes that skirt
The horseshoe stairs. Triumphant then to a sluice,
With Brownian movement down the giggling water drops
Past haunches, over ledges, out of mouths, and stops
In a still pool, but, by a plumber's ruse,
    Rises again to laugh and squirt
      At heaven, and is still

    Busy descending. White
Ejaculations leap to teach
How fertile are these nozzles; the streams run
Góngora through the garden, channel themselves, and pass
To lily-padded ease, where insubordinate lass
And lad can cool their better parts, where sun
    Heats them again to furnace pitch
      To prove his law is light.

    Marble the fish that puke
Eternally, marble the lips
Of gushing naiads, pleased to ridicule
Adonis, marble himself, and larger than life-sized,
Untouched by Venus, posthumously circumcised
Patron of Purity; and any fool
    Who feels no flooding at the hips
      These spendthrift stones rebuke.

    It was in such a place
That Mozart's Figaro contrived
The totally expected. This is none
Of your French topiary, geometric works,
Based on God's rational, wrist-watch universe; here lurks
The wood louse, the night crawler, the homespun
    Spider; here are they born and wived
      And bedded, by God's grace.

    Actually, it is real
The way the world is real: the horse
Must turn against the wind, and the deer feed
Against the wind, and finally the garden must allow
For the recalcitrant; a style can teach us how
    To know the world in little where the weed
    Has license, where by dint of force
      D'Estes have set their seal.

Góngora] literary, euphuistic style associated with Spanish poet, Luis de Góngora y Argote
(1561–1627)

Their spirit entertains.
And we are honorable guests
Come by imagination, come by night,
Hearing in the velure of darkness impish strings
Mincing Tartini, hearing the hidden whisperings:
'*Carissima*, the moon gives too much light',
Though by its shining it invests
Her bodice with such gains

As show their shadowed worth
Deep in the cleavage. Lanterns, lamps
Of pumpkin-colored paper dwell upon
The implications of the skin-tight silk, allude
Directly to the body; under the subdued
Report of corks, whisperings, the *chaconne*,
Boisterous water runs its ramps
Out, to the end of mirth.

Accommodating plants
Give umbrage where the lovers delve
Deeply for love, give way to their delight,
As Pliny's pregnant mouse, bearing unborn within her
Lewd sons and pregnant daughters, hears the adept beginner:
'*Cor mio*, your supports are much too tight',
While overhead the stars resolve
Every extravagance.

Tomorrow, before dawn,
Gardeners will come to resurrect
Downtrodden iris, dispose of broken glass,
Return the diamond earrings to the villa, but
As for the moss upon the statue's shoulder, not
To defeat its green invasion, but to pass
Over the liberal effect
Caprice and cunning spawn.

For thus it was designed:
Controlled disorder at the heart
Of everything, the paradox, the old
Oxymoronic itch to set the formal strictures
Within a natural context, where the tension lectures
Us on our mortal state, and by controlled
Disorder, labors to keep art
From being too refined.

Susan, it had been once
My hope to see this place with you,
See it as in the hour of thoughtless youth.
For age mocks all diversity, its genesis,
And whispers to the heart, '*Cor mio*, beyond all this
Lies the unchangeable and abstract truth',
Claims of the grass, it is not true,
And makes our youth its dunce.

Therefore, some later day
Recall these words, let them be read
Between us, let them signify that here
Are more than formulas, that age sees no more clearly
For its poor eyesight, and philosophy grows surly,
That falling water and the blood's career
Lead down the garden path to bed
And win us both to May.

(1968)

Michael Hamburger
1924–

197   *Weeding*

I

HERE I am again with my sickle, spade, hoe
To decide over life and death, presume to call
This plant a 'weed', that one a 'flower',
Adam's prerogative, hereditary power
I can't renounce. And yet I know, I know,
It is a single generator drives them all,
And drives my murderous, my ordering hand.

These foxgloves, these red poppies, I let them stand,
Though I did not sow them. Slash the fruit-bearing bramble,
Dig out ground elder, bindweed, stinging nettle,
Real rivals, invaders whose roots ramble,
Robbing or strangling those of more delicate plants.
Or perhaps it's their strength, putting me on my mettle
To fight them for space, resist their advance.

2

I stop. I drop the spade,
Mop my face, consider:
Who's overrun the earth
And almost outrun it?
Who'll make it run out?
Who bores and guts it,
Pollutes and mutates it,
Corrodes and explodes it?
Each leaf that is laid
On the soil will feed it,
Turning death into birth.
If the cycle is breaking
Who brought it about?

3

I shall go again to the overgrown plot
With my sickle, hoe, spade,
But use no weedkiller, however selective,
No chemicals, no machine.
Already the nettles, ground elder, bindweed
Spring up again.
It's a good fight, as long as neither wins,
There are fruit to pick, unpoisoned,
Weeds to look at. I call them 'wildflowers'.

(1977)

198   *Garden, Wilderness*

GREEN fingers, green hand, by now green man
All through, with sap for blood,
Menial to it, gross nature,
And governor of a green tribe
No law can tame, no equity can bend
From the sole need of each, to feed and seed,
Unless, refined beyond resistance to a blight
More grasping than their greed,
Rare shoots evade the keeper's pampering.

He goes to referee
A clinch of lupin, bindweed, common cleavers
And stinging nettle — each with a right to be
Where if one thrives the other three must weaken;

And with his green hand, kin to tendril, root,
Tugs at the wrestlers, to save, to separate
Although his green heart knows:
While sun and rain connive,
Such will the game remain, such his and their estate.

More rain than sunshine: his green lungs inhale
Air thick with horsetail spore,
Grass pollen; his legs trail
Trains of torn herbage, dragging through swollen growth
Twined, tangled with decay.
For his green food he gropes,
To taste his share, bonus of fruit and berry,
Tribute for regency,
Sweet compensation for defeated hopes
Or dole despite the drudgery, the waste.

A garden of the mind,
Pure order, equipoise and paradigm
His lord, long far away and silent, had designed,
With bodies, never his, indifferent machines
To impose it and maintain
Against the clinging strand, the clogging slime;
And best invisible, as now that lord's become
Whose ghost the green man serves; that contemplated flower
Whose day of stillness filled all space, all time.

(1982)

Lauris Edmond
1924–

199   *Jardin des Colombières*

IT's the country of childhood
authentic fairyland—walled garden
silent under cypresses
wild violets, primroses awake
in a delicate wood, stone bridge
spanning the legendary stream
marble pillars, dim heraldic halls.

I am the child of exiles who dreamt
of the lost garden. Here it is earth
and boundaries—it is property;
the eyes at the shapely window
are sharp with calculation. You pay
six francs to enter; the other, more
melancholy, cost I do not know.

(1983)

Ian Hamilton Finlay

1925–

200   *Garden Poem*

u r n
u r n
u r n
u r n
umn
c o l
umn
c o l
umn
c o l
umn
c o l
umn
c o l
umn

(1986)

Charles Tomlinson

1927–

John Maydew, or The Allotment

RANGES
   of clinker heaps
      go orange now:
through cooler air
   an acrid drift
      seeps upwards
from the valley mills;
   the spoiled and staled
      distances invade
these closer comities
   of vegetable shade,
      glass-houses, rows
and trellises of redly
   flowering beans.
      This
is a paradise
   where you may smell
      the cinders
of quotidian hell beneath you;
   here grow
      their green reprieves
for those
   who labour, linger in
      their watch-chained waistcoats
rolled-back sleeves—
   the ineradicable
      peasant in the dispossessed
and half-tamed Englishman.
   By day, he makes
      a burrow of necessity
from which
   at evening, he emerges
      here.
A thoughtful yet unthinking man,
   John Maydew,
      memory stagnates
in you and breeds

a bitterness; it grew
    and rooted in your silence
from the day
   you came
      unwitting out of war
in all the pride
   of ribbons and a scar
     to forty years
of mean amends . . .
   He squats
     within his shadow
and a toad
   that takes
     into a slack and twitching jaw
the worms he proffers it,
   looks up at him
     through eyes that are
as dimly faithless
   as the going years;
     For, once returned
he found that he
   must choose between
     an England, profitlessly green
and this—
   a seamed and lunar grey
     where slag in lavafolds
unrolls beneath him.
   The valley gazes up
     through kindling eyes
as, unregarded at his back
   its hollows deepen
     with the black, extending shadows
and the sounds of day
   explore its coming cavities,
     the night's
refreshed recesses.
   Tomorrow
     he must feed its will,
his interrupted pastoral
   take heart into
     those close
and gritty certainties that lie
   a glowing ruse
     all washed in hesitations now.

> He eyes the toad
>   beating
>   in the assuagement
>   of his truce.

(1963)

Juliet's Garden

*J'ai connu une petite fille qui quittait son jardin bruyamment,
puis s'en revenait à pas de loup pour 'voir comment il était quand
elle n'était pas là.'* (Sartre)

SILENTLY . . .
she was quieter than breathing now,
hearing the garden seethe
behind her departed echo:

flowers merely grew,
showing no knowledge of her:
stones hunching their hardnesses
against her not being there:

scents came penetratingly,
rose, apple, and leaf-rot,
earthsmell under them all,
to where she was not:

such presences could only
rouse her fears,
ignoring and perfuming
this voluntary death of hers:

and so she came rushing back
into her garden then,
her new-found lack
the measure of all Eden.

(1972)

202 epigraph] 'I knew a little girl who would leave her garden noisily, then tiptoe back "to see what it was like when she wasn't there" '

203   *In the Borghese Gardens*

EDGING each other towards consummation
On the public grass and in the public eye,
Under the Borghese pines the lovers
Cannot tell what thunderheads mount the sky,
To mingle with the roar of afternoon
Rumours of the storm that must drench them soon.

Cars intersect the cardinal's great dream,
His parterres redesigned, gardens half-gone,
Yet Pluto's grasp still bruises Proserpine,
Apollo still hunts Daphne's flesh in stone,
Where the Borghese statuary and trees command
The ever-renewing city from their parkland.

The unbridled adolescences of gods
Had all of earth and air to cool their flights
And to rekindle. But where should lovers go
These torrid afternoons, these humid nights
While Daphne twists in leaves, Apollo burns
And Proserpine returns, returns, returns?

Rome is still Rome. Its ruins and its squares
Stand sluiced in wet and all its asphalt gleaming,
The street fronts caged behind the slant of rain-bars
Sun is already melting where they teem:
Spray-haloed traffic taints your laurel leaves,
City of restitutions, city of thieves.

Lovers, this giant hand, half-seen, sustains
By lifting up into its palm and plane
Our littleness: the shining causeway leads
Through arches, bridges, avenues and lanes
Of stone, that brought us first to this green place—
Expelled, we are the heirs of healing artifice.

Deserted now, and all that callow fire
Quenched in the downpour, here the parkland ways
Reach out into the density of dusk,
Between an Eden lost and promised paradise,
That overbrimming scent, rain-sharpened, fills,
Girdled within a rivercourse and seven hills.

                                        (1987)

Anne Sexton
1928–1974

Noon Walk on the Asylum Lawn

THE summer sun ray
shifts through a suspicious tree.
though I walk through the valley of the shadow
It sucks the air
and looks around for me.

The grass speaks.
I hear green chanting all day.
I will fear no evil, fear no evil
The blades extend
and reach my way.

The sky breaks.
It sags and breathes upon my face.
in the presence of mine enemies, mine enemies
The world is full of enemies.
There is no safe place.

(1960)

Adrienne Cecile Rich
1929–

Versailles (Petit Trianon)

MERELY the landscape of a vanished whim,
An artifice that lasts beyond the wish:
The grotto by the pond, the gulping fish
That round and round pretended islands swim,
The creamery abandoned to its doves,
The empty shrine the guidebooks say is love's.

What wind can bleaken this, what weather chasten
Those balustrades of stone, that sky stone-pale?
A fountain triton idly soaks his tail
In the last puddle of a drying basin;
A leisure that no human will can hasten
Drips from the hollow of his lifted shell.

When we were younger gardens were for games,
But now across the sungilt lawn of kings
We drift, consulting catalogues for names
Of postured gods: the cry of closing rings
For us and for the couples in the wood
And all good children who are all too good.

O children, next year, children, you will play
With only half your hearts; be wild today.
And lovers, take one long and fast embrace
Before the sun that tarnished queens goes down,
And evening finds you in a restless town
Where each has back his old restricted face.

(1955)

Thom Gunn
1929–

206   *Last Days at Teddington*

THE windows wide through day and night
Gave on the garden like a room.
The garden smell, green composite,
Flowed in and out a house in bloom.

To the shaggy dog who skidded from
The concrete through the kitchen door
To yellow-squared linoleum,
It was an undivided floor.

How green it was indoors. The thin
Pale creepers climbed up brick until
We saw their rolled tongues flicker in
Across the cracked paint of the sill.

How sociable the garden was.
We ate and talked in given light.
The children put their toys to grass
All the warm wakeful August night.

So coming back from drinking late
We picked our way below the wall
But in the higher grass, dewed wet,
Stumbled on tricycle and ball.

When everything was moved away,
The house returned to board and shelf,
And smelt of hot dust through the day,
The garden fell back on itself.

(1971)

207   from *Breaking Ground*

LANK potato, darkening
cabbage, tattered raspberry
canes, but the flower beds
so crammed there is
no room for weeds
    fiercely aflame all August
when I sniff at the bergamot
the fruity-sage smell is like
a flower sweating

she's too old now to
dig, too old to move
that barrow of cuttings
by the shed, some
nephew can move it

barrow of cuttings, of
grasses not yet hay, fresh
green of redundant
branch, and nasturtium
only rusted a little at
edges of hot yellow

going down to earth, that's
what I can't accept
her kind hand, her
grey eyes, her voice
intonations I've known
all my life—to be
lost, forgotten in
an indiscriminate mulch, a
humus of no colour

(1974)

Peter Porter
1929–

208 ### *After Martial, XII. xxxi.*

THIS phalanx of pines, these demi-fountains,
this subtle pleaching, this irrigation system
ductile as a vein (water meadows under mountains),
and my twice-blooming roses richer than Paestum's,
the rare herb-garden—even in January, green—
my tame eel that snakes about its pond,
white dovecote outshone by its birds—I've been
a long time coming home and you, my fond
benefactress, dear Marcella, gave all this
to me. A miniature kingdom to do
with as I please. If Nausicaa with a kiss
should offer me her Father's gardens, you
need not worry: to everything that's grown
I give one answer, *I prefer my own.*

(1972)

209 ### *Pope's Carnations Knew Him*

BUT they knew they were on duty, replacing
the Rose of Sharon and the lilies of the field
for a gardener who never put a foot wrong.

208 Nausicaa] daughter of Alcinous (see no. 49), who befriended Odysseus

It was their duty to rhyme in colour,
to repeat their reds and pinks and shield
the English rose with their Italianate chiming.

He had such a way with the symmetry
of petals, he could make a flower yield
an epic from its one-day siege. His rows

of blooms had their grotesques but they
took the place of music. They bowed, they kneeled,
they curtseyed, and so stood up for prosody.

No wonder Smart learned from their expansive
hearts that they loved the ordered, the well-heeled
and ornate, the little poet with the giant stride.

Each gossipy morning he sniffed their centres
and they saw him: the lines of paradise revealed.
God make gardeners better nomenclators.

(1972)

210   *An Australian Garden*

HERE we enact the opening of the world
And everything that lives shall have a name
To show its heart; there shall be Migrants,
Old Believers, Sure Retainers; the cold rose
Exclaim perfection to the gangling weeds,
The path lead nowhere—this is like entering
One's self, to find the map of death
Laid out untidily, a satyr's grin
Signalling 'You are here': tomorrow
They are replanting the old court,
Puss may be banished from the sun-warmed stone.

See how our once-lived lives stay on to haunt us,
The flayed beautiful limbs of childhood
In the bole and branches of a great angophora—
Here we can climb and sit on memory
And hear the words which death was making ready
From the start. Such talking as the trees attempt

Smart] the poet Christopher Smart (1722–71)

Is a lesson in perfectability. It stuns
The currawongs along the breaks of blue—
Their lookout cries have guarded Paradise
Since the expulsion of the heart, when man,
Bereft of joy, turned his red hand to gardens.

Spoiled Refugees nestle near Great Natives;
A chorus of winds stirs the pagoda'd stamens:
In this hierarchy of miniatures
Someone is always leaving for the mountains,
Civil servant ants are sure the universe
Stops at the hard hibiscus; the sun is drying
A beleaguered snail and the hydra-headed
Sunflowers wave like lights. If God were to plant
Out all His hopes, He'd have to make two more
Unknown Lovers, ready to find themselves
In innocence, under the weight of His green ban.

In the afternoon we change—an afterthought,
Those deeper greens which join the stalking shadows—
The lighter wattles look like men of taste
With a few well-tied leaves to brummel-up
Their poise. Berries dance in a southerly wind
And the garden tide has turned. Dark on dark.
Janus leaves are opening to the moon
Which makes its own grave roses. Old Man
Camellias root down to keep the sun intact,
The act is canopied with stars. A green sea
Rages through the landscape all the night.

We will not die at once. Nondescript pinks
Survive the death of light and over-refined
Japanese petals bear the weight of dawn's first
Insect. An eye makes damask on the dew.
Time for strangers to accustom themselves
To habitat. What should it be but love?
The transformations have been all to help
Unmagical creatures find their proper skins,
The virgin and the leonine. The past's a warning
That the force of joy is quite unswervable—
'Out of this wood do not desire to go.'

In the sun, which is the garden's moon, the barefoot
Girl espies her monster, all his lovely specialty

Like hairs about his heart. The dream is always
Midday and the two inheritors are made
Proprietors. They have multiplied the sky.
Where is the water, where the terraces, the Tritons
And the cataracts of moss? This is Australia
And the villas are laid out inside their eyes:
It would be easy to unimagine everything,
Only the pressure made by love and death
Holds up the bodies which this Eden grows.

(1971)

Peter Jones

1929–

211   *In the Park*

WHAT to do with salvias?

They are piled high
in the gardener's wheelbarrow
still blood-red-pyramids
of too many presentiments
to go unnoticed; trundled past
the playground and the pond
where children laugh at the ducks
and mothers scheme futures
that take no account of the stars

(1972)

212   *In the Formal Garden*

ALMOST a child again
She rocks the swing; one toe-heel
Holds the tilting world. Stone leaves
Greener than ivy overtip her dry
Fountain; weeds cushion the terraces.
Only a fresh knot in the swing's old arm
Strains.
          She toes spilled marigolds,
Dropped fruit, surf of grass caught
Between neap and spring.

Almost a child again
She swings free of wilderness; raises her head;
Casts white shoes at the sun.

—her hands last possess
A stone geranium. Sparrows unpick the dew,
Let fall a jewel.

(1977)

John Hollander
1929–

213   *Instructions to the Landscaper*

I.   YOU must have the Garden respond to all seasons by showing, in its aspects, significant versions of the meaningless blossoming, the cold, grave slumber, the fall and all that, versions of what is happening to what generally grows at these latitudes.

II.   At the entrance, one must be made to pass through a representation of the whole Garden, but so placed that it is only while leaving it all, deliciously wearied by walking in the heats and shades, that one sees the entrance again in the new light of what it had always stood for—as if to have given a point to exiting.

III.   Of the carved fountains, placed wherever they are to be at the centers of open spaces, or up at one end of them, at least one must be shaped in an antique myth of Eloquence, and at least one must embody a fable of Helplessness. In neither case, then, will they look contrived.

IV.   There must be a stream, and a winding, ascending path along a slight rise that crosses and recrosses the stream on tiny stone bridges several times, vanishing into rocks and foliage in between the crossings. This is in order that, when one emerges from a state of shadow into a sudden openness, a wide glance around cannot fail to include a glimpse of where one had already been, at an earlier time, heading unthinkingly into the more recent darkness.

V.   If there are to be ornamental gates representing Virtues, paths of ancient Rightness, temples to the spirits of time and place, then let each one, half-hidden from many viewpoints in the luxuriance of green, afford a prospect of one of the others: from one side of the rounded Temple of Honor, for example, it is appropriate that one should see, perfectly framed by two of the fluted columns, huddling in the rocks by the long water, the Grotto of Fear.

VI.   In our climate, one may be plagued by hordes of starlings, and some recommend heroic measures against them. If they do gather, roosting nastily at sundown in the pine grove, making the needly floor stink with their droppings and the damp air shrill with their squawks, then wait, so they say, until a day when one's garden is closed to visitors. Torture one of the wretched creatures, we are told; record its woeful cries on a recirculating tape, and play it back continuously through small loudspeakers in the echoing grove: the others will all depart. But do not do this. Starlings will avoid the well-tended garden in any case. If they do come, you must abandon the whole place, for everything else will, in fact, have failed as well.

VII.   If the Garden has been properly laid out, there need not be a maze in it. For the quest, the puzzlement, the contingency of the place of rest with its bench and rosebushes in the center of it all, the ease of entrance and its welcoming entrapment, the problems of homing, will all have been provided by the Garden itself. And the maze's parable, unrolling beneath the hurrying feet of the last wanderers on a summer evening that now chills and darkens—the parable of how there can be no clarity of truth without puzzlement, no joy without losing one's way—will be propounded by the Garden's final perfection, namely, that in it is no trace of the designer, that no image of him can ever be found. He—you—will have disappeared into the ground of the place that had been made.

(1981)

Robert Druce
1929–

214   *Apropos of Garden Statuary: A Disquisition upon a Minor Genre*

APROPOS of garden statuary, sir,
    now the first April sunshine
  has beckoned you out of doors, might I venture
    a gnome's eye vision? I speak

for my tribe, who still await that occasion
        when scholarly attention
is paid to a species which, admittedly
        vulgar, nevertheless is

virtually ubiquitous, above all
        in suburbia, for there
no paradisal *hortus conclusus* you
        or those of your bent create

seems complete unless one or other of us
        is on hand to people it.
And if, sir, we cannot pretend to greatness
        there are precedents enough

to justify a mention. Kingly landscapes
        or merely seigneurial
spawn their massy heroes: bronze and hollow-horsed
        they command the horizons,

or in a pentelic glitter, rioting
        with dryads and demi-gods,
clutter the prospect with their unseemly brawls.
        These are studied, are they not?

Must we be precluded because of our scale?
        A moment's thought will suggest
that figures of a size to assert themselves
        among cedars, would appal

the eye in a suburban plot. But we, sir,
        like you, will never admit
the megalomaniac view. Discreetly
        the lupins overarch us

and silvery-fluted on our far skyline
        your palely-gleaming dustbin
is a lofty belvedere: that is romance
        enough for such pastoral

comedians as we are, whom you may trust
        not to make a lupanar
of your lawns. With our kind you may be at ease:
        unbuttoned, shirtless even,

hortus conclusus] enclosed garden, from the Latin version of the Song of Solomon: see no. 2

your own master, while we your creatures appear
    to labour about your feet
in honoured propinquity to your dwelling.
    Lacquered to resist, as bronze

and marble are not, the air's acidity,
    we make a splash of colour.
A laudable fault, I submit: handed down
    two hundred years. We arrived

with that Victorian penchant for Gothick,
    and are of equal date with
Christmas trees and cuckoo clocks. Our pedigree
    can be seen to mount at least

to the Kobolds, those legendary delvers
    who with water and fire-damp
wrought such Grimm mischief; nor should you overlook
    all the achondroplastics

of the Spanish and Salzburg courts; remember
    Velasquez, and that mankind
defines itself by the monsters at its edge,
    if Bacon's notion hold good.

But we are not freaks: Disney has seen to that.
    And you may safely ignore
the neo-Freudian contention (observing
    our hirsute and upthrust ears

our crimson caps) that we are merely phallic.
    If our Blucher boots hide hoofs
or tiny members bristle in our breeches,
    they are nothing to disturb

even your children's peace: sir, our womenfolk
    keep out of sight at all times.
Regard us, rather, breeched and bonnetted gules
    and jerkined azure, as a

valid, albeit minor, heraldic type.
    Watch us, wheelbarrowed passant
regardant, over your enamelled mead, or
    couchant by the puddle's edge

not at all peccant: we never gaff the fish.
    Hefting a sack, we can pass
for Santa Claus. And in the nightmare garden
    such kindliness should be prized.

Ours is a harsh world: nightly the rush of wings
    and the shrew's screams attest it.
Dandelions foul the air with ethylene,
    and each forwandered snail is

Prometheus to the passing thrush. Daisies
    shyly garotte their neighbours.
I see acts that far outstrip *your* cruelties.
    If we lack rank or breeding,

at least we put a brave face on those horrors,
    anthropologize nature.
Our role, sir, is cogent, numinous even.
    Critics who call us folk-art,

debased and commercial, do us ill-service;
    let the sociologists,
if art history be silent, speak their minds.
    Sir, I must not hector you,

but we are here in our millions, are we not?
    My only fears, I confess,
are that when you go, a less gentle master
    will be moved to banish me

to the backdoor steps and the ancient fishy
    stench of the cat-bowl, that Seb
will choose to pepper me with airgun pellets
    or I be a bugaboo

for Mandy's dollies, while spaniel Caliban
    daily piddles upon me,
wetly asserting his territorial claims.
    Spare me those indignities.

As for the broader issues, you would do well
    to say a word in season
in the proper critical quarters. Sir, I
    honour you for your concern.

Might I suggest, then, a learned article?
No?
    Or a footnote?
        Verses?

          (1985)

Richard Eberhart
1930–1986

215   *The Garden God*

STYLE is the water out of Homer,
  The way it flows. It never flows
    The same from the stone orifice
    Down into the garden pool.

Mark then that majestic head
  And fount of heavenly declension,
    The bubbles in the basin
    Making a merry noise and music.

Style is large and god-like, as if
  An elegance made life-like, and
    It seems to be an absolute,
    Curly locks, blind eyes, and sound.

Yet every day the water plays
  Differently from Homer's mouth.
    Each time I look thereon
    New enticement amazes me.

The winds of time will play the tune,
  A bird will come to sip alone,
    A cat will change the water-scene
    With arch and ritual concern.

I do not see our Homer plain.
  I see him melodious or restive,
    I feel the tensions of the day,
    The quick alarms, acclaims of change.

Style is magical despair
  Lest from the fount and source and power
    A single drop or grain
      Should lose itself from life's rich main

And it is plain for each to see
  In dream and consequence,
    The order of the oak and grass,
      The waving water's sound.

Or so I think replete
  With multitudinous harmonies
    On any day in summer here
      In the garden where our Homer is.

                (1960)

Alasdair Aston
1930–

216   *Everything in the Garden is Lovely*

EVEN the fat slug
That drags its belly nightly
Over dank paving
And into the heart of the lettuce
Is lovely.
And the seething myriads in the ant-hill
Are lovely.
The stealthy, disruptive mole,
The grubbing, wet-nosed hedgehog
Are lovely.
And the millipede,
The centipede,
The sexually reproductive woodlouse
Are lovely.
The dung fly and the dung beetle
Are doubly lovely.
The burying beetle, the emmet,
The devil's coach-horse, the dor
Are lovely.

Bean blight, leaf scab, club root,
Rose canker, cuckoo spit, wireworm
Cutworm, carrot fly, codlin,
Woolly aphis, apple weevil,
Leaf curl, algae,
Big bud, brown spot,
Rust, smut and mildew
Are all of them lovely.
And the flowers are lovely, too—
Nightshade, broomrape, henbane,
Love-lies bleeding and dead-men's fingers,
Viper's bugloss, red-hot poker,
Wormwood, woundwort, rue.
And the gardener himself is lovely—
With one eye on the stable clock
And the other on lovely nothing,
Flat on his back where he fell.
The lovely flies walk in his lovely mouth.
Everything in the garden is lovely.

(1975)

M. R. Peacocke
1930—

Railway Allotments

NEAR blackened alcoves
just where the sun's cut off
and peers through grilles
at fantasies of sooted brick
(English bond meticulously ordered),
clear of the frassy tunnels
where diesels bore and cough
and the electric engines sigh,
outside Birmingham Exeter Sheffield Stoke
retired men nurtured
upon implacable texts gingerly unbend
above their linear gardens bordered
with creosoted sleepers,
and shrug their coats and stand
watching for the express to saunter through.

Then turning to their loves,
their strips of peas crosshatched,
Maris Piper stitched in knots of green
along the steady rows, they contemplate
their manuscripts of common prayer
made brilliant with shallots; intercede
that Autumn King and Greyhound may mature,
each white Musselburgh
stand in its paper collar
like a marble pillar, ruby red Detroit
grow thick and firm,
the Stuttgart Giants raised from seed
be slender in the neck and touched
with gold, while the three twenty runs to time
each leisured afternoon.

(1988)

Robert Layzer
1931–

218   *The Lawn Roller*

Too many summers out of the way of a trowel
Has given the clover and dandelion a feast,
And now it's as easy to temper the whim of the soil
As argue the sun into crouching from west to east.

Down at the end of the street a sun-glazed man
Has three hundred pounds of water inside a drum
Rolling and pressing a naked torso of lawn
Into flat perfection, ripe for the gardener's thumb.

The bare and close is where I began, but somehow
Only wild things grew out of my ministries,
Or extravagant tame. Astonished, I watched them swallow
The plot like Africans eating their enemies

Not out of malice but a respect for kinship.
What could succeed? The peony changed a bed
Of oil and ease for a fierce alien worship,
The rose lay down beside the ragweed's head

And everything the lascivious earth raised up
From a cold slumber, threw off sheets of clay
To fold the sunlight in an amorous grip.
It was too late to prune the jungle away,

Or too injurious for the eye stained green
To crop an inch of greenness. The twentieth spring
Found me in this delirium eyeing the scene
With a lawn roller's contempt for rioting

Abundance, and a sunstruck tenderness.
I watched and waited. Later it seemed the moon,
Cold as the face of Helen in her distress,
Was looking through the branches, hard and alone.

(1957)

Alan Brownjohn
1931–

219   *In a Convent Garden*

In the convent vegetable garden the nuns
Have erected a scarecrow in front of the runner beans,
And it has an old wimple on its head.

In the spring the beans will climb and climb
But the crows are coming:
The wimple will chase them away.

In the convent vegetable garden the nuns
Have erected a scarecrow alongside the cauliflowers,
And it has an old wimple on its head.

In the spring the cauliflowers will rise will rise
But the daws are deadly:
The wimple will drive them away.

In the convent vegetable garden the nuns
Have erected a scarecrow behind the marrow plants,
And it has an old wimple on its head.

In the spring the marrows will expand will expand
But the tits are terrible:
The wimple will turn them away.

In the summer the marrows will fructify completely,
And will be scrubbed under rubber-nozzled taps and peeled
And sliced and cored and stuffed with mutton,

And the scarecrow will be taken apart
And at the long tables in the cool refectory
The Mother Superior and the nuns and the novice nuns
　　and the symbolists will sit and
　　　　stuff themselves for a considerable
　　　　　　length of time.

(1972)

Peter Redgrove

1932–

220　　　　　*Negotium Perambulans . . .*

IF they can get across our garden they have eaten it,
Feeding off flowerfaces, creaming the innocent smiles,
Blooms disclosing tall heaven, each a feretory,
Subject to the rasps of ambulant grey-mackintosh pillows.

How I wish our garden were infested with swans!
Like serpent angels with white wings that thunder
And shout with power that is white and of all colours,
Swan like an electrical dream about a snake in my pillow.

The slug's movement is that of a bad snake made of plastic
Awarded artificial motion by an unnatural scientist
Who slips one under the head of all our flowers;
The pillow eats the head in the dreamy garden.
So I have employed a slug-danseuse to rid us of them;
She has occupied the garden hut with the balsam of her unwashed
Ghostteeshirts drenched with gymnastic meditations;
She fires a little pistol into the swarming bees to show me
The speed of some people's percipience; see,

220 title] Business (of) walking, with a possible pun on *negotium* being the opposite of *otium* (leisure), which the Romans associated with life in villas and gardens

None falls, none is shot, this gives me confidence;
She dances like a foetus twitching and they're gone.

(Whereas the polluted cities have unclean frost,
Filthy vernix, greasy as a dead-face,
Here we have thunderstorms and awe-inspiring slugs
Which are bigger than a human eye, swallowing the garden.)

(1989)

James Schuyler
1933–

221   *Roof Garden*

tubs of . . .
      memory
for a moment
   won't supply a name
       not portulacas
         (' . . . she had on her
         new dressmaker dress and
         spectator pumps . . .')
petunias
  tubs of pink petunias
a gray roof
    black when it's hot
light grays today
      green tubs of punctured glow
        before a glowing wall
all the walls reflecting light
at six on a summer evening
      the petunias shimmer in a breeze
a long, long time ago
      petunias
adorable, sticky flower

(1969)

Fleur Adcock

1934–

Trees

ELM, laburnum, hawthorn, oak:
all the incredible leaves expand
on their dusty branches, like
Japanese paper flowers in water,
like anything one hardly believes
will really work this time; and
I am a stupefied spectator
as usual. What are they all, these
multiverdant, variously-made
soft sudden things, these leaves?
So I walk solemnly in the park
with a copy of *Let's Look at Trees*
from the children's library,
identifying leaf-shapes and bark
while behind my back, at home,
my own garden is turning into a wood.
Before my house the pink may tree
lolls its heavy heads over mine
to grapple my hair as I come
in; at the back door I walk out
under lilac. The two elders
(I let them grow for the wine)
hang vastly over the fence, no doubt
infuriating my tidy neighbours.
In the centre the apple tree
needs pruning. And everywhere,
soaring over the garden shed,
camouflaged by roses, or snaking
up through the grass like vertical worms,
grows every size of sycamore.
Last year we attacked them; I saw
my son, so tender to ants, so sad
over dead caterpillars, hacking
at living roots as thick as his arms,
drenching the stumps with creosote.
No use: they continue to grow.
Under the grass, the ground

must be peppered with winged seeds,
meshed with a tough stringy net
of roots; and the house itself undermined
by wandering wood. Shall we see
the floorboards lifted one morning
by these indomitable weeds,
or find in the airing-cupboard
a rather pale sapling?
And if we do, will it be
worse than cracked pipes or dry rot?
Trees I can tolerate; they are why
I chose this house—for the apple tree,
elder, buddleia, lilac, may;
and outside my bedroom window, higher
every week, its leaves unfurling
pink at the twig-tips (composite
in form) the tallest sycamore.

(1971)

Peter Bland

1934—

223   *Notes for the Park Keeper*

THEY'VE put the park bench
too near the pond. Lovers could drown
if the drains backed up. There's
a touching Chinese look to the plants
bordering the council flats. Perhaps
the gardener's a Buddhist but
he's far too trusting. His bamboo patch
has been flattened into a speedway track
for chopper bikes. That bench

sometimes doubles as a raft. Kids
use it to fish for eels. They get
twenty pence each from Presto's so
they climb the railings at night
to gaff by flashlight and to carve
graffiti into the picnic logs—
DUFFY FOR CHELSEA . . . NIG-NOGS

GO HOME ... and, strangest of all,
PICASSO PAINTS WITH HIS COCK.

*   *   *

The park's Victorian wrought-iron gates
are beginning to look like a cage
(shades of old 'class barriers'). That
and the bandsmen's buttoned-up uniforms
(deck-chairs in regimental rows)
give the place a 19th-century ambience

that stiffens each evening as shadows spread
heavy gothic lines. A picket fence
could be less inhibiting
while a sprinkling of violins and bare arms
might add a small bohemian gesture
to the bandstand's blatant military blare.

*   *   *

Water's essential to the public's sense
of nature at peace with itself.
It's what we expect to see—
air, water, light, all meeting here
in 'a marriage of earth and sky'.

The fountain's gone in the new council cuts—
which limits both ear and eye
(and how the tongue loved something cool
coming straight out of the ground). But
if they pruned the plane trees further back

then a view of the river would linger on
past Harrods' Depository—the one
with the domes and union-jacks
that houses a dusty Empire
of forgotten furniture and cabin trunks.

(1985)

Chris Wallace-Crabbe

1934–

The Life of Ideas

i.m. A. F. Davies

ALOE, agave, portulaca, prickly pear,
How these remotely anthropomorphic shapes
Gathered around us in their martian rig
As we walked numbly through an afternoon
Of lessening grief.
                    The eye delighted
In such a weird fair of inflected shapes.

These were the forms I once made up and drew
In backs of exercise books during Latin:
Perhaps their freakishness is vaguely classical.
Rounded up, fed here in a garden of science,
All these pumped-up elbows, clubs and phalloi
Articulate a system clear as Latin

But which I cannot do much more than glimpse,
Reading these plots as barbarous inspiration.
Yes, I'd pillage these monsters for a drawing,
Preferring not to know, in order to
Sneak up on knowing from another tack,
The calligraphic dance of inspiration.

The Life Force has come to a mardi gras,
Stagey bumpkins dressed up in quilted gear
Stuck full of arrows like Sebastian,
Or else ratbag knights from an amateur production
Of *Murder in the Cathedral*, pissed as newts.
How could nature have tricked out all that gear?

Bearing in mind (whatever may be mind) that
Language is the language of languages,
We ought to learn from this taxonomy
Something at least. Such plump allusions to
Plebeian cabarets or rustic orgies
Hide symptoms of the damaged languages.

Damage is where we start from. We survive
Displacing down a value-gradient
The itsy-bitsy fragments of our childhood.
The signified is all that is the case
But what rich slips got buried down the garden?
Grease, grace, gravy, Grandma, gradient . . .

Just naming them will conjure something up,
At best a truth: whatever that may be;
Say, something planted in the numinous
On which the sun leans with particular grace
Like it would on a dancer. What green piercing music
Coerces our shards of happening to *be*?

It is raw grief can lock us into process,
The linkage also grown from the forgetting
As uncollected plants may haunt this rockery.
Some of these succulents are jokes about
Utter non-being —
                                    I don't know why I said that.
I feel dreadful. I simply need forgetting.

We build from what we're given early on,
Keeping a child's original box of paints.
Freedom finds room amid taxonomy
And calls renunciation civilized,
Though barmy Nietzsche felt that pride and wit
Could reinvent the colours of the paints.

Language is limited but inexhaustible;
Our bodies are the grounds for metaphor
But forebears tell us how to name our bodies.
The double-bind suckles a double mind
With which we wander through Botanic Gardens
Negotiating them by metaphor.

Names for these shapes?
                                    Why, anthropoid,
Globulous, falgate, serrulated, drab,
Robust, rupestral, pyramidal, plump
And acutifoil. When we get a grip on the names
We take things into our mental block of flats,
Setting them up as crudely green and drab.

In this prodigious picnic of the cacti
Departures from a norm are the grand prize.
A new idea is always faintly monstrous,
Its novelty being what constitutes
The warp or bulge. It is the spanking new
Reversal of an axiom that we prize;

It is the opposite that's good for us,
Taking the dog of habit for a stroll
On the Big Dipper . . .
                        Heart then trips a beat
Peering into unguessed taxonomies:
Kekulé, dreaming of the benzene ring,
Let fantasy tell reason where to stroll.

Reason, the dream of dreaming centuries,
Listened to what prodigious Sigmund said,
Dwindling back to a tense meniscus: dread
And traumata beat against that skin,
Language papers vainly over the top —
Try it again with a Not in it, you said.

                              (1990)

Ronald Johnson
1935–

225   from *The Book of the Green Man*

WILLIAM Stukeley made his own Stonehenge, ·
a Druid Temple 'formed out of an old ortch-
ard'. 'Tis thus', he writes—'there is a circle of
tall filberd trees in the nature of a hedg, which
is 70 foot diameter & round it a walk 15 foot
broad, circular

too, so that the whole is 100 foot diameter.
The walk from one high point slopes each
way, gradually, till you come to the lowest
point opposite, & there is the entrance to a
temple, to which the walk may be esteemed as
porticoe. When one enters

225 William Stukeley] antiquarian and gardenist (1687–1765)

into this innermost circle or temple, one sees,
in the center, an antient appletree oregrown
with sacred mistletoe. Round it is another
concentric circle of a 50 foot diameter made
all of pyramidal greens, at an equal interval,
that appear as verdant

when fruit trees have dropt their leaves. The
pyramidals are in imitation of Stonehenge's
inner circles. The whole of this is included
within a square wall on every side, except the
grand avenue to the porticoe, which is an
appletree avenue. The

angles are filled in fruit trees, plumbs, pears,
& walnuts, & such are likewise interspersed in
the filberd hedg & borders, with some sort of
irregularity to prevent any stiffness in its
appearance & make it look more easy &
natural. At that point,

where is an entrance from the porticoe to the
temple, is a tumulus, but I must take it for a
cairn, or celtic barrow. I have sketched you out
the whole thing as it is formed. These are
some of the amusements of country folk,
insted of conversation'.

Alexander Pope: 'I have sometimes
had the idea of planting an old gothic
cathedral. Good

large poplars with their white stems
(cleared of their boughs to a proper
height) w'ld serve well for columns,
& might form

the aisles or the peristiliums by their
different distances &

heights. These w'ld look very well
near, & a dome rising all in a proper
tuft in the middle w'ld look well at a
distance'. This is the man whose
parodies

of topiary were inimitable, who deplored the
fantastical & wished for 'unadorned
Nature'. But the 'Gothick' was in fashion & has

since been destroyed as
the formal topiary before it—to serpen-
tinize brooks, to make vistas.

Now, the obelisks are toppled,
labyrinth & maze are uprooted to pasture
& ivies hide the Folly.
The giantesque animals, lop-sided arches & cones
& pyramids, have been allowed, now,
to grow into ghosts of shapes they once had.

'A laurestine bear in blossom, with a juniper hunter
in berries. A pair of giants, stunted. A lavender pig
with sage growing in his belly. The Tower of
Babel. St. George in box, his arm

scarce long enough, but able to stick the dragon by
next April—the dragon, also of box, with ground-
ivy tail. A pair of maiden-heads in fir, in great
forwardness. A quickset hog, shot up

to a porcupine, by its being forgot a week in rainy
weather. Noah's ark in holly, Adam & Eve in
yew—the serpent flourishing. Edward the Black
Prince in cypress, an old maid in wormwood'.

(1967)

Patrick Hare
1936–

226   *Deceit in the Park*

THE reason why the Park is closed
To All Persons from nine p.m.

Because persons might discover
There is no mansion there. Because
Someone might just hide and challenge
The uniformed men, unmasking
Apparent bandsmen and keepers.

There is endless garden and no house.
Paths lead only to other paths.
Thousands eat their miraculous
Picnics and roam in the sunshine
Of admission and audience.

By nine p.m. lovers have left.
Dogs on elastic go sideways
Over the turf, nosey but too
Animal to smell out reasons.
The late stroller wonders why
Ordinary trees have names like
Library books chained on display.

All Persons are locked out because
Someone might discover the truth.
Apparent bandsmen and keepers
Have done away with the mansion,
Constructed fanfares and flowers
Where the original sun
Struck a thousand admired windows.

(1975)

Neil Curry
1937–

227   *Gardens*

We smiled together
over the precepts in that old herbal,
vowing, as we valued our eyesight,
            never to gather
        the fruit of the peony
            save at dead of night
and thus 'all unseene of the woodpecker',

    noted too that powdered
periwinkle and earthworm, if taken
at mealtimes, does rekindle a wife's
        love for her husband;
        strange that they would tolerate
            such wild beliefs
in days when heretics, not weeds, got burned.

But what gardeners they were:
what arbours of trellis work; embroidered
intricacies of bright nosegay-knots;
    thrift and lavender-
    scented walks of evergreen;
      what salves and syrops
of simple herbs for health and provender;

    what workers for Eden.
Though few of us today would freely voice
our dream of unicorns and rosebuds,
    their secret garden
    has alleyways that may yet
      outpace all our thoughts.
What our lives lack is what our hands fashion.

    The Moghul emperor,
Babur, blazed and butchered his way across
the steppes of Asia, then called a halt
    while his warriors
    erected walls around one
      cool sequestered spot
where lilacs shaded white shawls of water.

                 (1988)

Dom Moraes
1938–

228   *Gardener*

WHEN they moved into the house it was winter.
In the garden a sycamore stood.
No other root nor shoot, but wild nettles
Good only for a bitter soup. He planned
Flowers around the sycamore for summer,
The great splayed rose, the military tulip,
All colours, smell of sun, himself with spade
Drinking cold beer with his wife. Spring came.
He rooted up the nettles with his hands.
He burnt them all, stamped on the clotted ash,
Tamping new seeds in, fingering stones aside.

This work he wanted, his hands came alive.
They wanted flowers to touch. But from his care
Only the tough nasturtiums came. They crawled
In sullen fire by the wall a week.
But the soil was sour, the roots went unfed.
Even they ceased to clutch, their heads fell forward.

All summer was the same. He fed the soil,
Flicking out stones, plucking the few sparse shoots.
The trapped flowers were trying to escape,
Bud died in their cells, and winter came.

Next year he planted early. Spring brought up
Over fussed tussocks, a green scanty surf.
Then it receded, but a tidewrack stayed
Of shrivelled leaves, shoots like dead dragonflies.
Then nettles crawled back. Now he didn't care.
His hands were useless, the earth was not his.
It did things to him, never he to it.
He watched the nettles with a little smile.

Then in the snowdrift of a summer bed
He planted himself, and a child came—
News that he knew early one winter day.
He came home dumbly from the hospital.
The garden gate was open. He went out,
Stood by the sycamore, watched the clouds moult,
Stood in the chilly and falling feathers
Under the sycamore, and not knowing why,
He felt his hands become alive, and touched
The tree's smooth body with a kind of joy,
Thinking next summer it would have new leaves.

(1987)

Wes Magee
1939–

A British Garden

The SPRING garden is *Irish* green,
its forty shades ranging
from the emerald stems of tulips
to the lawn's striped lemon and lime.
Already the garden is looking spruce,
a daffodil buttonhole on its jacket.
At gloaming see the crocus candles,
tiny flames of azure and crimson.

The SUMMER garden is *Welsh* dragon-red,
roses vivid as blood blots in the borders
while sunflowers beam down on leeks.
We lie beneath leafy trees slowly toasting,
first salmon-pink then lobster.
Red hot pokers stoke up the heat.
At evening look westward,
see how the sky runs with cochineal.

The AUTUMN garden is *Scots* tartan,
a blend of russet, gold and blue.
The trees wear plaid overcoats.
Soon, bonfires at garden ends,
then skirls of smoke, kilts of flame.
The clans gather for roast chestnuts,
watch fireworks shed their silver stars.
The children squeal and screech like bagpipes.

The WINTER garden is *English* white,
a cool bride who prepares herself
for a ceremony of pure cold.
Her snow gown dazzles with frost sequins.
The garden waterfall is iced like a
many-tiered wedding cake. A silence,
before the guests celebrate.
Children hurl white meringues against walls.

(1989)

Kelly Drake

1940–

230   *Genius Loci: Akrai, Sicily*

THEY trespassed on his land to see the gods
Carved on his rocks; they stole
His nectarines and figs, yet could not plunder
The images of meaning.

And he, jealous maybe of their interest,
Or thinking that the deities
Spoke more to strangers, so smashed the stone
Beyond the malice of the weather

That we, hushed in the fecundity of grove,
In the recovered hortus of bird
And rabbit, cannot trace their lineaments—
Presiding spirits of this place he loved.

(1973)

Tony Lucas

1941–

231   *A Town Garden*

THE minted flesh of leaves
    against the garden wall crisps
into printed paper, and begins
    to fall in drifts, that silt up
short-stubbed blades of iris
    and the hardening clumps of
daisies with their eyes gone out.

The best thing in the garden
    is the strength of sunlight
on the yellowed bricks, the shine
    of fresh white window frames.
Our swing lies where it has fallen,
    berries moulder, and the grass
will go without its final cut.

We have grown tired of rural games:
   autumn will strike new fires
and put the lights back on.
   Fresh air and flowers have had
their day; we close the door
   and leave them vegetating on
the cold dank consequences of decay.

                (1983)

D. M. Black
1941–

232   *Kew Gardens*

(in memory of Ian A. Black, died January 1971)

DISTINGUISHED scientist, to whom I greatly defer
(old man, moreover, whom I dearly love),
I walk today in Kew Gardens, in sunlight the colour of honey
which flows from the cold autumnal blue of the heavens to light these
   tans and golds,
these ripe corn and leather and sunset colours of the East Asian
   liriodendrons,
of the beeches and maples and plum-trees and the stubborn green
   banks of the holly hedges—
and you walk always beside me, you with your knowledge of names
and your clairvoyant gaze, in what for me is sheer panorama
seeing the net or web of connectedness. But today it is I who speak
(and you are long dead, but it is to you I say it):

'The leaves are green in summer because of chlorophyll
and the flowers are bright to lure the pollinators,
and without remainder (so you have often told me)
these marvellous things that shock the heart the head can account for;
but I want to sing an excess which is not so simply explainable,
to say that the beauty of the autumn is a redundant beauty,
that the sky had no need to be this particular shade of blue,
nor the maple to die in flames of this particular yellow,
nor the heart to respond with an ecstasy that does not beget children.
I want to say that I do not believe your science
although I believe every word of it, and intend to understand it;

that although I rate that unwavering gaze higher than almost everything
there is another sense, a hearing, to which I more deeply attend.
Thus I withstand and contradict you, I, your child,
who have inherited from you the passion which causes me to oppose
    you.'

(1991)

233   *For and Against the Environment*

I HAVE come out to smell the hyacinths which again in this
North London garden

have performed a wonderful feat of chemistry and hauled
that delectable perfume

out of the blackish confection of clay and potsherds which
feebly responds when I name it flower-bed;

and so wet was the Spring that I clipped the grass with
shears, to prevent the mower sliding in mud,

and my attempt to dig the beds to enhance their fertility
foundered caked with clods.

But today the April sun blazes from a cloudless sky, and
the lawn, drenched with raindrops

like an utterly saturated sponge has unfurled and surrendered
its freight,

and—where do they come from?—the small pert insects
emerge onto the skin of dryness

like Noah's prospecting pigeon and at once they are up to
all sorts of business,

and the buds you had thought paralyzed if not embalmed are
surely discernibly plumper

and purpler or pinker than you remember them yesterday, and
the hum of potential life

swells with its distinctive excitement to just short of the
threshold of actual audibility

through which it bursts, perhaps, by way of the throat of
that unceasing ingenious blackbird

poised on my neighbour's gutter against the blue of the
sky. O, wonderful world!

and here are two absolute flowers, new as babies:

they have bowed their heads for weeks in their bashful,
fleecy pods,

but today they stare up at me bravely, giving all they have
got

and making at last no pretence they are anything else but
anemones

and this is their hour, and if they don't impress now they
will never impress,

but they do, and to support my judgment a small fly is
clambering deliberately over the organ stops of their stamens

making, I do not doubt, marvellous music. O, wonderful
world!

And the ant is rushing at immense speed over the lifeless
plains of the rose-bed

which are not plains to her but ridged and crested with
salts and terrible canyons

and she winds every which way through them but never forgets
her sense of direction

for she is not such a fool as to think, but attends to the
sun and the earth's magnetism

and I am shocked by my own thought, that my own thought

may be a blind lobe on the body of the great creature of
evolution,

an experiment which does not carry the future. And meanwhile
here is this ant,

only the most distant relation of Mozart and Shakespeare, yet
unmistakably designed for survival,

nosing about through the clods like an exceptionally fleet
piece of earth-moving equipment

and not in the least reciprocating the warm concern she has
evoked in me,

and the same is true of the blackbird, whose song I salute,
and the anemone

whose sleek pods I have fondled, and the clods which I have
rendered more fertile,

and at this moment, speaking now as one of the Lords of
Creation,

speaking as one of the Shepherds of Being, unique bearers of
conscious and self-conscious life,

I have to declare my preference within all the sparkling
welter

(O, wonderful world!) and I do, keeping the ant firmly fixed
in my gaze:

great and more fragile is man than ant or earth or anemone

and in or out of the glass-house of nature, let him above all
not be seduced.

(1991)

Douglas Dunn
1942–

234 Gardeners

England, Loamshire, 1789

A gardener speaks, in the grounds of a great house,
to his Lordship

GARDENS, gardens, and we are gardeners ...
Razored hedgerow, flowers, those planted trees
Whose avenues conduct a greater ease
Of shadow to your own and ladies' skins
And tilt this Nature to magnificence
And natural delight. But pardon us,
My Lord, if we reluctantly admit
Our horticulture not the whole of it,
Forgetting, that for you, this elegance
Is not our work, but your far tidier Sense.

Out of humiliation comes that sweet
Humility that does no good. We know
Our coarser artistries will make things grow.
Others design the craftsmanship we fashion
To please your topographical possession.
A small humiliation—Yes, we eat,
Our crops and passions tucked out of the view
Across a shire, the name of which is you,
Where every native creature runs upon
Hills, moors and meadows which your named eyes own.

Our eyes are nameless, generally turned
Towards the earth our fingers sift all day—
Your day, your earth, your eyes, wearing away
Not earth, eyes, days, but scouring, forcing down
What lives in us and which you cannot own.
One of us heard the earth cry out. It spurned
His hands. It threw stones in his face. We found
That man, my Lord, and he was mad. We bound
His hands together and we heard him say—
'Not me! Not me who cries!' We took away

315

That man—remember, Lord?—and then we turned,
Hearing your steward order us return,
His oaths, and how you treated us with scorn.
They call this grudge. Let me hear you admit
That in the country that's but half of it.
Townsmen will wonder, when your house was burned,
We did not burn your gardens and undo
What likes of us did for the likes of you;
We did not raze this garden that we made,
Although we hanged you somewhere in its shade.

(1979)

David Ashbee

1945–

235   *Open Day at Stancombe Park*

THE man who takes our coins on the gravel track
is perched with a polythene box upon his knees;
another, strolling, hands behind his back,
keeps one eye on a comical Great Dane
that trots among the geometric trees.

made for a stage set: all part of the plot
pretending this is just another scheme
to raise funds for the Red Cross, a spot
where ladies who like claiming, naming things
take tea and cuttings, strawberries and cream.

But what mind dreamed these twisting boulevards?
How can we prove the well-repeated tale
that a love-sot built this folly only yards
from his betrothed bed? For still the house keeps
a blind silence; there are no guides for sale.

From these windows, no union might be guessed:
all routes submerged in a junction-box of brick
where girls emerge from tunnels, looking perplexed,
and couples ask 'is this where we came in?',
unwitting victims of a twilight trick.

Is it a whale's rib, or distressed wood
That shocks us as we round a sudden bend?
The rest is a threadbare maze from childhood,
half recollected, a crazy pilgrimage
of which the outset is forgotten, the end

never quite believed in. Recurring figures snake
above our heads or beyond a gurgling stream
that slides from oblong holes to a distant lake
where fat goldfish, like scattered mosaics,
nose through lily-pads, in some other dream—

drowned souls perhaps, or ancient overlords
saved by knowing the right path from the wrong,
who stepped as we do now, over quaking boards
to a leaky boat and summer-house, where, lost
and loath to rebegin, we long to belong.

(1989)

Wyatt Prunty
1947–

236   *The Vegetable Garden*

NEEDLED by death for change, for simple change,
We turn the soil,
                    another season's crop
Growing from seed, from rain and last year's rot
Into a fruit we never arrange:

The lettuce outgrows our appetite,
While fences smother with towering beans
And tomatoes swell from the dark of their roots;
All tactile reaching for decay turns green

And hangs in the spray of a garden hose.
Dripping with light, the leaves must bow,
Darkening under shadows we cast
Walking among each picked, each weeded row.

Seasons are canned into lines along shelves,
Are named and dated while vinegar boils,
Filling the house with an acrid smell,
And vines are turned beneath themselves:

Our garden is a form that answers cost,
And, growing out of hand with constant care,
Distinctions bloom, ripen, rot and bear
Into the gathering grasp of something lost.

(1982)

Robert Minhinnick
1952–

237   *Grandfather in the Garden*

DIGGING was always my worst work.
After ten minutes I would blow
My scalding hands and watch him fork
Quite effortlessly the rain-heavy clay
Of a new garden, meticulous and slow
Labour that soon tired a boy.

All his life a cultivator
Of the soil's best things, ingenious
Exterminator of what opposed his sure
Design. Summers wet or dry found him
Aware of deep conspiracies of earth
To damage or destroy the year's triumph.

Thus he squared his jaw, donned ancient
Clothes, and set to digging out his
Fears. Late evenings I'd be sent
To call him in, a dark and elemental
Shape by then, the ruins of a young man's face
Still visible behind the years, the toil.

A labourer and architect,
He taught patience in slow lessons
And one man's dedication to a craft.
From his cracked hands I watched the brittle seed
Cast surely for the future, the unborn;
Those acts of affirmation his deep need.

(1979)

Brad Leithauser
1953–

In a Japanese Moss Garden

After a night of rain
   this garden so
fragile it's never raked, but swept,
   lies on a bed
soft as itself, and all the morning, fed
by the rain banked richly below,
   bathes in a glow

   gentle as candle-light.
      Variety's
ascendant in this lowland where
   a hundred-plus
plush samples of the like-velutinous—
star-shaped mosses, amulets, keys,
   bells, snowflakes—ease

   toward freshly minted greens
      which have no one-
word names: rust- or russet-green, pump-
      kin-tangerine-,
copper- and pewter-, frost- and fire-green . . .
No land was ever overrun
   more mildly, none

   yielded with more repose:
      an intertwined,
inclusive, inch-by-inch advance
      built this retreat
where stones are put to rest beneath a sheet
of nap, where limbs are under-lined,
   and where the mind

   meets not tranquillity
      merely, but some
dim image of itself—the rounded
      mounds, the seams dense
with smaller seams, the knit, knobbed filaments
all suggesting the cranium,
   as witnessed from

within. But now this web
of imagery
bends with a newcomer the colours
of an unripe
tomato who, beast of another stripe,
untended and rootlessly free,
apparently,

runs, runs, runs without rest.
His body gleams
with those pellucid lusters found
within a night's
last vistas, when a dyeing dawn alights
upon your lids, flooding your dreams,
until it seems

your inborn sights and pigments
outshine the day;
it's morning in a Japanese
moss garden and
a creature blazing like a firebrand
now makes its episodic way
between a grey

stand of toadstools that lean
like headstones, through
a swampy heel-print, up a fallen
leaf (and then back
down when it proves an airy cul-de-sac),
across a root, a stump, a dew-
drenched avenue

of shorter moss that looks
and feels like felt . . .
Inanimate, the garden may
better have met
the thoughtful ends on which its lines are set,
but if its motionlessness must
come to a halt,

what cause more fitting than
this zigzag creature,
bizarre as anything in Nature,
whose home's a firma-

mental network, a plane of lifelines pitched
upon a random set of reference
   points, a maze which in its

   closed-in stringiness makes
     a self-portrait?
One might view him as captive, too,
     like any prey
inside his web, yet still take heart at the way
he runs to the task, as if to say,
   Today's the very

   day for weaving finally
     a tapestry
at once proportionate and true.

(1987)

Reginald Arkell
1882–1959

239   *What is a Garden?*

WHAT is a garden?
Goodness knows!
You've got a garden,
I suppose:

To one it is a piece of ground
For which some gravel must be found.
To some, those seeds that must be sown,
To some a lawn that must be mown.
To some a ton of Cheddar rocks;
To some it means a window-box;
To some, who dare not pick a flower—
A man, at eighteen pence an hour.
To some, it is a silly jest
About the latest garden pest;

To some, a haven where they find
Forgetfulness and peace of mind . . .

What is a garden
Large or small
'Tis just a garden,
After all.

(1934)

NOTES AND REFERENCES

No references in the notes are given to poems by authors whose collected works are easily available. Texts of many poems from the seventeenth and eighteenth centuries are to be found in A. Chalmers, *The Works of the English Poets* (1810). For details of poems still in copyright, see the Acknowledgements.

3. 'The Parliament of Fowls', ll. 169–217; wr. *c.*1380, printed 1497–8.

4. *The Romance of the Rose*, ll. 1,349–438; trans. *c.*1360, pub. 1532.

5. John Lydgate: *Poems*, ed. J. Norton-Smith (Oxford, 1966), ll. 36–84, st. 6–12.

6. *Middle English Lyrics*, ed. R. T. Davies (1963), 158.

7. *The Kingis Quair*, ed. W. M. Mackenzie (1939), st. 31–3.

8. John Gardner, *Archaeologia*, 54 (1894), ll. 1–20; wr. 1440–50.

9. *The Flower and the Leaf*, pub. 1532; ed. D. A. Pearsall (1962), ll. 22–77.

10. *The Assembly of Ladies*, pub. 1532; ed. D. A. Pearsall (1962), ll. 1–14 and 47–70.

11. *The Passetyme of Pleasure*, ed. W. E. Mead (1928), ll. 2,008–30.

12. *Yale Studies in English*, 69 (1925), 393–4.

13. *A Hundred Good Points of Husbandry*, ed. W. Payne and S. J. Herrtage (1876; repr. 1984), 100–1.

14 and 15. *A Hundreth Sundrie Flowres* (1573).

16 and 17. *The Faerie Queene*, II. xii. st. 42–4 and 50–63; III. vi. st. 29–46.

18. *Poems*, ed. Joan Grundy (1960).

19. *The Divine Weekes* . . ., ed. Susan Snyder (1979), 330–2; 'Eden', ll. 497–582.

20. From 'Spectacles', *The Complete Works*, ed. A. B. Grosart (Edinburgh, 1880), ii. 300.

21. *Richard II*, III. iv. 34–73.

22. *Salve Deus* (1611), fo. H2 recto–H3 recto.

24. *Complete Poems* (1876), 13–15; st. xxv–xxxiii.

26. *Poems*, ed. E. Robinson (1914).

27. *Occasional Issue of Unique or Very Rare Books*, ed. A. B. Grosart, 10 (1879), 153–6. Cabinets of curiosities were often associated with gardens.

28 and 29. Texts from Chalmers, vol. viii.

31 and 32. *Paradise Lost*, IV. 205–68 and IX. 385–454.

33. *The Minor Poems*, ed. E. Robinson (1914).

34. *Essays, Plays and Sundry Verses*, ed. A. R. Waller (1906), 422–8.

37. 'Upon Appleton House', ll. 281–368.

38. *Amanda* . . . (1923).

39. *Poems* (1958), 87–93 (ll. 1,245–475).

40. *The Complete Poems*, ed. D. M. Vieth (1974), ll. 21–32.

41. Text from 1673, pt. III, pp. 144–7, 151–4, 157–63.

42. Edition of 1682, pp. 12–13 (January) and 251–2 (December).

43. *Poems*, ed. Myra Reynolds (Chicago, 1903).

44. 'My Lady's Lamentation and Complaint against the Dean', ll. 173–86.

45. *The Genius of the Place: The English Landscape Garden 1620–1820*, ed. John Dixon Hunt and Peter Willis (Cambridge, Mass., 1990), 198–203. As yet no critical edition of this poem has been published.

46. From 'Of the usefulness of snails in Medicine', *Posthumous Works* (London, 1728), 31–2.

47. *The Works of Monsieur Boileau*, ii (1711), 117–22, 125.

48. *The Works*, 2nd edn. (1754).

49. Pope's translation of the *Odyssey*, VII. 142–75.

50 and 52. *Minor Poems* volume of the Twickenham Edition (1954), 225–6 and 47–8; the latter, written *c.*1722, was printed in various forms between 1737 and 1803.

51. *Epistle to Lord Burlington*, ll. 39–126; here using the 1744 revised text.

53. *Miscellaneous Works*, iii (London, 1778), 203.

54. *The Genius of the Place*, 228–32, with one correction.

55 and 56. *The Seasons*, ed. James Sambrook (Oxford, 1981), Autumn, ll. 1,037–80 (first pub. in slightly different form in 1729), and Spring, ll. 516–55 (first pub. 1728).

57. *Stowe*, ll. 55–100.

58. *Various Pieces in Verse and Prose* (1791).

59. *On Richmond Park, and Royal Gardens* (1731), 78–80.

60. Osborn Collection, in the Beinecke Rare Book and Manuscript Library, Yale University: Lee Papers (Poetry Box 1).

61. *London Magazine*, 7 (Jan. 1738).

62. *Hymns* (Shrewsbury, 1755), 213.

63. *The Triumphs of Nature*, ll. 204–87.

64. *The Art of Preserving Health*, III ('Exercise'), ll. 102–36.

65. *Edge-Hill*, I. 422–89.

66. Whitehead, text from Chalmers, vol. xvii.

67. Lord Holland's seat at Kingsgate, near Margate, was decorated with representations of classical edifices and ruins.

68. *Poetical Works* (1805), II. 134.

69. *Poems on Several Occasions* (Dublin, 1749).

70. *The Enthusiast*, opening lines; verses on Kent added to 1744 text in 1748.

71. *The Rise and Progress, etc*, 17, 29–91.

72. *Miscellaneous Poems* (1771), 3–7; written before Shenstone's death in 1763.

73 and 74. Written 1772; edition of 1783, I. 407–91; IV. 173–231.

75. *The Genius of the Place*, 323–4, 325.

76. *Poems* (1796–7), III, p. 73.

77. *The Botanic Garden*, IV. 561–86.

79 and 80. *The Task*, both passages from Book I.

84. *Poetical Works* (1774), i. 42–6.

85. Langhorne, opening lines; text from Chalmers, vol. xvi.

86. *Works* (1810).

87. *Cottage-Pictures; Or, the Poor* (3rd edn., 1803), ii. 42–4.

88. *The Landscape*, opening of Book II.

89. Canto II, sec. 6, pp. 129–32.

91. Canto III, pp. 58–61.

94. *Poetical Vagaries* (1816).

95. Issued as broadsheet in Waterford (British Library shelfmark 11622.b.30(5)).

96. Pub. 1887.

97. *The Excursion*, I. 713–56.

101. 'Kubla Khan', opening lines.

102. 'The Story of Rimini', III. 1–40.

103. 'The Sensitive Plant', ll. 1–40.

104. From *Early Poems* (Oxford, 1989), ll. 105–89.

105. From *Poetical Works*, ed. H. H. Waggoner (Boston, 1975). Originally composed in 1882 as a hymn for the American Horticultural Society.

106. First pub. 1830.

108. 'The Gardener's Daughter', ll. 105–40.

109. *The Princess*, Prologue, ll. 49–95.

111. *Maud*, pt. I, sec. xxii.

112. *Sordello*, IV. 111–71.

114. Whitman; first published in 1856 with title 'Poem of Wonder at the Resurrection of the Wheat'; first appeared in *Leaves of Grass* in 1860; much reworked, this title given it in 1867.

116. *Lyrical Poems* (1871).

117. Text from *Collected Poems* (1900); written 1875.

119. *Poems and Ballads*, first series (1866).

122. From F. E. Hardy, *Early Life of Thomas Hardy* (1928); written 1857–60.

125 and 126. *Collected Poems* (1897).

128. This music-hall song was most associated with Gus Elen.

129. From the *New Oxford Book of Victorian Verse*.

130. From MSS in the County Record Office, Clwyd, and the version given by

Merlin Waterson, *The Servants' Hall* (1980), 156–8; probably 1882, the year after Phillips's death.

134. *The Rainbow and the Rose* (1905).

135. *Poems* (1924), ii. 212; Verlaine's poem was published in his *Fêtes Galantes* (1869).

136. First poem in a sequence entitled 'Meditations in Time of Civil War'.

139. *English Poems* (1900).

141. Originally untitled.

182. Written in 1931 and only published forty years later.

184. First published in the *Times Literary Supplement*, with no translator named.

186. Broadcast, then published in *The Listener*.

192. Written in 1971 as a 'Found Poem' from William Cowper's *Letters*.

ACKNOWLEDGEMENTS

THE editor and publisher are grateful for permission to include the following copyright material in this volume.

Fleur Adcock, from *Selected Poems*, © 1971 OUP. Reprinted by permission of Oxford University Press.

Reginald Arkell, extract from 'What is a Garden?' from *Green Fingers*. Reprinted by permission of Random House UK Ltd. on behalf of the Estate of Reginald Arkell.

Alasdair Aston, first published in *New Poetry I*. © Alasdair Aston.

W. H. Auden, from *W. H. Auden: Collected Poems*, edited by Edward Mendelson. Copyright 1951 by W. H. Auden. Reprinted by permission of Faber & Faber Ltd., and Random House, Inc.

George Barker, from *Collected Poems*. Reprinted by permission of Faber & Faber Ltd.

[Mary] Ursula Bethell, from *Collected Poems*, edited by Vincent O'Sullivan, Auckland, Oxford University Press, 1985. Reprinted by permission of the Estate of Ursula Bethell.

Elizabeth Bishop, from *The Complete Poems 1927–1979*, © 1979, 1983 by Alice Helen Methfessel. Reprinted by permission of Farrar, Straus & Giroux, Inc.

D. M. Black, from *Collected Poems 1964–87*. Reprinted by permission of Polygon.

Peter Bland, from *Times Literary Supplement*, Jan. 1985. © Times Supplements Ltd. Used with permission.

Edmund Blunden, from *Collected Poems* (Macmillan). Reprinted by permission of the Peters Fraser & Dunlop Group Ltd.

Alan Brownjohn, from *Collected Poems* (Hutchinson, 1988). Reprinted by permission of the author.

Michael Bullock, 'Garden'. © the author.

Leonard Clark, first published in *The Hearing Heart* (Enitharmon, 1974). Reprinted by permission of The Literary Executor of Leonard Clark.

Hart Crane, from *Complete Poems and Selected Letters of Hart Crane* (Liveright).

Neil Curry, from *Ships in Bottles*. Reprinted by permission of Enitharmon Press.

Donald Davie, from *Collected Poems 1950–1970*. Reprinted by permission of Carcanet Press Ltd.

Walter de la Mare, reprinted by permission of The Literary Trustees of Walter de la Mare and The Society of Authors as their representative.

Robert Druce, first published in *Journal of Garden History*. Reprinted by permission of the author.

Douglas Dunn, from *Barbarians*. Reprinted by permission of Faber & Faber Ltd.

Lawrence Durrell, from *Collected Poems 1931–1974*, edited by James A. Brigham. © 1980 by Lawrence Durrell. Reprinted by permission of Faber & Faber Ltd., and Viking Penguin, a division of Penguin Books USA Inc.

ACKNOWLEDGEMENTS

Richard Eberhart, 'The Garden God' from *Collected Poems 1930–1986* (OUP, Inc.).

Lauris Edmond, from *New and Selected Poems*, Auckland, Oxford University Press, 1991. Reprinted by permission of the author.

William Empson, from *Collected Poems of William Empson* copyright 1949 and renewed 1977 by William Empson. Reprinted by permission of Random Century Group on behalf of the Estate of William Empson and Jonathan Cape as publisher and Harcourt Brace Jovanovich Inc.

D. J. Enright, from *Collected Poems*. Reprinted by permission of Watson Little Ltd., Authors' Agents.

Ian Hamilton Finlay, 'Garden Poem', © 1993 Ian Hamilton Finlay. Reprinted by permission of the author.

Robert Graves, from *Collected Poems 1975*, © 1975 by Robert Graves. Reprinted by permission of Oxford University Press, Inc., and A. P. Watt Ltd. on behalf of The Trustees of the Robert Graves Copyright Trust.

Horace Gregory, from *Collected Poems*, © 1964 by Horace Gregory. Reprinted by permission of Henry Holt & Co., Inc. Published in the UK by MacIntosh, McKee & Dodds.

Geoffrey Grigson, from *Collected Poems* (Cape). Reprinted by permission of David Higham Associates.

Thom Gunn, from *Jack Straw's Castle*, © 1976 by Thom Gunn. Reprinted by permission of Faber & Faber Ltd., and Farrar, Straus & Giroux, Inc.

Michael Hamburger, from *Collected Poems* (Carcanet, 1985). Reprinted by permission of the author.

Patrick Hare, 'Deceit in the Park', first published in *New Poetry 1*. © Patrick Hare.

Anthony Hecht, from *Collected Earlier Poems* (Knopf; OUP, 1991) © 1990 by Anthony E. Hecht. Reprinted by permission of Alfred A. Knopf Inc.

Phoebe Hesketh, first published in *Prayer For Sun* (Hart–Davis, 1966) and reprinted in *Netting the Sun: New and Collected Poems* (Enitharmon Press, 1989). Reprinted by permission of Enitharmon Press.

John Hollander, from *Harp Lake*, © 1988 by John Hollander. Reprinted by permission of Alfred A. Knopf, Inc.

Randall Jarrell, from *The Complete Poems*, © 1969 by Mrs Randall Jarrell. Reprinted by permission of Farrar, Straus & Giroux, Inc., and Faber & Faber Ltd.

Ronald Johnson, from *The Book of the Green Man*, in *Tales of Mystery and Imagination*, edited by Roland John. Reprinted by permission of Longman Group UK.

Peter Jones, from *The Garden End*. Reprinted by permission of Carcanet Press Ltd.

Patrick Kavanagh, 'The Long Garden' is included by kind permission of the Trustees of the Estate of Patrick Kavanagh, c/o Peter Fallon, Loughcrew, Oldcastle, Co. Meath, Ireland.

Robert Layzer, reprinted in *New Poets of England and America*, edited by D. Hall (Meridian, 1957).

Richard Le Gallienne, reprinted by permission of The Society of Authors as the literary representative of The Estate of Richard Le Gallienne.

Brad Leithauser, from *Between Leaps*, © Brad Leithauser 1987. Reprinted by permission of Oxford University Press.

Cecil Day Lewis, from *Collected Poems* (Cape).

Robert Lowell, from *For the Union Dead*, © 1962, 1964 by Robert Lowell. Reprinted by permission of Faber & Faber Ltd., and Farrar, Straus & Giroux, Inc.

Tony Lucas, first published in *New Poetry 9* (Hutchinson/Arts Council, 1983). © Tony Lucas 1983. Reprinted by permission of the author.

Wes Magee, from *Morning Break and Other Poems* (Cambridge University Press). © Wes Magee. Reprinted by permission of the author.

Robert Minhinnick, from *The Native Ground*. Reprinted by permission of Christopher Davies Publishers Ltd.

Dom Moraes, from *Later Poems*. Reprinted by permission of the author and Penguin Books India Pvt. Ltd.

Edwin Morgan, from *Collected Poems*. Reprinted by permission of Carcanet Press Ltd.

Howard Nemerov, from *The Collected Poems of Howard Nemerov* (University of Chicago Press). Reprinted by permission of Margaret Nemerov.

Alfred Noyes, from *Collected Poems*. Reprinted by permission of John Murray (Publishers) Ltd.

Octavio Paz, from *Times Literary Supplement*, 20 July 1989. © Times Supplements Ltd. Used with permission.

M. R. Peacocke, 'Railway Allotments', © M. R. Peacocke from *Marginal Land* (1988). Reproduced by permission of Peterloo Poets.

Ruth Pitter, 'The Diehards' from *The Rude Potato* (Cresset, 1941), 'Other People's Glasshouses', first published in *The Rude Potato* and reprinted in *Collected Poems* (Enitharmon Press, 1990). Reprinted by permission of Enitharmon Press.

Cole Porter, from *Hitchy-Koo*. Reproduced by permission of Warner Chappell Music Ltd.

Peter Porter, from *Collected Poems*, © Peter Porter 1983. Reprinted by permission of Oxford University Press.

Wyatt Prunty, from *The Times Between*. Reprinted by permission of The Johns Hopkins University Press.

Herbert Read, 'Garden Party' from *Selected Poetry* (Sinclair Stevenson). Reprinted by permission of David Higham Associates.

Peter Redgrove, from *The First Earthquake* (Secker). Reprinted by permission of David Higham Associates.

Adrienne Cecile Rich, from *Collected Early Poems, 1950–1970*. Reprinted by permission of W. W. Norton & Co. Inc.

Theodore Roethke, all copyright 1948 by Theodore Roethke from *The Collected Poems of Theodore Roethke*. Used by permission of Doubleday, a division of Bantam Doubleday Dell Publishing Group, Inc., and Faber & Faber Ltd.

Vita Sackville-West, extract from *The Land*, copyright 1927 Vita Sackville-West, and extract from *The Garden*, copyright 1946 Vita Sackville-West. Reprinted by permission of the Curtis Brown Group Ltd.

Siegfried Sassoon, from *Collected Poems*. Reprinted by permission of George Sassoon.

James Schuyler, from *Selected Poems*, © 1969, 1988 by James Schuyler. Reprinted by permission of Carcanet Press Ltd., and Farrar, Straus & Giroux, Inc.

Anne Sexton, from *To Bedlam and Part Way Back*. © 1960 by Anne Sexton. Reprinted by permission of Houghton Mifflin Company. All rights reserved.

Osbert Sitwell, 'In the Potting Shed' from *Five Drawings of Mr Hague* and 'In the Winter' from *Villa L'Allegria*. Reprinted by permission of David Higham Associates.

A. H. Snow, from *Times Literary Supplement*, 3 Dec. 1982. © Times Supplements Ltd. Used with permission.

Muriel Spark, from *Going Up to Sothebys* (Granada). Reprinted by permission of David Higham Associates.

Margaret Stanley-Wrench, 'Hinterland'. Reproduced with permission.

Wallace Stevens, from *Opus Posthumous*, published in the USA in *Collected Poems*, © 1957 by Elsie Stevens and Holly Stevens. Reprinted by permission of Faber & Faber Ltd. and Alfred A. Knopf, Inc.

Arthur Symons, extract from 'Fetes Galantes: L'Allee' from *Collected Poems* (Secker, 1924). Reprinted by permission of Mr Brian Read, MA (Oxon.).

Dylan Thomas, from *The Poems* (Dent). Reprinted by permission of David Higham Associates.

Charles Tomlinson, 'John Maydew, or the Allotment' and 'Juliet's Garden' from *Collected Poems*, © Charles Tomlinson 1985; 'In the Borghese Gardens' from *The Return*, © Charles Tomlinson 1987. Reprinted by permission of Oxford University Press.

Arthur Waley, from *Chinese Poems* (Unwin Hyman) and *One Hundred Seventy Chinese Poems* (Knopf). Copyright 1919 and renewed 1947 by Arthur Waley. Reprinted by permission of Unwin Hyman, now an imprint of HarperCollins Publishers Ltd. and Alfred A. Knopf, Inc.

Chris Wallace-Crabbe, from *For Crying Out Loud*, © Chris Wallace-Crabbe 1990.

Dorothy Wellesley, from *Early Light* (Hart Davis, 1955). Copyright the Trustees of Dorothy Wellesley's Will Trust.

Richard Wilbur, 'Caserta Garden' from *The Beautiful Changes and Other Poems*, copyright 1947 and renewed 1975 by Richard Wilbur. *A Baroque Wall-Fountain in the Villa Sciarra* from *Things of This World* © 1956 and renewed 1984 by Richard Wilbur. Reprinted by permission of Harcourt Brace Jovanovich Inc.

William Carlos Williams, 'The Tulip Bed' from *The Collected Poems of William Carlos Williams, 1909–1939, Vol. I*, copyright 1938 by New Directions Publishing Corp.; 'The Mental Hospital Garden' and 'The Italian Garden' from *The Collected Poems ... 1939–1962, vol. II*, © 1944, 1948, 1962 by William Carlos Williams. Reprinted by permission of New Directions Publishing Corporation.

ACKNOWLEDGEMENTS

W. B. Yeats, 'Ancestral Houses' copyright 1928 by Macmillan Publishing Company, renewed 1956 by Georgie Yeats; 'Coole Park and Ballylee, 1931', copyright 1933 by Macmillan Publishing Company, renewed 1961 by Bertha Georgie Yeats, both from *The Poems of W. B. Yeats: A New Edition*. Reprinted by permission of Macmillan Publishing Company.

Philip Yorke, 'Our Gardener at Erdigg'. Reproduced by permission of The National Trust for Places of Historic Interest or Natural Beauty.

Although every effort has been made to establish copyright and contact copyright holders prior to printing this has not always been possible. If contacted, the publisher will be pleased to rectify any inadvertent errors or omissions.

INDEX OF FIRST LINES

The references are to the numbers of the poems

INDEX OF AUTHORS

The references are to the numbers of the poems

OXFORD

MORE OXFORD PAPERBACKS

This book is just one of nearly 1000 Oxford Paperbacks currently in print. If you would like details of other Oxford Paperbacks, including titles in the World's Classics, Oxford Reference, Oxford Books, OPUS, Past Masters, Oxford Authors, and Oxford Shakespeare series, please write to:

UK and Europe: Oxford Paperbacks Publicity Manager, Arts and Reference Publicity Department, Oxford University Press, Walton Street, Oxford OX2 6DP.

Customers in UK and Europe will find Oxford Paperbacks available in all good bookshops. But in case of difficulty please send orders to the Cash-with-Order Department, Oxford University Press Distribution Services, Saxon Way West, Corby, Northants NN18 9ES. Tel: 0536 741519; Fax: 0536 746337. Please send a cheque for the total cost of the books, plus £1.75 postage and packing for orders under £20; £2.75 for orders over £20. Customers outside the UK should add 10% of the cost of the books for postage and packing.

USA: Oxford Paperbacks Marketing Manager, Oxford University Press, Inc., 200 Madison Avenue, New York, N.Y. 10016.

Canada: Trade Department, Oxford University Press, 70 Wynford Drive, Don Mills, Ontario M3C 1J9.

Australia: Trade Marketing Manager, Oxford University Press, G.P.O. Box 2784Y, Melbourne 3001, Victoria.

South Africa: Oxford University Press, P.O. Box 1141, Cape Town 8000.

OXFORD BOOKS

Beginning in 1900 with the famous *Oxford Book of English Verse*, the Oxford Books series now boasts over sixty superb anthologies of poetry, prose, and songs.

'These anthologies—along with digests and reference books—are exactly what the general reader needs.'
Auberon Waugh, *Independent*

THE NEW OXFORD BOOK OF
IRISH VERSE

Edited, with Translations, by Thomas Kinsella

Verse in Irish, especially from the early and medieval periods, has long been felt to be the preserve of linguists and specialists, while Anglo-Irish poetry is usually seen as an adjunct to the English tradition. This original anthology approaches the Irish poetic tradition as a unity and presents a relationship between two major bodies of poetry that reflects a shared and painful history.

'the first coherent attempt to present the entire range of Irish poetry in both languages to an English-speaking readership'
Irish Times

'a very satisfying and moving introduction to Irish poetry'
Listener

Also in Oxford Paperbacks:

The Oxford Book of Travel Verse
edited by Kevin Crossley-Holland
The Oxford Book of Contemporary Verse
edited by D. J. Enright
The Oxford Book of Late Medieval Verse and Prose
edited by Douglas Gray

POETRY FROM OXFORD PAPERBACKS

Oxford's outstanding range of English poetry offers, in a single volume of convenient size, the complete poetical works of some of the most important figures in English Literature.

WORDSWORTH
Poetical Works

This edition of Wordsworth's poetry contains every piece of verse known to have been published by the poet himself, or of which he authorized the posthumous publication. The text, which Thomas Hutchinson based largely upon the 1849–50 standard edition, the last issued during the poet's lifetime, was revised for the Oxford Standard Authors series by Ernest de Selincourt.

The volume preserves the poet's famous subjective arrangement of the Minor Poems under such headings as 'Poems Referring to the Period of Childhood', 'Poems Dedicated to National Independence and Liberty', and 'Sonnets Upon the Punishment of Death'. *The Prelude* is given in the text of 1850, published shortly after Wordsworth's death, and *The Excursion* as it appears in the 1849–50 edition. Two poems of 1793 are included, 'An Evening Walk' and 'Descriptive Sketches', and a group of other pieces not appearing in the standard edition. The text reproduces Wordsworth's characteristic use of capital letters and in most cases his punctuation, though spelling has been regularized. The poet's own Notes to the 1849–50 edition, as well as to some earlier editions, are reprinted, along with his Prefaces.

The edition also contains a chronological table of Wordsworth's life, explanatory notes on the text, and chronological data for the individual poems.

Also in Oxford Paperbacks:

The Prelude   William Wordsworth
Poetical Works   John Keats
The Golden Treasury   Francis Turner Palgrave

OXFORD POETS

Oxford Paperbacks' well-established and highly regarded series of contemporary poetry includes the work of some of the world's most important poets, amongst them Fleur Adcock, Joseph Brodsky, D. J. Enright, Roy Fisher, Thomas Kinsella, Peter Porter, and Craig Raine.

A PORTER SELECTED

Peter Porter

This selection of about one hundred of Porter's best poems is chosen from all his works to date, including his latest book, *Possible Worlds*, and *The Automatic Oracle*, which won the 1988 Whitbread Prize for Poetry.

What the critics have said about Peter Porter:

'I can't think of any contemporary poet who is so consistently entertaining over such a variety of material.' John Lucas, *New Statesman*

'an immensely fertile, lively, informed, honest and penetrating mind.' Stephen Spender, *Observer*

'He writes vigorously, with savage erudition and wonderful expansiveness . . . No one now writing matches Porter's profoundly moral and cultured overview.' Douglas Dunn, *Punch*

Also in Oxford Poets:

Possible Worlds   Peter Porter
Shibboleth   Michael Donaghy
Orient Express   Grete Tartler
Selected Poems 1990   D. J. Enright